STUDIES IN AMERICAN LITERATURE

Volume XXI

ROBERT PENN WARREN AND HISTORY

"The Big Myth We Live"

by

L. HUGH MOORE, JR.
Georgia Institute of Technology

1970

MOUTON

THE HAGUE · PARIS

LIBRARY OF CONGRESS CATALOG CARD NUMBER: 76-98470

Printed in The Netherlands by Mouton & Co., Printers, The Hague.

To Mary, Hutch, and Mimi

ACKNOWLEDGEMENTS

I am deeply indebted to Professor William B. Dillingham and Professor Floyd C. Watkins for their interest, guidance, and encouragement. Their unselfish, willing, and expert help always goes far beyond my excessive demands upon their knowledge and experience. The manuscript was also improved by Professor Albert E. Stone, Jr. who offered many helpful suggestions.

CONTENTS

I

INTRODUCTION

No subject is more central to the work of Robert Penn Warren than is the subject of history, and no topic subsumes so many of his other major themes. No one can adequately understand Warren without carefully considering the influence of history upon him and his use of it in his works, especially his novels. Warren has himself said that an awareness of history is central to all of his works.[1] Although critics are increasingly coming to focus on this aspect of Warren's work after almost completely neglecting it for many years, there is no topic in Warren that is more deserving of study, that better repays close attention, or that seems as inexhaustible in its ramifications. Part of the reason for critical neglect of this important subject derives, perhaps, from the complexity of some of his ideas and his occasional ambiguous presentation of them. But as he publishes more it becomes increasingly apparent that he is genuinely and deeply involved with historical facts and their meaning.

Many things have conspired to create in Warren an abiding interest in the past, especially the American and in particular the Southern past. First, he is a Southerner, and for him the past seems to be more alive in the South than in other regions; then, too, because of economic and political conditions and because of a love of tradition, which Warren calls "piety", the past in the South reaches vitally into the present. As a boy Warren was imbued with a love of history from the folklore and stories he heard

---

[1] "The Art of Fiction XVIII: Robert Penn Warren", in *Writers at Work: The Paris Review Interviews*, ed. Malcolm Cowley (New York, 1958), p. 188.

from his grandfather and other old-timers around Guthrie, Kentucky, and while quite young he read widely in Macauley, Gibbon, Buckle, and "a good deal of American history".[2] At sixteen he began his long association with the Fugitives at Vanderbilt, whose most obvious similarity lies in a re-examination and re-evaluation of their common Southern heritage and the concern with history which this implies. Allen Tate, Donald Davidson, and especially John Crowe Ransom confirmed and quickened Warren's early interest in history; he said that they gave him "in a very concrete way a sense of how literature can be related to place and history".[3] This concern with history and respect for the past have not slackened throughout his career. Warren is interested, first, in the facts and details of the past; his novels thus have remarkable historical accuracy and verisimilitude. He is also interested in the meaning of history; he has worked out and effectively dramatized a coherent philosophy of history that is quite apparent in his novels and poetry. Deriving from his philosophy of history is his strong conviction of the necessity of tradition and the need for myth. In *Wilderness* (1961) Warren has provided the critic with an excellent dramatization of these ideas as well as a concrete example of his imaginative confrontation with the historical event which he regards as the most important in American history and our society's best subject for a historical myth – the Civil War.

Robert Penn Warren was a historian before he was a novelist or a poet. His first book was a historical biography, *John Brown: The Making of a Martyr* (1929), an attempt to reinterpret the Northern abolitionist myth centering on Brown. One of his latest works, *The Legacy of the Civil War* (1961), is an astute analysis of the causes and consequences of the war. And *Who Speaks for the Negro?* (1965), an exhaustive and detailed job of research on and interpretation of the Civil Rights Movement, makes him one of the foremost historians of the Negro revolution. In between he has written well-researched articles such as "Remember the

---

[2]   "Autobiographical Notes", *Wilson's Bulletin*, XIII (June, 1939), p. 652.
[3]   *The Paris Review Interviews*, p. 192.

Alamo!" and "How Texas Won Her Freedom". The facts of the
past as well as their meaning are, then, quite important to Warren.
A mastery of historical facts – physical details as well as social
and political issues – and their meaning and significance is also
central to the method of composition he follows in his novels, four
of which are clearly historical, while the other three recreate and
document a more recent past. Although from the worthy beginnings of this genre in Scott and Thackeray the historical novel
has declined in importance and seriousness (as the romantic
escapism of such novelists as Hervey Allen, Taylor Caldwell, and
Frank Yerby amply documents), Warren has taken this time-
worn, cliché-ridden form and made it again a literary form capable
of serious use.

Warren is never content with vagueness or historical inaccura-
cy. Few American writers can match Warren in learning, in the
sheer bulk of facts he has at his command, and none can surpass
his imaginative grasp and control of these historical facts. To him
the people and issues involved in the replevin controversy in
Kentucky in the 1820's, or the New Orleans riots of 1866, or
Louisiana politics in the 1930's are not shadowy abstractions.
Because he has intellectually mastered his historical facts, his
novels are extremely specific. As C. Vann Woodward has said,
"his novels quicken and vivify our consciousness of history in a
way that conventional historical novels, as well as many bona
fide histories, do not".[4]

Warren's practice in his novels of amassing a large number of
details has thematic as well as stylistic justification. History and
human experience, he maintains, are enormously and overwhelmingly complex. In formulating ideals, values, and ideas from the
past one must keep in mind the tremendous number of details
that contribute to the complexity of history. This is the tentative,
skeptical state of mind which he praises in Conrad. Like Jack
Burden and Jeremiah Beauchamp, many of his characters learn
that knowledge can be salvation. The more one knows of history

the more valuable will be one's ideas and ideals; Warren would
have man as well as the artist proceed inductively rather than
deductively, working from the facts of the past toward generalizations valid for himself and his time. Knowledge even of the evil
of history, of horrible events like the gory butchering of a slave,
has value. Such horrible facts, first, help the individual confront
his own sinful nature. And, second, optimistic illusions perish in
the fire of history, for the facts of the past will correct any such
delusions. Finally, the facts will free one from a dependence on
history, on the notion that things will work out well, that life is
not a tragedy; this realization throws one back on his own human
resources. As Hamish Bond says, you want to know "the worst
that can happen, then you feel free".[5]

With his historian's love of the documented past and with his
philosophical emphasis on the necessity of considering an enormous number of details in formulating one's ideas, it is not surprising that in his own works Warren amasses a great number of
facts and that his novels posesss an amazing solidity of specification. But his development as artist and historian has been toward
a more selective, more philosophical use of the facts of the past
rather than a piling of example on top of example. He has
mastered his total recall. As a philosophical novelist Warren has
increasingly concerned himself with the meaning, not just with
the facts of history, and the relation of history to man's other
concerns – psychological, social, artistic, economic, spiritual, and
moral. In his early works such as *Night Rider* (1939) and "Prime
Leaf" (1931) Warren seemed to be mainly intent upon vividly
and abundantly documenting a particular time and place. *Wilderness*, however, has much less material that can be considered pure
documentation. In it Warren has been more selective, and he is
much more interested in theme, meaning, and philosophy than
in just facts of which he has, as always, an abundance. His poetry
reveals the same development; it has become increasingly philosophical, complex, and symbolic. All of his work has become

---

[5] *Band of Angels* (New York, 1955), p. 163. All references in the text
are to this edition.

more intensive – "a talent exhaustively aware of the immediate richness and implication of the single scene" – rather than extensive, an approach which "works by accumulating illustration",[6] as Warren defines these terms. *At Heaven's Gate* (1943), replete with facts and details, is his best example of an extensive novel, while *Wilderness* pruned and compact, is his best example of an intensive one. Warren has also become decreasingly dependent upon historical characters and events to use as models. Warren's use of the facts of the past, in other words, has become more selective, more imaginative, more that of an artist than that of a historian.

A consideration of Warren's use of historical detail leads one to his definition of history and his philosophy of history. First, he frequently uses the term "history" in relation to the individual's personal past and his family heritage, both of which one must accept and come to terms with. This aspect of his use of the term merges into general human history. Warren believes in the dual nature of man. Man is capable of nobility, dignity, bravery, selflessness, and love, and he can, through struggle, formulate worthy ideals. Part of history involves, then, a study of this aspect of human history – the nobility some individuals have been able to achieve in the past. The examples of such men as Abraham Lincoln and Robert E. Lee can, of course, inspire us today to strive to be like them. This is the example of the past that can rebuke and correct modern man – the example of men striving to live by worthy and humane codes of conduct or of men trying to create such codes. Warren believes that in the past people were more likely to be concerned with concepts of honor, truth, and justice, rather than merely with success and progress.

But man has also the potential to be evil and irrational, for Warren believes that a part of man's nature is depraved. History, then, is also a record of this aspect of man's nature, an aspect reflected in deeds of incredible violence, evil, and irrationality, deeds which Warren does not hesitate to record in vivid detail.

---

[6] "The Fiction of Caroline Gordon", *Southwest Review Book Supplement*, XX (January, 1935), p. 5.

This portion of human history then merges with non-human history which consists of the forces of nature, such as floods, storms, droughts, famines, earthquakes, and other forces which grow out of social interaction but which are beyond human control, like some economic and political forces. Part of human history and all of non-human history, therefore, Warren considers to consist of a blind ruck of events, a mindless clash of forces, non-rational, and dependent upon chance, not plan. This aspect of history is without meaning or significance until it impinges upon the rational side of man's character. Jack Burden is right when he finally realizes that "History is blind".[7] But he also learns that man is not, for man faced with overwhelmingly complex and blank forces must make human, moral sense of them, must form his own ideals and values while keeping always in mind the tremendous complexity of the material he is shaping. And this is a never-ending process; through an imaginative, creative, moral involvement with the blind side of history man must continue to validate his human ideals anew.

To add to man's enormously difficult and hazardous task these blind historical events are complexly and illogically interrelated in time; history, as Jack Burden says, is like a spider web. Man, just by being born, touches the web and sets up vibrations that he cannot foresee or understand in the whole fabric of the web. This theory of historical interrelatedness should not be interpreted as implying a moral plan to the universe, for there is nothing orderly, logical, planned, or predictable about the operation of the web of history. Warren, however, argues that this web necessitates man's acceptance of complete responsibility for his every act beyond any rational intention and for the mere fact of his existence, for in Warren's world-view even the best of intentions can bring about disastrous consequences. Man is responsible, for Warren believes man's will is free; he rejects behaviorism as an explanation of man because it denies him a moral choice. But man's free choice may have little or no effect upon the physical

---

[7] *All the King's Men* (New York, 1946), p. 462. All references in the text are to this edition.

world of non-human history; the tumults of the past can show us some people who oppose their wills to the ruck of forces and who accept their responsibility, but it cannot guarantee that such people have had any effect other than to offer us a noble example.

History, further, should be recorded in all its abundant detail, for if no one can predict the consequences of any act, how can one distinguish between the important and the trivial without the aid of historical perspective? The affair between Amantha and Hamish in *Band of Angels* (1955), Amantha says, is "as much History as any death-cry at the trench lip or in the tangle of the abatis" (p. 135). Warren's theories increase his effectiveness as a novelist, poet, and critic; they encourage looking at the whole picture and discourage premature or dogmatic judgments. C. Vann Woodward, testifying to Warren's skill as a historian, states that Warren looks for the meaning of the present in the past because to Warren "the present is a fleeting segment of the cumulative past". Like the historian he sees the individual "as inextricable part of a living history and community, attached and determined in a thousand ways by other wills and destinies of people he has only heard about".[8] In the realm of aesthetics, Warren's composition of his novels in accord with his theory of historical interrelatedness of time enriches each individual moment, each thought, and even each gesture and makes them more truly significant by a constant reference to past times. Any sight or any idea in Warren's novels is a lane leading directly into the past. Many of his characters are like the adult in "Boy's Will, Joyful Labor Without Pay, and Harvest Home (1918)" who thinks of his past: "And the years go by like a breath or eye blink,/ And all history lives in the head again,/ And I shut my eyes and I see that scene. . . ." [9] The effect is frequently a sense of grandeur of perspective, a richness and depth, and a feeling of the sweep of time achieved only in great literature – for example in *Absalom, Absalom!* and *Ulysses*.

The structure of Warren's works, as well as the detail, reflects

---

[8] Woodward, pp. 37-39.
[9] *Promises: Poems 1954-1956* (New York, 1957), p. 81.

his ideas about history. He makes frequent use of irony to illustrate the disparity between the two aspects of man's nature and the distance between man's ideals and the blank historical process. Paradox and ambiguity point up the tremendous complexity of the task of creating worthy moral values from history. By the very plotting of his novels he expresses his belief in the interrelatedness of people and events, the convergence of all history and time at any one moment or in any one event. The plot of *All the King's Men* (1946) perfectly illustrates this: the man whom Jack helps Willie to blackmail turns out to be his own father, and hence Jack is responsible for his death. Furthermore, Warren seldom uses a straightforward, chronological arrangement; rather he goes backward and forward in time, indicating that the past is never really dead.

Because Warren believes that man is guilty of Original Sin and hence capable of any evil, he emphasizes man's need of a tradition, a code of conduct to guide him, to help him to realize the best side of his own humanity more fully and completely. Left to his own devices, man, because of the blackness of his motives, conscious and unconscious, falls into sin and error. Because he believes, further, that the blind neutrality of history threatens human values, Warren feels that history requires a myth to accommodate it to man. Ideally, the tradition and the myth are one, for the myth explains, justifies, and embodies the tradition. An interest in tradition implies an interest in history, a willingness to learn from what people in the past have done and to profit from their errors. This attitude is present in Warren's respect for tradition in literature. He has used time-honored forms creatively. In choosing a structure he says "I think more of trying to find what there is valuable to us, the line of continuity to us and *through* us." [10] As an artist he thus sees himself as a user and bearer of the literary tradition much as T. S. Eliot does, believing that the artist like the individual must try to learn all he can from the past: "I don't know what is meant by the word 'experiment'." [11]

[10]   *The Paris Review Interviews,* p. 195.
[11]   *Ibid.,* p. 198.

In his poetry and his novels he works with an explicit awareness of the traditions of both English and American literature, and he creatively builds upon them.

It is perhaps ironical that Warren, despite his great concern for history and for literary tradition, is known as one of the New Critics who rescued literature from the stifling confinement of historical criticism. The New Criticism, however, has in Warren's theory and practice never been a denial of history or the value of the past and tradition. Rather, it has been an attempt to get literature accepted and appreciated for its own sake, not for the information it communicated or for what it revealed about the author who created it or about the age in which it was created. Far from commending a criticism which slights history and tradition, Warren merely holds that when the critic has exhausted historical concerns in an analysis of a work of art, he has not exhausted the work of art. Slim Sarrett states the point in his paper on Shakespeare: "But the business of criticism is ultimately to disengage itself from the historical accident which, I grant, can only be achieved by mastery of the historical accident." [12] The critic, then, should know his history just as the artist should know the literary traditions, and both should be instructed by them.

Warren in his novels portrays three main groups of characters who have healthy attitudes toward tradition, who offer examples of a purposeful adaptation to life. The agrarians humbly follow the life of their fathers, hard labor growing crops. Associated with this life are the values of integrity, responsibility, submission to a harsh, Old Testament God, honesty, and respect and genuine concern for the rights and welfare of others. Secondly, there are the orthodox Christians, those who submit fully to the will of God and who love their fellow men. These two groups occur almost invariably in the exempla, and they are not completely involved in the main stream of the life depicted in the novel. The third group is made up of those who respect tradition but who realize that change is a necessary aspect of the historical process.

---

[12] *At Heaven's Gate* (New York, 1943), p. 194. All references in the text are to this edition.

These characters, the Hugh Millers and the Cassius Forts, use the traditions of the past creatively and imaginatively and modify them to suit changing times and needs. Completely ignoring the law and tradition as Jeremiah Beaumont does or modifying it at will to suit one's needs of the moment as Willie Stark does are always wrong and dangerous.

Because history is full of danger for man, he needs a myth. Since much of history has no meaning inherent in it, man must make sense of it. The sense he makes of it is part of the myth, and today the burden of our time is that with the old values and beliefs destroyed by science and the ideal of progress we must each construct our own myths. But myths are also needed to explain and justify traditions. Finally, we need them to help us bear the horror of historical reality, for man cannot bear too much brutal truth and maintain his sanity. Myths should go counter to the facts of history only to meet an urgent human need; myths are justified in ordering the facts to make them more bearable or in filtering out some of the horror of existence. Like Ibsen in "The Wild Duck", Warren sees the value of illusions and the "true lie", true, that is, to human values even if false to the brute facts of the historical process. Myth is not superstition, but "a fiction, a construct which expresses a truth and affirms a value". It "defines the myth-maker's world, his position in it, his destiny, and his appropriate attitude".[13] Myth is also total communication appealing to the imaginative, emotional, and spiritual side, and not just to the intellectual; hence it is better able to make its values readily available and more capable of inspiring action than any other type of communication. The artist's greatest task and highest function, Warren believes, is the creation of a valid, usable historical myth for society as a repository of worthy, humane values. He has expended much effort upon the criticism and debunking of historical myths which he considers false to the complex facts of history or ones which he feels embody unworthy values; he has engaged himself especially with those myths that have grown up around the Civil War.

[13] "John Crowe Ransom: A Study in Irony", in *Selected Essays* (New York, 1958), p. 96.

Warren sees the Civil War as the historical event that is most likely to yield a national historical myth. "It is", he has said, "an overwhelming and vital image of human and national experience. We instinctively feel that we can best understand ourselves and our country by it." [14] Most important for Warren's purpose, the Civil War is our only "felt" history [15] – the only history vitally alive in the minds and imaginations of the entire American society. The Civil War thus comes to the artist as a subject already partly mythologized, ready for the artist to shape it creatively and make it even more available.

Wilderness is Warren's attempt to make sense of the blind, coiling mass of complex event and overwhelming detail of the war, a function the novel shares with the historical analysis of *The Legacy of the Civil War*. But the novel goes further than the history: it attempts to embody worthy values, to dramatize them so that they appeal to the emotional, imaginative, and spiritual sides of man. *Wilderness* is thus in many respects similar to myth, sharing its main purpose and functions. Indicative of the novel's kinship with myth is the large number of mythic elements – superstition and mystery, legends, stylized details, the odyssey-like structure, and allusions to myths and mythical characters. At the Fugitives' reunion in Nashville in 1956 a recurring question was why, with all their promise, none of the group had attempted an epic, the creation of a myth for society, the task Homer performed for the Greeks. It cannot be maintained that Warren in *Wilderness* has created a full-fledged native historical myth, the most ambitious goal a writer can set for himself. He does, however, seem to be preparing the way for such a myth by showing the kinship of the Civil War with the stuff from which myths are made, by mythologizing the historical material, that is, throwing over the subject an aura of myth, and by performing well the same task as myth – to dramatically embody worthy values in an appealing story in such a way as to make these values immediate-

---

[14] "The Second American Revolution", *Virginia Quarterly Review*, VII (April 31, 1931), p. 282.
[15] *The Legacy of the Civil War* (New York, 1961), p. 4.

ly available to the audience, so available that they carry over into the reader's own life.

There are other valid reasons for a close study of *Wilderness*. This novel represents the culmination of the trend in Warren away from the technique of proliferation of detail toward a more selective use of facts. It forms a striking contrast with his other novels such as *At Heaven's Gate* and *World Enough and Time*, which are approximately four times as long. Yet unlike the relatively short novel, *The Cave* (1959), *Wilderness* contains all of his major themes in effective and original dramatizations. *Wilderness* illustrates that throughout his career Warren has become more openly and seriously philosophical and concerned with meaning. Fortunately, this tendency toward a concentration on meaning beyond mere faithful reproduction of historical detail has not injured the literary worth of his novel as it well could have done, as a similar concentration has done to the works of Faulkner and Hemingway. Warren is far too concerned with physical presence to neglect factual development and verisimilitude. In fact, *Wilderness* is one of Warren's most artistically successful novels, particularly if we apply one of Warren's favorite critical dicta to it – the effective dramatization of themes in the work of art. Although Warren would allow the writer to deal with any theme whatsoever, even social protest or politics, he believes that the writer must wed his theme "with the concrete projection in experience, that is, his subject".[16] He must imaginatively assimilate his ideas. Theodore Dreiser in *An American Tragedy* was often able to absorb his theme imaginatively so that form and idea became one.[17]

A philosophical novelist such as Warren runs this risk of lack of assimilation of theme to a great extent; if he fails to avoid the risk he may become merely a propagandist. This has been one of Warren's knottiest problems, and he has not always solved it satisfactorily. In 'The Ballad of Billie Potts", for example, the

---

[16] "Literature as a Symptom", in *Who Owns America: A New Declaration of Independence*, ed. by Herbert Agar and Allen Tate (Boston and New York, 1938), p. 279.

[17] "An American Tragedy", *Yale Review*, LII (October, 1962), p. 5.

narrative and the commentary split apart. As Floyd C. Watkins states, the simple folk story is inadequate to bear the weight of philosophical commentary with which Warren loads it.[18] Confronting the same problem – the necessity to comment upon the action – in *Night Rider, All the King's Men,* and *Band of Angels* (1955), Warren has relied upon the device of an inserted exemplum, a story within a story. Although these exempla, which carry much of the philosophical burden of the novels, are adequate and even excellent as short stories – all were published separately – they are intrusions and represent an admission that the novelist was unable to dramatize his ideas in his main narrative. *The Cave* has no exemplum, but it also lacks much of the philosophical and historical richness characteristic of the other novels. *Wilderness* is the first novel in which Warren has been able to dispense with such intrusions, and it is also one of his most notable successes in the blending of theme and subject into an artistic whole. With *Flood* (1964) he continues this success.

Just as the philosophical novelist faces the danger of a split in narrative and commentary, the historical novelist, writing in one of the most abused genres, runs the risk of descending into melodrama. Again, Warren has not always avoided this pitfall. *Band of Angels* is as full of outrageous examples of stagey, unconvincing melodrama as a second-rate Victorian novel, Hollywood epic, or popular magazine short story. There is, for example, the slave auction scene, in which noble old Hamish Bond gracefully and easily intimidates and disarms the vulgar young dandy who tries to examine poor little Manty cowering on the block. Even technicolor, wide screen, and Clark Gable could not do full justice to such a scene. This is, of course, Warren at his worst. *Wilderness,* however, is almost completely lacking in such melodramatic scenes. He avoids melodrama first by originality, by avoiding triteness. Historical novels from those of Scott to those of Howard Fast almost invariably contain at least some sex; it is to be expected. Yet *Wilderness* is nearly sexless. We expect dramatic

---

[18] Floyd C. Watkins, "Billie Potts at the Fall of Time", *Mississippi Quarterly*, XI (Winter, 1958), pp. 26-27.

and often sentimental confrontations and partings such as the scene between Jack Burden and his mother or those in *War and Peace*. Yet Adam leaves the farm of Maran Meyerhof without even a goodbye. We expect also impressive scenes, but Warren keeps the large battles, the dramatic fighting and dying in the background. Despite the title, the Battle of the Wilderness never comes center stage. It is there, and the reader is always aware of it, but it comes to him as it comes to Adam, as a muffled roar. *Wilderness* also well illustrates that Warren's concern with and interest in the facts of the past and the meaning of history – the concerns of a historian – have not hindered him artistically; just the opposite is true, for his use of history and of the related subjects of tradition and myth is one of the best aspects of his novels and contributes significantly to the success of much of his poetry.

II

THE FACTS OF THE PAST

Robert Penn Warren is both a historian and a historical novelist. He has used the events of American history, particularly Southern history, in his novels, poems, short stories, and in occasional books and articles on history. In his historical studies he does much the same as in his fiction – he documents and interprets the facts of the past with careful scholarship and uses them to generalize from. Much of the success of his histories and his historical novels derives from his respect for facts and details and his inclusive method. This respect for factual details is a direct result of his philosophical and critical theories. Abstractions, he believes, represent a particularly dangerous trend of modern, secular, scientific society. History and fiction not grounded in the specific, vitalizing details lack life, warmth, interest, and emotional and imaginative appeal. His method of exhaustively cataloging facts and details derives from his belief in the complexity of history and human life and the danger of a partial, oversimplified view. The facts of history gleaned from books, diaries, journals, newspapers and eyewitnesses' accounts, then, are to Warren extremely valuable and important in fiction, but they alone are not all-important. Since he believes that the mere facts cannot give the whole truth, he goes beyond them. And facts must, in fiction, do more than re-create in detail an historical event or era. They should participate organically in the form by affording revealing vignettes or by rising to the status of symbol. Warren is extremely careful with the realistic surface of his novels, as can be seen in his exacting historical research, his writing about a region and its history which he knows intimately, and his meticulous factuality and accuracy. But he uses accurately observed details creatively. By selection and control he gives them significance and appeal. A study of Warren's historical writings, his use of historical facts in his novels, and his philosophical and critical justification of his use of these details, reveals that his development has been toward a more selective and creative use of the facts of the past, less pure documentation, and less reliance upon actual historical situations. This trend, however, has not been accompanied by less respect for the value of facts, nor has, in general, the verisimilitude of his novels suffered.

1

Beyond his use of history in his creative work, Robert Penn Warren has proved himself to be, for the most part, a competent historian in the conventional history he has written. His first published book, *John Brown: The Making of a Martyr* (1929), is a historical biography of this fanatical abolitionist. "The Briar Patch', his contribution to *I'll Take My Stand*, touches upon many of the same themes. In *The Legacy of the Civil War* (1961) he analyzes the causes, consequences, and meaning of the great American conflict. *Segregation: The Inner Conflict in the South* (1956) documents a problem in social history as it manifests itself in the present, and Warren here sets the racial conflict in a historical context, thus giving it added perspective. *Who Speaks For the Negro?* is his remarkable attempt to make sense of the confusion of shifting loyalties, goals, and leadership in the Civil Rights Movement. His historical articles include "The War and the National Monuments", a scrupulous documentation of the removal of the chief American documents such as the Constitution and the Articles of Confederation from the Library of Congress to Fort Knox during World War II, and a detailed history of the elaborate care they were given. "Remember the Alamo!" and "How Texas Won Her Freedom" are stirring narratives of some of the most dramatic events in the history of Texas. In these historical studies we can see his scholarly attention to the facts of history and his careful interpretation and evaluation of the events he is studying. Without sacrificing richness of detail, Warren in his histories has become more concerned with interpreting the past rather than with massively documenting it. He has, also, become a better historian, less biased and much surer in his handling of fact and meaning. And his attitude has become more tentative and questioning, the best attitude for a historian desiring to present several sides of the issues, the complexity of events, and the multiplicity of the facts of the past which must be kept in mind in reaching generalizations.

Surprisingly, *John Brown: The Making of a Martyr*, written while Warren was a graduate student at Yale, is a failure both as a history and as an assessment of Brown, although it is successful in re-creating the historical period. Ignoring sound scholarship, Warren even resorts to the fictional device of reading Brown's mind, revealing his thoughts and emotions for which there is no documentary evidence. But the worst fault of the book is his bias, which glares forth from almost every line. As in "The Briar Patch" Warren views the Negro as a simple, happy, fun-loving creature fitted only for small farming and domestic service, who "never bothered his kinky head about the moral issue [of slavery] and for him the matter simply remained one of convenience or inconvenience".[1] And he is all too obviously trying to discredit Brown and his supporters, to burn them in effigy, as Leonard Casper says,[2] rather than trying to present the past in all its complexity and ambiguity; he indulges in immature and bitter iconoclasm at the expense of sound historical research. His prejudice reaches almost comical proportions at times, and he even ignores evidence that he himself has given. After stating that Brown steadfastly refused to implicate others at Harper's Ferry, that he would not plead insanity to save his life, and that he refused any escape attempt, Warren makes much over the fact that the condemned man devoted his last days to securing financial

---

[1] *John Brown: The Making of a Martyr* (New York, 1929), p. 348.
[2] Leonard Casper, *Robert Penn Warren: The Dark and Bloody Ground* (Seattle, 1960), p. 90.

assistance for his wife and family. This proves, Warren asserts, that Brown was using the abolition crusade to make money.[3]

In addition to the fault of its bias, Warren's interpretation of Brown is logically inconsistent. Depending upon the whim of the moment, he treats Brown as either a shrewd but dishonest mercenary or a completely irrational madman. In *John Brown*, then, Warren is guilty of the very things he has warned against, a one-sided attack, ignoring the tremendous complexities which he believes inhere in any historical event or any human motivation. He is as guilty of writing propaganda as any of the liberal or proletarian writers he attacks. Yet all is not lost in Warren's first book. Even in this biased work his historical imagination – the ability to enter imaginatively into the life of a past age and the ability to bring it to life for the reader – and his love of accuracy of detail are in full evidence. He has brilliantly documented the world through which Brown moved, and reproduced what John L. Stewart calls the "texture" of that age.[4] In presenting Brown's involved financial affairs, for example, Warren exhibits a considerable detailed knowledge of the wool business and the financial practices of the time – an understanding that a writer less interested in the complexity of details which make up history could easily have ignored. Also, one remembers the big scenes that Warren makes come alive, such scenes as the brutal Pottawatomie massacre and the tenseness and exaltation as old Brown and his men await the resolution of their fanatical dreams in the little farm house outside Harper's Ferry.

Though less ambitious than *John Brown*, Warren's three main historical articles are less biased and more scholarly. His next piece of historical writing required little interpretation, for it is almost entirely reportorial. While editor of *The Quarterly Journal of Current Acquisitions* in 1944 at the Library of Congress, Warren wrote a detailed account of the removal of America's most precious documents, the Articles of Confederation, the Declaration of Independence, and the Constitution, from

---

[3] *John Brown*, pp. 429-30.
[4] John L. Stewart, "Robert Penn Warren and the Knot of History", *ELH*, XXVI (March, 1959), p. 104.

Washington to Fort Knox, where they would be safer from the threat of enemy bombing. In this article, "The War and the National Monuments", Warren is performing two functions: he is preserving for posterity a detailed account of an important event, and he is writing the history of the care of these documents through the years prior to their removal. No piece of writing better evidences his love of accuracy and his eye for details and facts, for the minutiae of experience:

The task of packing was completed by five o'clock. Immediately the cases were loaded into an armed and escorted truck of the Bureau of Engraving and Printing, and driven to the Union Station. There the cases were transferred to compartment B, car A-1 (Pullman sleeper "Eastlake"), of the "National Limited" of the Baltimore and Ohio Railroad. The compartments adjoining and interconnecting on each side were occupied by Messrs. Shannon and Moriarity of the U.S. Secret Service, and by Mr. Clapp, Director of the Acquisitions Department of the Library. The secret service guards were armed. In fact, the entire responsibility for the protection of the documents in their travels was borne by the Secret Service of the Treasury Department.[5]

The two related articles "Remember the Alamo!" and "How Texas Won Her Freedom" analyze the meaning of the events and their modern relevance. He attempts in these to give a full, detailed account of the struggle and to set it in historical perspective. He gives battle plans, formations, and tactics as well as the ancestry and future of the characters. He illustrates the tremendous complexity and ambiguity inherent in any historical event.

As a social history, *Segregation: The Inner Conflict in the South* (1956) is a sensitive and fair presentation and interpretation of a long-standing American social problem. Warren recorded his conversations with fellow Southerners during a tour of the South after the Supreme Court's decision declared segregation in schools unconstitutional. He tries to document and interpret the South's attitude in all its various manifestations and in all its complexity. He frankly states that he himself is for desegregation

---

[5] "The War and the National Monuments", *Library of Congress Quarterly Journal of Current Acquisitions*, II (September, 1944), p. 70.

as rapidly as practicable, but here he is more objective and tentative than in *John Brown*, and he does not let his own views control his evidence and interpretations. The views the people represent do not control the way in which Warren describes them. Indeed, some less objective critics who should agree with him missed his point. L. D. Reddick, a Negro critic, claims that Warren is no better than the mobs of racists howling outside Southern schools.[6] But Warren presents both sides fairly and sympathetically, and he never passes judgment. In *Segregation* he attempts to allow the fully documented moment of history to speak for itself. As a historian Warren has come a long way since *John Brown*.

The Legacy of the Civil War (1961) studies the historical event in the American past to which Warren attaches the most importance – the Civil War. This work marks the culmination in Warren's historical writing of an emphasis on philosophy rather than on the facts of the past. Here, rather than telling the story of this event or some part of it, he analyzes the causes and consequences of the War, concerning himself mostly with what modern America can learn from this bloody event in its past. It is more of a comment upon the meaning of the events than a history of them. As Warren sees it the chief cause of the War was the two irreconcilable states of mind: the "higher law" attitude of the North which led to a denial of compromise, because the abolitionists and transcendentalists who held this view believed themselves privy to God, and the legalistic state of mind of the Southern leaders, which resulted in a denial of change, even gradual change. Warren's originality and profundity is most in evidence in his description of the legacies, the problems resulting from the war. From the war and Reconstruction the South developed "the Great Alibi", which excuses everything, including laziness, hate, and prejudice on the basis that they are victims of history; the North developed "the treasury of virtue" which absolves them of everything – including such evils as exploitation

---

[6]   L. D. Reddick, "Whose Ordeal?", *New Republic*, CXXXV (September 24, 1956), pp. 9-10.

and greed – because they believe they fought a just, noble war for the ideal of human freedom. Warren presents neither side as more noble or more villainous than the other; both, he knows, share the guilt and responsibility for causes and results. Although he suggests the social, political, and economic results of the war, such as the growth of big business and finance capitalism, mass production, the westward expansion, the solid South, centralization in New York and Washington, he attaches more importance to the psychological and moral effects of the conflict, what it has done to the national mind, the rationalization and hate that came as a result. Warren in this study writes as a philosopher of history considering such questions as the meaning of the past and its lessons for the present. These are the questions the serious historian must ultimately ponder. But he must first, Warren knows, master the facts and details. He must ground his observations, his philosophy, in the concrete in order to make them meaningful to the reader; Warren has done this in *The Legacy of the Civil War*. The following passage on the South's unionism illustrates how well Warren has derived the general from the particular and how well he has made the meaning live by clothing it with human details.

This unionism was, we must remember, particularly ferocious in the South, as the old Jackson, the young Calhoun, and many a Whig planter, even in 1860, would testify. We can recall with what reluctance Jefferson Davis or Stonewall Jackson took the step toward disunion, and lately some historians find the corrosive of a crypto-unionism deep in many a Conferedate breast less eminent than that of General Lee. When General Pickett, leading his division on the road to Gettysburg, passed a little Dutch girl defiantly waving the Federal Flag, he took off his hat and bowed to her. Asked why he had saluted the flag of the enemy, he replied: "I did not salute the enemy's flag. I saluted the heroic womanhood in the heart of that brave little girl, and the glorious banner under which I won my first laurels." True or not, the tale, reported by LaSalle Corbell Pickett, points to a truth. Shared experience of the past and shared hopes for the future could not easily be expunged; and I myself have heard an old man who had ridden three years with Forrest, and never regretted that fact, say that he would have sadly regretted the sight of this country "Balkanized." [7]

[7] *Legacy*, pp. 5-6.

The lessons Warren would have us learn from the event are not the obvious ones, certainly not the ones the author of *John Brown* derived from it. Now Warren states that "the events of Tuscaloosa, Little Rock, and New Orleans are nothing more than an obscene parody" of Southern history, and asks "Can the man howling in the mob imagine General Robert E. Lee, CSA, shaking hands with Orval Faubus, Governor of Arkansas?" [8] Beyond this particular lesson, the study of the Civil War, Warren believes, in all its complexity affirms "the possibility of the dignity of life" – a "tragic dignity". And a contemplation of this grand story may result in some of its grandeur rubbing off on us.[9] That is to say, an imaginative, full study of the war in all its confusion and ambivalence may provide modern America with a goal for which to strive – a goal more real because of the fact that the ideal once, in our past, strove to become flesh at least in the hearts of many of its participants. As a historian Robert Penn Warren thus exhibits the originality and learning that are so much in evidence in his fiction, criticism, and poetry. His best work is fair and unprejudiced, and all his historical writing exhibits the style, the eye for the exact, telling detail, and the narrative ability apparent in his best novels. And while progressing from more of a concern with meaning than with documentation, he has simultaneously become a better, a more impartial historian. In *Who Speaks for the Negro?*, Warren is present as a skilled interviewer leading his subjects to reveal themselves more fully than most imagined possible. Here he never comments directly, but his presence is felt by the calm rationality and good will shown in his questions.

Because of his love of the past and his scholarly interest in it, Warren quite naturally turned to the writing of historical novels, one of the dominant genres of the thirties when he began his novelistic career. Of his seven novels, *Night Rider*, *World Enough and Time*, *Band of Angels*, and *Wilderness* are clearly historical in that they re-create a past time. *At Heaven's Gate*, *All the*

[8]   *Ibid.*, p. 57.
[9]   *Ibid.*, p. 109.

King's Men, The Cave, and *Flood* confront the same problems
but have as subjects the characters and events of the more recent
past. Warren has said that the writing of *At Heaven's Gate*
whetted his appetite to compose "a highly documented picture of
the modern world",[10] a picture which he gave in *All the King's
Men.*

2

Michel Mohrt accurately describes these novels as "chronicles
of an era in which the imagination is guided and limited by
historical themes".[11] Indeed, so great is his "romantic kind of
interest" in the facts of the past [12] that he frequently admires
works that provide a strong insight into a particular historical
time or event, paying little attention to the question of literary
merit. He finds, for example, Theodore Dreiser's novels admirable for their "documentary value" which gives "the color of a
period".[13] He says of *An American Tragedy*:

We also feel, in this book, the burden of a historical moment, the
moment of the Great Boom which climaxed the period from Grant to
Coolidge, the half century in which the new America was hardening
into shape and its secret forces were emerging to dominate all life. In
other words, *An American Tragedy* can be taken as a document, both
personal and historical, and it is often admired, and defended, in
these terms.[14]

The historical novel gives Warren ample scope for this love of
historical documentation, whether he describes the organization
and rituals of the Tobacco Grower's Asociation, the intricacies
of the world of high finance, Southern statehouse politics, a New
Orleans slave auction, "High Juba" in the slave quarters, small

10 "A Note to *All the King's Men*", *Sewanee Review*, LXI (Summer,
1953), p. 478.
11 Michel Mohrt, "Robert Penn Warren and the Myth of the Outlaw",
Yale French Studies, No. 10 (1953), p. 74.
12 *The Paris Review Interviews*, p. 188.
13 "An American Tragedy", p. 3.
14 *Ibid.*, p. 5.

town life in modern Tennessee, or the intense boredom of soldiers in winter quarters during the Civil War.

There are several good reasons for Warren's use of the historical novel. An awareness of history, he has said, is central in his work,[15] and he indicates this awareness by dealing with his ideas on history within a historical context. Speculations about the meaning of history thus arise naturally from consideration of the particular historical event he writes of. Subject and theme reinforce one another. Fiction, Warren has stated, has two poles: history and idea. And the writer must validate his thematic considerations ("idea") in terms of circumstance and experience ("history") never in the poverty of statement.[16] In most of his works, poetry included, the abstract, the general, the universal are related to the particulars of a localized historical setting, characters, and events. His method is to take a historical event, record it with heavy documentation, and extract from it philosophical meaning. Like Shakespeare he looks to stories from the past from which to derive timeless, universal messages.

Finally, Warren finds in historical events effective counterparts to his ideas – so effective that frequently the past event can serve as a symbol for his theme. The romantic trappings of Jeremiah Beauchamp's *Confession*, for example, suggested to Warren a historical novel in which these paraphernalia could be ironically commented upon. Part of his theme thus inheres in the historical story itself. In *Segregation* he has said that the race question in the United States becomes "a total symbolism for every kind of issue",[17] and in *The Legacy of the Civil War* he sees the war as a mirror of the deep conflicts within the individual. These issues and events in his novels counterpoint his themes. In *Band of Angels* the vivid background of confusion – military campaigns, riots, the political, social, and economic chaos of the war – suggest and emphasize the disorientation and inner turmoil of the characters. And Manty's failure to confess her Negro blood is em-

---

[15] *The Paris Review Interviews*, p. 188.
[16] "Irony with a Center: Katherine Anne Porter", in *Selected Essays*, p. 155.
[17] *Segregation: The Inner Conflict in the South* (New York, 1956), p. 155.

blematic of the failure of man to admit his own guilt and sin. Of *All the King's Men* Warren has said: "Politics merely provided the framework story in which the deeper concerns, whatever their final significance, might work themselves out".[18] Corrupt politics mirror individual and social corruption. Warren, then, has chosen the historical novel as the chief vehicle for his themes because of his interest in the facts of the past, because the meaning of history is in itself a major theme, and because in the events of the past he has been able to find vivid stories to embody his thematic concerns.

Warren has also been concerned with the art of the historical novel, with what it should and should not be, and his comments add up to a thoughtful critique of his most usual genre. He is not impressed with the historical novel as it is usually written. Criticizing the unimaginative exploitation of local color by second-rate novelists who neglect meaning for manners, Warren similarly objects: "The historical novel, as ordinarily conceived, is equally deficient in the same respect; manners tend to be substituted for value, and costume and decor for an essential relationship between man and his background both natural and social. The result is another form of the quaint, again incomplete and un-philosophical." [19] Documentation and scholarship by themselves will not guarantee the success of a work of art. "You don't 'work up' literature." "You can't research to get a book. You stumble on it, or hope to. Maybe you will if you live right." [20] The historical novel, then, must be concerned with meaning as well as fact, costume, and decor. Warren has stated that he put Jack Burden into *All the King's Men* to keep it from being a straight naturalistic novel,[21] the kind Hamilton Basso and John Dos Passos wrote using the same subject.

Warren has also been highly critical of those historical novelists who are deficient in the historical imagination – the ability to

---

[18] "A Note to *All the King's Men*", p. 480.
[19] "Not Local Color", *Virginia Quarterly Review*, VIII (January, 1932), p. 154.
[20] *The Paris Review Interviews*, pp. 196-97.
[21] "A Note to *All the King's Men*", p. 478.

project oneself into the past and to see it as different from an extension backward in time of the present and the talent to make it come vividly alive. The historical novels of T. S. Stribling, Warren maintains, are merely extensions of his contemporary sociology. His historical sense is deficient because he has failed to understand the special historical contexts in which he sets his novels.[22] The writer must enter into the past imaginatively and creatively; he must shed his modernity. Warren has done this so well that he has become increasingly impatient with the limitations of historical fact, the actual record. *Brother to Dragons*, for example, although it deals with a real event and historical characters, portrays a meeting which never took place. It is set in "no time" and "no place". "This would", he explains, "allow me, I hoped, to get out of the box of mere chronology, and of incidental circumstantiality." [23] That he has been able to do this has become increasingly more evident in his novels.

In his early novels, poetry, and short stories Warren looked to the past for events and characters as well as atmosphere. His historical imagination seemed to require the stimulation of actual people and events. In his poetry and short stories the past he re-creates is often his own personal one. Many of the early pieces in *Selected Poems*, for example, are partly autobiographical; and the accuracy with which he evokes the Southern background, mostly Kentucky, Tennessee, and Louisiana, owes a great deal to personal experience and observation. This is especially apparent in such poems as "Bearded Oaks", "The Return: An Elegy", and "Kentucky Mountain Farm". The impulse behind his fine short story "Blackberry Winter", Warren has said, was a nostalgic reminiscence of his past: "Hunting old bearings and bench marks, if you wish. Trying to make a fresh start, if you wish. Whatever people do in their doubleness of living in a present and a past." [24]

---

[22] "T. S. Stribling: A Paragraph in the History of Critical Realism", *American Review*, II (February, 1934), p. 476.
[23] "The Way It Was Written (*Brother to Dragons*)", *New York Times Book Review* (August 23, 1953), p. 60.
[24] "How a Story Was Born and How, Bit by Bit, It Grew", *New York Times Book Review* (March, 1959), p. 5.

The portrait of the father in the story is a tribute to his own father, and the boy, who is initiated into life in rural Tennessee, is modeled after himself. "Prime Leaf", "Testament of Flood", "The Love of Elsie Barton: a Chronicle", and "A Christian Education" were all inspired by his own early life; they show, according to Henry Nash Smith, "How his imagination has nourished itself upon Proustian exploration of a remembered world of childhood in Northwestern Tennessee".[25] His first book, *John Brown*, was, however, a step toward fiction because he exercised his historical imagination upon facts gleaned from research and historical themes he had long been interested in – the period leading up to the Civil War. Also, his unpublished novel *God's Own Time* (1931-1933) was based on historical research rather than personal experience, for the book deals with the life and career of Thomas Hardy.

But in *Night Rider* personal experience is combined with careful scholarship to produce an effective historical novel. The tobacco wars, a violent clash between the growers who were attempting to get a fair price for their tobacco and the huge companies who had banded together to set prices ruinously low, took place between the years 1904-1911 in Warren's boyhood and centered around his home town of Guthrie, Kentucky, the heart of the dark-fired tobacco region. One of his earliest memories is of troops stationed in Guthrie to keep the farmers from blowing up the company warehouses. So immediate are the events of the conflict to Warren, that he does not regard *Night Rider* as a historical novel.[26] And he denies any but a minimal connection with the historical events: "Although this book was suggested by certain events which took place in Kentucky in the early years of the century, it is not, in any strict sense a historical novel. And more particularly, the characters in this book are not to be identified with any actual persons, living or dead, who participated in those events."[27] J. Letargeez, however, has shown that Warren

[25] Henry Nash Smith, "Proustian Exploration", *Saturday Review of Literature*, XXII (January 31, 1948), p. 14.
[26] *The Paris Review Interviews*, p. 182.
[27] *Night Rider* (Boston, 1939), frontpiece. All references in the text are to this edition.

has added to personal recollection a detailed knowledge of James O. Nall's *The Tobacco Night Riders of Kentucky and Tennessee*,[28] the most authoritative source of information about these dramatic events from Southern history. Despite Warren's denial the entire outline of the novel is factual. And some of the characters are closely modeled after actual participants; Dr. MacDonald, for example, was suggested by Dr. David A. Amoss, one of the leading organizers of the night riders. The climactic event of both *Night Rider* and Nall's account is the raid on Hopkinsville and the blowing up of the warehouses. Even the route followed by Dr. MacDonald is the exact route taken by Dr. Amoss, which Nall gives in a map. The only significant departure from Nall's narrative is the shooting, which is Warren's addition, and the character of Perse Munn, who is almost entirely Warren's invention. Obviously then, the background, the setting and the narrative framework, and even some of the characters of Warren's first novel are based closely on history – both from his own memory and an authoritative source. Warren in *Night Rider* has obviously gone to history for more than just hints.

The next two novels, *At Heaven's Gate* (1943) and *All the King's Men* (1946), are closely related to historical events which had affected Warren personally. *At Heaven's Gate* is modeled quite recognizably on the career of the wealthy and unscrupulous financier, Luke Lea, who rose to the heights of wealth and political influence in Tennessee during Warren's undergraduate days at Vanderbilt. Along with Donald Davidson and Allen Tate, Warren while in college wrote for the book page of the Nashville *Tennessean*, one of Lea's papers. In the novel Lea becomes the monstrous, inhuman Bogan Murdock, who exploits the land and its people, turning them away from the soil to industry and finance capitalism. And in the career of both, the plot to buy up huge grasslands properties triggered their downfall. Private Porsum, the war hero, is drawn quite recognizably from Sergeant Alvin York. Even small details are taken from life. Slim's paper

---

[28] J. Letargeez, "Robert Penn Warren's Views of History", *Revue des langues vivantes*, XXII (1956), p. 540.

on Shakespeare, for instance, is an almost verbatim transcript of Professor Curry's lectures at Vanderbilt, according to several of Curry's former students.

Resulting from Warren's teaching at the Louisiana State University was *All the King's Men*, which owed much of its popular success to the journalistic relevance of its theme. Huey Long was governor while Warren was teaching at the university, and Long did not refrain from playing politics with the school and meddling in its affairs. In fact it was Long's generous financial support that made possible one of the most distinguished of literary magazines, *The Southern Review*, which Warren helped to edit. Warren was of course not a hireling of Huey Long as Robert Gorham Davis implies,[29] but his position did give him a unique opportunity to observe Long and his world in operation. The plot of the novel closely follows Long's career. Warren admits: "Certainly, it was the career of Long and the atmosphere of Louisiana that suggested the play that was to become the novel. But suggestion is not identity." [30] Willie Stark is in part Huey Long, and Adam Stanton is based partly on the actual assassin, Dr. Weiss, who had a number of grievances against Long, none of which, however, closely resembles the motives behind Adam's acts. Most of the other characters, including the main one, Jack Burden, are Warren's invention. Indeed, the actual history of Long and his regime is important primarily as it affects Jack, the narrator. And he experiences it fully because he was part of it, and as a historian and an aware intellectual he can logically comment upon the meaning of the bit of history he has lived through. Jack got in the novel, according to Warren, to keep it from being a purely naturalistic work. "The impingement of that material [the Willie Stark story], I thought, upon a special temperament would allow another perspective than the reportorial one, and would give a basis for some range of style." "And the story, in a sense, became the story of Jack Burden, the teller of

---

[29] Robert Gorham Davis, "Dr. Stanton's Dilemma", *New York Times Book Review* (August 18, 1946), p. 3.
[30] "A Note to *All the King's Men*", p. 480.

the tale." [31] Thus in *All the King's Men* Warren, with the use of a historian narrator, can both document the Huey Long regime and comment naturally upon its meaning and significance.

In his next novel, *World Enough and Time*, Warren turned to the more distant past, the Kentucky of the 1820's, for his story. This novel offers the best opportunity for a comparison with the historical sources from which it derives, since it closely follows Beauchamp's *Confession* and the famous Sharp-Beauchamp murder trial which also inspired such writers as Poe and Simms. Warren's statement that he spent five minutes reading the *Confession*, which Katherine Anne Porter showed him at the Library of Congress, and six years composing the novel is belied by the close similarity between the novel and the *Confession*, newspapers, diaries, letters, and official records which Warren as a good historian examined with obvious care. His love of examining the past through its records found ample material here, for even before Beauchamp was hanged in 1826 the affair, because of its melodrama and sentimental appeal, and background of politics, had not only received much newspaper publicity but had also become a frontier legend with ballads and stories based upon it. The novel's plot closely follows the historical narrative. Most of the incidental events were suggested by the records, and even most of the minor characters were at least mentioned in the *Confession*. The elaborate preparations of Jeremiah to murder Fort, plans which Warren describes with minute detail, are factually accurate. And James H. Justus concludes that there is at least some support in the *Confession* for the philosophy and morals in Warren's novel.[32]

Furthermore, Warren omits no actual history that bears upon the characters and events of his novel. He details such historical background material as the Blair-Williams decision by Judge James Clark, the political campaigns between members of the Old Court and those of the New Court, the depression of the

---

[31] *Ibid.*, p. 478.
[32] James H. Justus, "Warren's *World Enough and Time* and Beauchamp's *Confession*", *American Literature*, XXXIII (January, 1962), p. 501.

1820's and its effects on credit, financial speculation in Western lands, the intricacies of the law and the trial with a detailed discussion of Jerry's case by various newspapers, and the complicated political maneuverings of both parties. Yet Warren has freely departed from the facts he gathered from research. Rachel Jordan bears little resemblance to Ann Cook, who was ugly, brutal (she herself fought a duel), and a monomaniac about the revenge of her "honor". Warren alters her to make of her a more sentimental heroine, and he makes her less aggressive in order to increase Jeremiah's responsibility. The ending, however, is the most notable departure from strict historical accuracy. Beauchamp was hanged, but Beaumont escapes jail for an adventure in the malarial swamps of the Mississippi, the domain of the fantastic La Gran' Bosse, only to be decapitated by Wilkie's henchmen as he returns to accept responsibility for his deed. Since this change is dramatically anticlimactic as well as historically untrue, it was obviously made to confirm and extend the philosophical themes. At this stage of his career Warren no longer felt constrained to follow slavishly the historical record.

He narrates this novel as a historian, a non-participant, a scholar looking back on the events over a hundred years later, trying to decipher the record, to make it speak to modern man. This point of view adds another perspective, the modern one, to the material, and it allows Warren to philosophize upon the history; it also provides him with a reason for including background material and for going forward in time later than the story of Jeremiah Beaumont, as he did with Jerry's lawyers, for example. Hilton Hawgood, a noble Anti-Relief lawyer, offers his services to Jeremiah in the interest of justice. Warren does not merely give his background; he also follows his subsequent career. "He had great abilities, and at a tender age was to become Attorney General of Kentucky, and a Member of Congress. The abilities are remembered at least in the two or three paragraphs allotted to him in the histories of the Commonwealth, but the legend of his integrity lived for a time on the tongues of men as well as on the printed page." "Hilton Hawgood died very young at Washington, during his first session in Congress. He died of a fever after but a few days of illness." [33]

In his next novels, *Band of Angels* (1955) and *The Cave* (1959), as in his narrative poem *Brother to Dragons* (1953), Warren has departed much further from the historical record than ever before. In *Band of Angels* Warren, for the first time, does not base his plot upon any one historical event and does not model his major characters after any historical personages. But the background, including the siege of New Orleans, the New Orleans riots, the corrupt regime of General "Beast" Butler, and the temper of the Gilded Age, is accurately documented. The meticulous factuality of *Band of Angels* had its inception, Warren has said, in his historical research; he mentions particularly Winston Cateman's *Slavery Days in Kentucky*, Canot's autobiography, memoirs of officers on slave patrol, hearings in the British Parliament, and other documents from the Brown University and Yale collections.[34] The historical facts, however, are so absorbed into the terms of the life of the novel that the reader never feels that Warren is giving him a history lesson. We learn, for example, about the results of the passage of the Fourteenth Amendment from Amantha Starr, who has good cause to be bitter and ironic about the results of Northern legislation designed to free the Negro:

The Amendment didn't give the Negro the vote, but it was understood that it would get him the vote in the Rebel states. Failure to ratify, failure to give the vote, would mean the refusal of Congress to admit representatives. The happy fate of Tennessee made that clear. Tennessee ratified immediately and immediately in July, their representatives were seated in Washington.

But in Louisiana it was different. The legislature wasn't in session. No special session was called. The Democrats didn't want a special session because they still hoped, perhaps, that President Johnson would win, that the West would help him, that the Fourteenth Amendment would fail of general ratification. As for the Radicals, at least most of them, they didn't want a special session either, for

---

[33] *World Enough and Time: A Romantic Novel* (New York, 1950), pp. 281-82. All references in the text are to this edition.
[34] Casper, *The Dark and Bloody Ground*, note 28, p. 188.

ratification would, presumably, leave the present incumbents in office in the state.

No, they had a bolder plan. They would cut the present government off, root and branch, and cast it into the fire. (p. 294)

Warren derived the story of *Brother to Dragons* from the folklore of Kentucky and from accounts in old newspapers and abolition literature in the Library of Congress. His comments upon the composition of this poem indicate well how he has come to use historical events: "I am trying to write a poem and not a history, and therefore have no compunction about the tampering with facts", he says in his introduction. "But poetry is more than fantasy and is committed to the obligation of trying to say something about the human condition. Therefore, a poem dealing with history is no more at liberty to violate what the writer takes to be the spirit of history than it is at liberty to violate what the writer takes to be the nature of the human heart." [35] But the writer, Warren knows, must first master the historical facts before he can determine the spirit of his history. The gory butchering of the slave, George, in the meat house by Jefferson's nephews is a documented historical event, but Jefferson's reaction is entirely imaginary as is the meeting of all the characters, both the living and the dead, in "no time" and "no place". In other words, Warren here merely stimulates his imagination with the historical record and makes very little attempt to achieve complete factual accuracy, believing thematic considerations to be more important and a better way to get at the underlying "truth". In commenting on his poem he has said, for example, that theme rather than historical fact dictated Meriwether Lewis' suicide.[36]

Warren in *The Cave* (1959) relies even less upon historical record than in *Band of Angels* and *Brother to Dragons*. There is in this novel very little connection, beyond the generalized situation of a man trapped in a cave, with the story of Floyd Collins which occurred in 1925 when Warren was a student at Vanderbilt. And *The Cave*, like the almost wholly imaginary *Flood*

---

[35] *Brother to Dragons: A Tale in Verse and Voices* (New York, 1953), p. XII. All references in the text are to this edition.
[36] "The Way It Was Written", p. 6.

(1964), is set in modern Tennessee, not the Tennessee of the twenties. Throughout his career, then, Warren has moved further and further away from strict adherence to historical events and characters toward a more imaginative evocation of the past after mastering the facts from historical research.

In none of his novels, even those that closely follow a particular event, is Warren working only as a historian or a reporter. But his novels, especially *All the King's Men* because of its contemporary subject and setting and because of the violence with which many react to Huey Long, have often been interpreted in this way. Hamilton Basso, who also based a novel on Long's career, reads *All the King's Men* as an apologetic biography of Long and criticizes Warren for inventing characters and incidents, and for not adhering strictly to facts.[37] Warren correctly believes that the fact that he stimulates his imagination with real events, contemporary or historical, in no way effects their being classed as imaginative creations. Writing of Dreiser's *An American Tragedy*, Warren states that the fact that Clyde was modeled on a real person does not make him any less a creation. "Rather, it emphasizes that he is a creation" because of the contrast between "the dreary factuality of an old newspaper account and the anguishing inwardness of the personal story".[38] Literature, he has explained, does two things: "Literature looks out – it records a world. Literature looks in – it records a man." [39] Both processes, however, are controlled by the creative imagination, which gives a vision of form, so that the finished product is a living thing, neither history nor autobiography, though partaking of both. Just as a comparison of Shakespeare's plays with their sources in Holinshed and elsewhere reveals the magnitude of his imagination, a comparison of Warren's novels with their sources merely makes one realize the greatness of his achievement. His purpose is not to reconstruct history but to achieve universality within the

---

[37] Hamilton Basso, "The Huey Long Legend", *Life*, XXI (December 9, 1946), p. 121.
[38] "An American Tragedy", p. 6.
[39] "The Veins of Irony", *University: A Princeton Magazine*, Nos. 17-18 (Summer-Fall, 1963), p. 12.

context of the specific historical event. Hence, he refuses to identify any of his characters merely with Luke Lea, Huey Long, or Floyd Collins. He is in this way able to transcend the narrow limitation of historical fact.

3

Partly because of his respect for specific details and for physical presence, Warren is a regionalist, for as much as possible he writes about places and even events he has observed at first hand. His purpose, for example, in *All the King's Men* was to compose "a highly documented picture of the modern world – at least, as the modern world manifested itself in the only region I knew well enough to write about." [40] And he nearly always visits the places about which he writes in order to steep himself in the sights which the historical characters saw. He explored the ruins of the Lewis home near Smithland, Kentucky, for example, on two different occasions, once in summer and again in winter, while writing *Brother to Dragons*. If there is one aspect of Warren's fiction that stands out above all others, it is what Henry James called a "solidity of specification", an accumulation of facts and details which adds up to a completeness of presentation which can give the feeling, atmosphere, and mood of a particular time in the past. The physical details which Warren provides recreate past or contemporary times – nineteenth-century Kentucky, Civil War New Orleans, the Tennessee of the 1920's and 1950's, the Louisiana of the twenties and thirties – so that the reader is vividly aware of the closeness of history. Diana Trilling has observed that his method is analogous to that of great photography, such as that of Walker Evans, in the amassing of detailed scenes for a record of a time.[41] Like Swift in *Gulliver's Travels* Warren believes that verisimilitude is best fostered by the proliferation of specific detail. In this respect he uses the methods of naturalism just as did Dreiser, whom he admires for his "scrupulous accre-

---

[40]   "A Note to *All the King's Men*", p. 479.
[41]   Diana Trilling, *Nation*, CLXIII (August 23, 1946), p. 220.

tion of detail, small indications, and trivial events",[42] which give the feel of life being lived in all its urgency. Warren's almost photographic recording of facts allows him, perhaps best of contemporary novelists outside of Faulkner, to realize the aim of the historian, to present his characters in relation to the world in which they exist and which, at least to some extent, shapes their destiny. And, finally, just as he has become less reliant upon historical events and characters for his stories, he has become less dependent upon piling example upon example. He is still specific, but his use of facts has become more artistic, more selective, and more symbolic; he has learned how to let one detail suggest or stand for many more.

Warren's re-creation of a region and a time is evident even in his short stories, a form of art not usually suited to such a method, and it is especially apparent in his early novels. The last paragraph of "The Circus in the Attic", by merely listing highly specific facts, sums up the story and vividly depicts the life of the small Southern town of Bardsville and the life led by its inhabitants.

He [the dead Jasper] will go away where he belongs, to join the circus in the attic. He will join Seth Sykes and drunken Cash Perkins and all the heroes who ever died for all their good reasons, and old Lem Lovehart, who laid himself down amid birdsong at dusk and was scalped by a Chickasaw, and Simon Lovehart, with the wound and the prayer book as his truth, and Louise Bolton Lovehart with her dear, treacherous heart in her bosom, and the kitten little Louise Bolton flung from her window to thud on the paving bricks, and the bloodless arrowheads and the fading flag of Simon Lovehart's regiment and the song "Let the nearer waters roll," which they sang at the baptizing and the song they sang in the square the night of the armistice in 1918, and the painted animals carved from wood and the sinister ring master and the girl acrobat with the frivolous skirt and round blue painted eyes, and all the things by which Bardsville had lived and found life worth living, and died.[43]

Christopher Isherwood has said of *Night Rider*: "From the very

---

[42] "An American Tragedy", p. 6.
[43] *The Circus in the Attic and Other Stories* (New York, 1948), p. 61. All references to short stories in the text are to this edition.

first sentences you begin to hear and see and smell the Kentucky
of forty years ago." [44] Here Warren has exhaustively documented
the Kentucky of his youth. Not content with accurately describing
the land, the farms, the rivers, and the people, Warren also skillfully transcribes the speech of his characters, catching both pro-
nunciation and cadence. Only Faulkner equals Warren in the
ability to reproduce speech pattern. When the red-headed Dr.
MacDonald came to see Perse Munn, Munn's Negro hand, Old
Mac, on being asked who the visitor was, replies: " 'Hits a red-
headed gemmun,' . . . 'His head, you mought say hit incline to
red' " (p. 233). And the Negro accused of murder explains that a
bullfrog found the knife for him. "Yassuh . . . that big ole bullfrog. Shore, bos, I never knowed that knife was yore'n, I . . .
shore would a brung hit back and give hit to you. I never wants
nuthen not rightful and truly mine in God's sight, and I'd a-brung
hit back" (p. 75). Warren's stories, like those of Elizabeth Madox
Roberts, seem to "grow out of the life of the place and are told in
a language firmly rooted in that place".[45]

In *At Heaven's Gate*, Warren presents a detailed panorama of
life in Tennessee in the twenties from the plush world of finance
capitalism in Nashville to the rural life of Jerry's family to the
rustic world of the mountaineer Ashby Wyndham. In transcribing
Ashby's speech rhythms and highly detailed figures of speech,
Warren adds depth to our understanding of the life of the poor
whites in the mountain regions of the South. God's will in respect
to the former prostitute Pearl is to Ashby like a hunted fox:

She taken off one sin, lak a man his shirt sweat dirty, and flung it
down, but she has done swapped one Bible sin for anuther, and hate
in her heart, and the cold stone wall round and about where she lays
down. God's will it runs lak a fox with the dogs on him, and doubles,
and knows places secret and hard for a man's foot. (pp. 36-37)

The evil atmosphere of the city, however, dominates the novel

---

and influences the characters. And Warren heavily documents
city life, as in this long description of Sunday morning:

It was about half past ten, on Sunday morning, the day and the hour
when little children – the little girls in careful, pastel-colored ribbons
and cute dresses, clutching miniature purses, the little boys in belted
wool jackets and white collars, with plastered hair curling unrulily at
the ends and faces scrubbed until they have the appearance of being
varnished – set on hard chairs in the basements and annexes of
churches and scrooge and twist secretly and dangle their legs, and in
thin, uncertain voices raggedly repeat in unison the Golden Text.
When black limousines whisk, and a few sedate electrics amble, up the
sunlit, tree-lined avenues – the trees are bare now and a few final
colored leaves, just fallen, lie in the dry gutters and stir to the passage
of the cars – and the automobiles presently will stop before the great
piles of brick or still new-looking Gothic limestone, and old ladies
with the help of colored chauffeurs, will creakily descend and, with
the concealment of a lace handkerchief, place a peppermint drop upon
the tongue, which is dry and gray, and will go in to worship. When
Negro cooks take a look at the roast in the oven, and, knowing there
is no danger of the mistress bursting into the kitchen, spit into the
sink and boldly insert a gob of snuff on the lower gum. When laborers
stretch their feet, shoeless, toward the coal stove and belch with the
comfort of the late breakfast. When children scream in the slum street.
When newsboys congregate on the corner by the drugstore and scuffle
and exchange obscenities and hail passing cars. When red-faced,
tweedy men step out of cars at the country club and inhale deeply,
two or three times, the brisk air, then light cigars and, followed by a
caddie carrying the bag of clubs, stalk toward the locker entrances,
grinding the gravel under their cleated feet. When young lovers, free
for a whole day together, begin to prick themselves deliciously, half
consciously, in the deeps of the mind with the thought of dark hall-
ways or the car parked in the country lane. When the bedridden
invalid knows that before dark people will call, bearing too perfect,
ceremonial greenhouse blossoms, which will be disposed about the
room in an ironic prematureness. (pp. 348-49)

In *All the King's Men* he has again produced an accurately and
vividly detailed portrait of an age and its people. Better than the
other novels based on the career of Long, *All the King's Men*
captures the atmosphere of the Louisiana of the twenties and
thirties. This verisimilitude derives largely from the fact that Jack
Burden as narrator reported in detail the events he had lived

through and the people he had known. Jack seems always to visualize everything specifically, and this adds more facts to his narrative. To him the Yankee exploiters did not simply leave Mason City; rather he says, "The big boys were gone, with diamond rings on their fingers and broadcloth on their backs" (p. 5). The Cass Mastern story gives Warren a chance to reproduce the romantic high-flown Southern rhetoric of the nineteenth century which he also renders well in the political speeches of *Night Rider* and Jeremiah Beaumont's diary. Cass reflects on meeting Jefferson Davis: "I had observed how worn to emaciation was his face by illness and care, and how thin the skin lay over the bone." "Then my brother and I continued our promenade in silence, and I reflected that Mr. Davis was a good man. But the world is full of good men, and now reflect as I write these lines down, and yet the world drives hard into darkness and the blindness of blood . . ." (pp. 197-98).

World Enough and Time and *Band of Angels* are almost as factually detailed as the earlier novels. There are, however, fewer lists, less amassing of example upon example than in the first three novels. These later novels are just as long as the previous ones, but their length is as much due to an increased number of events and characters as to the careful reproduction of a region and time. Yet the atmosphere, the feel of the period is just as vividly alive in these works. But with *The Cave*, Warren is well on his way toward developing the method of using details that culminates in *Wilderness*. In *The Cave* Warren has become more selective and more symbolic, integrating his facts more closely into his narrative line and thematic considerations. No longer does he seem to be caught up in a desire to catalog sights and sounds. The panorama of the small towns, for example, arises naturally from the plot as Isaac escapes Johntown for Nashville and eventually New York. The details document a particular time and place, but they also characterize Isaac's attitude of disgust toward life in a small town. More subtly, they suggest the falseness and hollowness of Isaac himself:

He passed the settlements, sleeping exposed and shameless in their poverty, under the starlight, like an animal killed by a passing car and knocked to the roadside, and the towns, with their melancholy prosperity and sad pretension of new gas pumps and chrome and glass on store fronts. On the outskirts of Biggerstown he passed a new brick house, not big but with two stories and an awkward jackleg imitation of the classic white pillars of Confederate graciousness, and a spotlight on one corner of the house illuminating, even at this hour, a patch of newly installed lawn with a concrete fountain and a couple of painted wooden jigsaw herons standing guard beside it.[46]

Unfortunately Warren is not frequently as skillful as this in his use of detail in the novel, and the result is occasionally a thinness, a note that does not ring true. This is especially apparent in the exaggerated portraits, almost caricatures, of Wes Williams, the television announcer; the stupid country bumpkin, Jebb Holloway; and the committee of do-gooding matrons to raise funds for Jasper's pregnant girl friend, whose efforts the paper headlines:

WOMEN OF STATE RALLY
Mother's Committee formed to Guard Sweetheart
and Unborn Child of Trapped Hero Fund Tops $20,000   (p.369)

Generally, however, Warren has developed the ability to reconstruct a particular place and a past time with fewer details without giving up the suggestion of the urgency and complexity of life.

4

The philosophical justification for Warren's extensive use of particulars is that this method is related to one of his central ideas on the nature of history and human experience and to his idea of what literature and written history should be in order to reflect his concept of historical reality. His philosophical and critical ideas, that is, make the use of heavy documentation in his works imperative; specificity is a stylistic metaphor for his idea. History, Warren insists, is enormously complex; all ideals, values, and philosophical statements must be earned, derived inductively from an adequate consideration of the massiveness of experience.

[46] *The Cave* (New York, 1959), p. 365. All references in the text are to this edition.

For this reason written history must convey the complicating details in order to avoid the impression that it was ever a simple thing. Edmund Wilson's *Patriotic Gore*, a study of the Civil War, is, by Warren's standards, admirable because of the impure details and complicating facts that Mr. Wilson is able to comprehend in his book; this work contains, as all written history should, "all the density, paradoxicality, and ambiguity of felt life".[47] Warren's idea here carries over into his evaluation of contemporary social issues. He states in *Segregation*, for example, that no social problem can be solved without reference to its historical context, which in itself will make one aware of the complicating factors. This should dissuade the mind hot for certainties. Warren goes on to urge appreciation of life and history in all their variety, difference, and complication. "Basically the issue isn't to 'solve' the 'race problem or the sex problem.' You don't solve it, you just experience it. Appreciate it." [48] Liberal literature of protest, he feels, is so busy rushing headlong after answers that it fails to appreciate the enormously complicated details that make up history. And solutions to any social issue must be arrived at, Warren maintains, by a consideration of them within their historical context and with an awareness of the complicating facts and details.

Protest *qua* protest denies the texture of life. The problem is to permit the fullest range of life into racial awareness. I don't mean to imply that there's nothing to protest about, but aside from the appropriate political, sociological, and journalistic concerns, the problem is to see the protest in its relation to other things. Race isn't an isolated thing – I mean as it exists in the U.S. – it becomes a total symbolism for every kind of issue. They all flow into it and out of it. Well, thank God – it gives a little variety to life.[49]

To add to the difficulty of knowing the past, we do not even have all the facts of the past, and those we do have we cannot be sure of. We especially lack the facts that, in their affirmation of

[47] "Edmund Wilson's Civil War", *Commentary*, XXIV (August, 1962), p. 157.
[48] *The Paris Review Interviews*, p. 203.
[49] *Ibid.*, pp. 203-04.

the essential humanity of the characters, are more apt to tell the truth than is the factual record. Bolton Lovehart of "The Circus in the Attic", thanks to his tireless scholarship in dredging up the facts of the past from records, newspapers, and survivors, knew most of the facts for his history of Carruthers county. But he did not know that the first settler, his ancestor the hard backwoodsman, Old Simon Lovehart, when he first came to the area that is now Bardsville, had sat down and wept amid birdsong at dusk on a spring day. This fact, which Warren regards as the most significant event about the history of the county, would, of course, not be recorded in the official records, and since it went unobserved, no one else could know of it and pass it on. How, then, Warren seems to ask in this short story, can the true historical reality be known?

The fanatics and idealists whom Warren portrays in his novels err in trying to force history into a pattern which suits their own needs and in interpreting it too narrowly. By draining it of complicating particulars they make it too abstract and too simple. Quite frequently these idealists want their history refined of the evil and the ugly. In *Brother to Dragons* Warren comments ironically upon the D.A.R.'s monument to Lucy; the plaque does not mention that "she/ Gave suck to two black-hearted murderers". "But let that pass, for to the pious mind/ Our history's nothing if it's not refined" (p. 21). Similarly, in "The Circus in the Attic", he calls the U.D.C. "the defenders of ancient pieties and the repositories of ignorance of history" (p. 5).

This refining of historical facts through the small sieve of one's own ideas is a manifestation of the dissociation of sensibility – the disparity between fact and idea, which Warren sees as the special disease of modern times. Perse Munn, for example, in giving his allegiance to the association's ideal, a partial view because it cannot account for all the details that impinge upon him and because it ignores the historical context and Munn's own personal history, is led not only to destroy tobacco plant beds, but to commit adultery and murder. If a man can ignore facts that bother him, he can then do what he wishes. Adam Stanton is, Jack says, a romantic; ". . . he has a picture of the world in his head, and when the world doesn't conform in any respect to the picture, he wants to throw the world away. Even if that means throwing out the baby with the bath" (p. 262). Unable to accept his father's complicity in the evil of history, Adam violently rejects him and the past. Jack says, "he has lived all his life in the idea that there was a time a long time back when everything was run by high-minded handsome men wearing knee breeches and silver buckles or continental blue or frock coats, or even buckskin and coonskin caps, as the case may be . . . who sat around a table and candidly debated the good of the public thing" (p. 262). But Willie Stark's coarsening of history is just as partial and oversimplified. He ignores the dignity and nobility of the past, which, Warren believes, are there just as surely as ugliness and evil. Willie puts his view of history succinctly: "I bet things were just like they are now. A lot of folks wrassling round" (p. 72). In *World Enough and Time* it is Percival Skrogg who disowns the world for an ideal, a good cause; the world, Warren tells us, "shriveled to nothing in the blaze of his justice" (p. 82). And Jerry for most of his life is contemptuous of the facts: "He had thought that the idea in and of itself might redeem the world" (p. 459). In *Brother to Dragons* Jefferson, ignoring the evidence of history, proclaimed the goodness and perfectibility of man. He had not earned his dream of innocence by reference to the evils of the past. He had failed his history lesson, for, as R.P.W. tells him, the dream of the future can be no better than the fact of the past.

Just as ignoring the details of the past can bring blindness, a full, intelligent contemplation of the fully documented historical reality can lead man to understanding. Because of the complexity of history, a proper study of it can rescue man from a one-sided, abstract view of life. One should first arrive at values inductively and then re-submit these to the test of facts. This process is evidenced in the education of Jack Burden and Jeremiah Beaumont, as well as many of Warren's other characters, as they try to account in full for the part of history they have observed and participated in. Jack tentatively arrives at theories, such as the Great Twitch and a twisted idealism, then rejects them as life presents him with new evidence, new facts. Although he does not reach Jack's position in time to save himself, Jeremiah undergoes a similar educative process, rejecting partial generalizations – such as the idea as all and the world as all – as he lives longer, experiences more, and gathers more facts. Their final position can accommodate nearly all the facts that history can give them.

"Knowledge and the Image of Man" is Warren's clearest statement of the idea prevalent in most of his work that the end of man is knowledge, that knowledge is salvation. Only by knowledge of the facts of history and human experience can man achieve identity. The knowledge to be derived from the study of history, its facts as well as its meanings, is important in helping man gain a true image of himself, because man has a foreground and a background; he is "in the world with continual and intimate interpenetration, an inevitable osmosis of being, which in the end does not deny, but affirms, his identity".[50] Knowledge of the world thus leads man to distinguish himself from the world; and beyond personal experience, which is also history, the best way to learn of the world in all its complexity is to study the fully documented and re-created past. Professor Strugnell sees Warren's main theme as the arrival at self-understanding through a contemplation of one's past. "The retelling of history is our attempt to break through to a new understanding of human ambition and human error." [51] This is the impetus behind Jerry Beaumont's journal; he is trying to understand himself and mankind by a study of the part of history he has lived through. His conclusion is that man does not need happiness, peace, or salvation, but only knowledge, which is better than any of these.

In his novels Warren portrays characters moving from ignorance and innocence toward a knowledge that comprehends all the facts and details. He initiates his characters into respect for the necessity of a knowledge of the complicating facts and details, which they arrive at through a contemplation of their personal

---

[50] "Knowledge and the Image of Man", *Sewanee Review*, LXIII (Winter, 1955), p. 186.
[51] John R. Strugnell, "Robert Penn Warren and the Uses of the Past", *A Review of English Literature*, IV (October, 1963), p. 102.

past and of history. Jack Burden at first actively side-stepped knowledge: "The world was full of things I didn't want to know" (p. 151). But as a historian he comes to believe that life is motion toward knowledge and that "The truth shall make you free" (p. 276). Knowledge, that is, confirms the complexity of history and the tragic possibility of life. After all the violence and turmoil which Jack Burden has lived through, he decides that the knowledge paid for in blood saved his mother, Judge Irwin, and himself. Judge Irwin's suicide saved Jack and his mother by showing them both that she was capable of a deep human love. The knowledge that his past evil was known saved Irwin in that it forced him to quit living a lie and to sacrifice himself. Jefferson in *Brother to Dragons* calls knowledge "the bitter bread", and says "All truth is bought with blood, and the blood is ours,/ Or we shall have no truth, and only the truth can make us free" (p. 10). Jefferson learns of the evil that man, even his own flesh and blood, is capable of, and faced with the overwhelming facts he modifies his premature assumptions. In *The Cave,* the knowledge of themselves and their capacity for good and evil paid for by the death of Jasper, prepares many of the characters for salvation. Knowledge of facts frees them from their chains so that they can see not shadows but reality.

In his use of facts, Warren insists upon meticulous accuracy. The individual in the complexity of the historical process impinged upon by a myriad of facts must form his ideas, values, and generalizations inductively from this complexity. In literature the artist must do the same thing, and in order to be effective he must show the reader at least some of the concrete facts that led to his generalizations. Warren permits the novelist an interest in philosophy, but the artist should never relinquish his grasp on the actual world and its facts. The philosophical novelist is "one for whom the documentation of the world is constantly striving to rise to the level of generalization about values, for whom the image strives to rise to symbol, for whom images always fall into a dialectical configuration, for whom the urgency of experience, no matter how vividly and strongly experience may enchant, is the urgency to know the meaning of experience. This is not to say that the philosophical novelist is schematic and deductive. It is to say quite the contrary, that he is willing to go naked into the pit, again and again, to make the same old struggle for his truth." [52] What he struggles with is the mass of documented facts from history and his own experience. The artist, like the historian, Warren says, should approach his task with no preconceived interpretation, for the facts themselves must provide their own meaning. If the writer is to be honest, he will not be able to ignore the sordid and the ugly, or ideas with which he disagrees. In fact, this confrontation of all aspects of experience involved in writing fiction led him to reverse his early segregationist stand which he took in "The Briar Patch". "If you are seriously trying to write fiction you can't allow yourself as much evasion as in trying to write essays." [53]

Just as literature should be factually accurate and detailed, it should also be comprehensive and inclusive in order to suggest the complicated nature of historical reality. Warren wants the writer to be faithful to the whole body of experience by detailing the historical context within which all problems should be solved. Great writers, such as Eliot and Faulkner, Warren contends, are those who have tried "to remain faithful to the complexities of the problems with which they are dealing, because they have refused to take the easy statement as solution, because they have tried to define the context in which, and the terms by which, faith and ideals may be earned".[54] In his poetry Warren tries "to get range and depth",[55] which he admires in the deliberately roughened lines of Melville's poetry. Again his goal is inclusion. In *Brother to Dragons*, for example, he includes the physical process of urination as well as the grisly episode of the butchering of the slave in the meat house. The lists of sense impressions, the many styles, voices, characters, and episodes are all methods that he uses in his novels to achieve inclusiveness.

[52] " 'The Great Mirage': Conrad and *Nostromo*" in *Selected Essays*, p. 58.
[53] *The Paris Review Interviews*, p. 195.
[54] "Pure and Impure Poetry", in *Selected Essays*, pp. 31-32.
[55] "Melville the Poet", in *Selected Essays*, pp. 187-88.

But the use of detail provides more than depth and completeness; literature, especially fiction, needs the specific to attract and
interest the reader. This idea underlies Warren's distinction between subject and theme. "The subject is the device used by the
writer to objectify the theme, to dramatize it, to realize it in
experience." [56] The subject, then, is not only the story, the plot
line, but it is also the surface, the facts – in a historical novel,
what one learns from research into the past – which should be an
integral part of the work. The theme consists of generalizations
about values, ideals derived inductively from the subject. The
aim of the artist is to effect "the true marriage of his convictions,
his ideas, that is, his theme, with the concrete projection in
experience, that is, his subject". [57] "We want", Warren states, "the
factual richness of life absorbed into the pattern so that content
and form are indistinguishable. ..." [58] If this fusion occurs
subject and theme will appear as experience, not as abstractions.
The subject is, then, the source of the vitality of fiction and poetry, the reason it engages the reader intellectually and emotionally.
These ideas on the relation of subject to theme are of course
related to the New Critical doctrine of the living quality of a
work of art, a quality that makes it more than just a sum of all its
parts. But Warren's characteristic application and modification of
this doctrine is to insist more upon the details, the specific facts,
which he feels can, better than any other aspect of a work of art,
make the theme available to the reader as experience.

5

But Warren believes that the facts alone are not enough for one
either to understand history or to compose successful fiction. We
cannot understand history merely by careful research into the
past, by detailed documentation, for it is greater than the sum of
its parts. Jack Burden has the facts of the Cass Mastern story

---

[56] "Literature as a Symptom", p. 269.
[57] *Ibid.*, p. 277.
[58] "Why Do We Read Fiction?", *Saturday Evening Post*, CCXXXV
(October 20, 1962), p. 84.

neatly recorded on his three-by-five cards, yet he fully realizes that he does not possess the truth. For this he has to be reborn in such a way that his historical imagination can more fully enter into the world in which Cass Mastern lived. Warren in *World Enough and Time* again and again reminds us that although we have the facts, we cannot be sure that we have the truth of this piece of history. "We have what is left, the lies and half lies and the truths and half truths. We do not know that we have the truth" (p. 3). And Jerry asks "what the men who wrote the histories ever knew when they gave the cold reasons?" (p. 268). Amantha Starr compares her own involvement in the New Orleans riots with the official history, *Report of The Select Committee on the New Orleans Riots in 1876*, which abounds in dusty facts. Warren's juxtaposition of Amantha's memories with the factual history forms an ironic comment on the inability of the facts alone to give the whole truth of the past. When, many years later, Amantha sees her daughter with the report, her heart almost stops. To the daughter, however, the book is merely something to hold; the facts so important to the mother mean nothing to the daughter. This is perhaps the main reason why Warren with his great interest in history, its facts and meanings, writes historical novels. He is trying to penetrate to a truth not available in the mere facts of the past, and he is trying to rise to generalizations about values. He can also in the novel make the past seem more alive and relevant than he could in a factual history without losing any of the details of the past in his presentation. And because of his conviction that the facts by themselves cannot reveal truth, he has become increasingly concerned with methods other than documentation to reveal the meaning of history.

Similarly in literature, scrupulous accuracy and careful scholarship do not insure the success of a work of art, for Warren believes that the novelist must be more concerned with truth than facts.[59] T. S. Stribling's preoccupation with the naturalistic surface of his novels is unfortunate because the details never add up to

[59]   Warren and Cleanth Brooks, Jr., eds., *Understanding Fiction* (New York, 1943), p. 27.

value.[60] The recorded facts should either rise to symbol or do something very similar – that is suggest a weight of meaning and implication behind them which gives a feeling of "mysterious depth".[61] Warren's goal in his fiction is that which he believes Caroline Gordon has achieved: "the observations, always accurate and compelling, sometimes carry a weight of implication that defies analysis, and she is exhaustively aware of the immediate richness and implication of the single scene".[62] Many of his own scenes are thus weighty with implication. In *Night Rider*, for example, the simple gesture of a hand raised by Captain Todd as he resigns from the association in protest against the violence takes on added significance when Munn recalls it six weeks later as he sees Todd's son, Benton, make the same gesture to join the night riders, those responsible for the violence. And Warren like Faulkner uses the phenomenon of stopped time, "freeze time", to imply and suggest. "The frozen moments" in Faulkner's work, Warren explains, harden up an event or detail and give it additional meaning by holding it fixed.[63] Because of its significance the moment is apotheosized, thus achieving an effect close to symbolism. In *Night Rider* the moment when the vigilantes brutally kill a dog as they prepare to rake a plant bed becomes emblematic of the senseless violence they are invoking in the name of a good cause. ". . . for an instant, the instant before the sodden crack of the impact of wood on flesh, the forms seemed to be almost merged in the darkness" (p. 193).

As his use of details has become more economical Warren has become more symbolic; in his later work he lets a few well-chosen, significant details do the work of many, to suggest more facts and details rather than to catalog them. The symbol is especially valuable, Warren states in his essay on "The Rhyme of the Ancient Mariner", because it yokes philosophy to the physical details from which it is derived,[64] thus fulfilling one of his major

60   "T. S. Stribling", p. 497.
61   "A Note to *All the King's Men*", p. 478.
62   "The Fiction of Caroline Gordon", pp. 5-9.
63   *The Paris Review Interviews*, p. 201.
64   "A Poem of Pure Imagination", in *Selected Essays*, p. 218.

requirements of literature. The first novels contain exhaustive documentation, which sometimes does little more than add verisimilitude. But these facts frequently both document and imply and suggest. The opening scene of *Night Rider*, for example, vividly describes Munn on a crowded train being pushed and shoved by the crowd as the cars lurch about. As documentation of a past time the scene is admirable; but it also serves to symbolize the way in which Munn throughout the novel is led almost against his will by the desires of other people. Because he lacks a center to his life and any significant moral convictions, he is easily moved by crowd pressure. But other facts, such as the long description of the type of man who could have written the letter threatening Munn to fire his Negroes or the description of a typical farm house, do not do more than document, though quite admirably, the world of rural Kentucky in the first decade of this century. The major imagery of *At Heaven's Gate*, that of disease, decay, deformity, filth, and ugliness, suggests Warren's judgment on the city with its moral sickness and the evil exploitation of finance capitalism. But the long lists of physical details do not rise to symbol.

In *All the King's Men* more, but by no means all, of the copious details become symbolic. Highway 58, for example, is accurately described, but it also symbolizes Willie's regime; it is a glittering example of modernity brought to the Southern backwoods; and it vividly contrasts the old and the new. By describing the small animals, the snakes and possums, which the cars kill, Warren has the highway represent a clash with the natural, a destruction of nature. In the next two novels symbols arise convincingly from the historical background. In *World Enough and Time* the recurrent images associated with the primitivistic blood ritual derive from the early history of Kentucky, which the Indians regarded as "the dark and bloody ground" where gods dwelled, and these images point up the sacrificial victim theme. The images associated with the high stage and romantic tragedy derive logically from the journal since Jeremiah, as a nineteenth-century romantic, saw himself as a tragic hero. Warren has said that race becomes a "total symbolism" for every kind of issue,[65] and in *Band of Angels* he associates whiteness with the intellect and blackness with the body and emotions. Manty's Negro blood, which she tries to deny, is also emblematic of the taint of Original Sin and guilt, which all must learn to bear.

With *The Cave*, however, Warren has become much more overtly symbolic; every detail seems to strain toward becoming symbol. But here the fault is exactly the reverse of the fault of *At Heaven's Gate*, for Warren now seems to be so interested in meaning and significance that the physical details occasionally seem to lack the vitality, the feel of life that in his other novels reinforce the verisimilitude. The cave itself, along with the re-current imagery of wells and boxes, is, on one level, admirable as a symbol for the desire to escape from the world into a place of constant temperature and total darkness; but, on another level, it suggests Plato's use of the cave image to mean that all men are prisoners within the cell of the self or within lies and false ideas and hence see reality only at third hand, as shadows against the cave wall. As a symbol the cave is as meaningful and as logically accurate as any in Warren. But as detailed naturalistic surface, as description of a particular place it is less admirable, for Warren leaves it vague and generalized; he fails to make it a bit of Tennessee regionalism as well as a symbolic cave. On the other hand, as Warren has come to use increasingly more symbols, he has also come to make his facts do more than document. In *Wilderness* this method is used successfully for the first time so that there is meaning and significance with no sacrifice of the illusion of reality.

Because of his abiding interest in history and his love of the past Robert Penn Warren has written well-researched, thoughtful histories in which he not only documents the facts of the past but also speculates upon the meaning and significance of those his-torical events he is working with. And he has written historical novels in which he does the same things and more. One of the chief reasons for his great ability to re-create a past time and to

---

[65]   *The Paris Review Interviews*, p. 205.

enter into history imaginatively is his respect for physical presence. This respect accounts for one of the chief values of his novels, their amazing verisimilitude, the quality that transports the reader into the past as no mere factual history can do. The use of facts, details, examples, the heavy documentation, in his novels is directly related to one aspect of his philosophy of history – his idea that history is so enormously complicated and complex that no one key can unlock its secrets. And, he further believes, man faced with the tremendous complications of history should proceed cautiously, tentatively; he should form his ideas, ideals, values and generalizations inductively, constantly referring to the facts in order to save himself from a narrow, one-sided idealism. The artist, too, should proceed cautiously and tentatively from facts to generalizations, and his work should by its factual density reflect the complexity of historical reality. But more than this, literature, especially fiction, must be specific and concrete if it is to be vitally engaging to the reader, if it is to come to him as felt experience, as though a part of history he himself has lived through. As Warren has matured as an artist he has come to rely less and less on catalogs, lists of physical details and facts to gain verisimilitude, to document an age, and to suggest the complicated nature of human experience. He has become more selective, more symbolic, attempting to let one fact, one detail do the work of many. Only in *Wilderness* does Warren exhibit his full mastery of this more artistic method. Yet in all of his novels, from *Night Rider* to *Flood*, Warren is working as a philosophical novelist, attempting to reproduce the historical moment in all its complexity and also to comment, to generalize about it. He is "one for whom the documentation of the world is constantly striving to rise to the level of generalization about values".[66] He has taken the historical novel, a badly hackneyed, stereotyped and trite form, and made it capable of carrying serious and complex philosophical themes. He is the only American writer to achieve greatness using this the most decadent of popular forms; indeed, some

---

[66] "Conrad and *Nostromo*", p. 58.

critics believe he has created an entirely new literary form.[67] The genre, however, is not new, for, typically, Warren has not been experimental; he has, however, greatly revitalized a type of novel already existing.

[67] William Wasserstrom, *Heiress of All the Ages. Sex and Sentiment in the Genteel Tradition* (Minneapolis, 1959), p. 114.

III

ROBERT PENN WARREN'S PHILOSOPHY OF HISTORY: "HISTORY IS BLIND, BUT MAN IS NOT"

Warren's great interest in history has long been apparent, and his major themes have been defined as the meaning of history or the relation of the past to the present and the future. But no one has defined accurately just what Warren's philosophy of history is, and on several major points where they have attempted to do so there are disagreements and confusions. Since history is the most pervasive theme in Warren's criticism, poems, short stories, and novels, since his treatment of it is always complex and frequently ambiguous, and since no theme in his work has been so variously interpreted and poorly understood, his philosophy of history represents perhaps the greatest challenge for the critic attempting to study Warren's thought.

One of the chief causes of difficulty in understanding Warren's philosophy of history is the great disparity between his ideas on history and his view of man. And one cannot understand his philosophy of history unless one understands his theory of the nature of man. His idea of history as morally neutral and blind is much like that of Dreiser's belief in history as a collision of blind forces. The critics who have called him a naturalist are then partially right. But his idea on the nature of man is in no way similar to that of Dreiser, who argued that because history is blind, virtue is impossible. To Warren this idea is the Great Twitch, a theory of the nature of man – not of the nature of history. Jack Burden learns that "History is blind", but he also learns that "man is not". Human history has two aspects, the first of which is the noble strivings by people of the past to live by worthy and humane codes of conduct. But Warren believes that part of man's nature is depraved. History, then, also records man's depravity, and this portion of human history merges with non-human history – the forces of nature as well as economic and political forces, forces such as the struggle between the tobacco growers and the companies, the Civil War and Reconstruction, and the Old Court versus the New in early nineteenth-century Kentucky. Part of history to Warren, then, is a mindless clash of forces, non-rational and dependent upon chance not plan – and he nearly always uses the term "history" in this sense. Jack's statement does not mean that history has no significance. It does mean that what significance it has is owing to man, as man confronts it with his human faculties. Non-human history and part of human history is a blind mechanical process with no moral meaning inherent in it, but the individual events in this blind process are complexly interrelated and interwoven. Hence man is responsible morally if not physically for any consequences of his acts, thoughts, or mere existence, even though frequently he cannot know or guess these consequences. Warren also believes in the freedom of the will, that man must live in an agony of choice. He is free to choose even though he cannot know the outcome of his choice and even though his choice may make little or no difference in the physical world; indeed, the result may be exactly the opposite of what he intended, although the more knowledge he has the less idealistic he is and the less history can surprise him. Man, because his will is free, is not merely a product of history. Warren is, thus, no believer in historical determinism, but like a good historian he looks for explanations and even causes in the past. Virtue, direction, meaning, values, significance are man's responsibility and do not reside in history itself. Man is a part of history and nature, but, Warren argues, if this is all he is, he is a nothing, a moral failure.

1

History, non-human as well as a great deal of human history, to Warren is a blank, morally neutral process. Man's contact with this process involves conflict, pain, suffering, and frequently tragedy, for history is something for man to oppose with his human qualities. And since history usually conquers the human, it is frequently evil as well as tragic. Several critics have noticed this aspect of his philosophy of history. Charles R. Anderson states that to Warren the world is violent, and history merely records this senseless violence.[1] Eric Bentley notices Warren's idea on man's responsibility in history: "the mere flux of events in history is in itself meaningless; meaning comes from man".[2] To obtain this meaning one must oppose one's will to the mechanical process of history, to try, like Warren's characters, to avoid being engulfed by the "tide of history".[3] History, however, nearly always wins in the end, and the best that man can hope for is the achievement of some human "glory" in defeat. Written history, then, records the constant though sometimes noble failure of man amid the blind rush of history. Edmund Wilson's *Patriotic Gore* exemplifies how Warren would have the historian view history. To Wilson history consists of "blank forces", "voracity against voracity", what Warren calls "the great anonymous forces of history".[4] And Wilson sees clearly the tragic problem of historical costs – all change is paid for in blood, a necessary condition of history.[5] *Patriotic Gore* is, finally, a book about individuals caught in a collision of blind forces of which they must make sense: [6] "*Patriotic Gore* does not say that history makes sense. But it clearly says that men must, in the end, make sense of history." [7] Warren in his own histories views the past in the same way that Edmund Wilson does. He looks to the past for examples of people opposing their wills to the forces of history. As he said at the Fugitives' Reunion: "The drama of the

---

[1]   Charles R. Anderson, "Violence and Order in the Novels of Robert Penn Warren", in *Southern Renascence: The Literature of the Modern South*, ed. Louis D. Rubin, Jr. and Robert D. Jacobs (Baltimore, 1953), p. 210.
[2]   Eric Bentley, "The Meaning of Robert Penn Warren's Novels", *Kenyon Review*, X (Summer, 1948), p. 413.
[3]   Strugnell, p. 100.
[4]   "Conrad and *Nostromo*", p. 51.
[5]   "Edmund Wilson's Civil War", p. 154.
[6]   *Ibid.*, p. 152.
[7]   *Ibid.*, p. 158.

past that corrects us is the drama of our struggles to be human" before the non-human forces of history.[8] He sees the Civil War as an example of "the glory of the human effort to win meaning from the complex and confused motives of men and the blind ruck of event", of the human grandeur amid the confusion and "brutal ambivalence" of history,[9] "the great a-moral economy of history".[10] And he sees in the war an image of historic reality, the horror, savagery, confusion, ambiguity, and evil that make up the past and with which man must come to terms.

Warren's view of history is clearly reflected in his ideas on art and the nature of the artistic process. In "Pure and Impure Poetry" he compares the writing of poetry to living in history – undergoing resistances, uncertainties, and conflicts to win the right to convictions.[11] The surface roughness and the use of discordant elements in Melville's poetry, Warren maintains, are admirably suited to convey the idea of history as complex and disordered.[12] But Thomas Wolfe's method is too much like history; that is, he records disordered, meaningless experience without the shaping power of the human mind and imagination.[13] Great writers present characters trying to impose order on historical reality and learning of the horror of history, the "grimness of fact".[14] Faulkner's characters, even the villains for the most part, are, in Warren's view, merely trying to break out of the meaningless "mechanical process" of history.[15] In his own poetic technique the rough lines, unpleasant images, and discordant elements suggest his idea of history as involving evil and ugliness. In "Summer Storm (circa 1916) and God's Grace" the poet is shocked and bitter over the rapacity of history which he symbolizes by the violent storm which destroyed the crops in a few short

[8]   Purdy, Rob Roy, ed., *Fugitives' Reunion: Conversations at Vanderbilt* (Nashville, 1959), p. 214.
[9]   *Legacy*, pp. 108-09.
[10] *Ibid.*, p. 66.
[11] "Pure and Impure Poetry", in *Selected Essays*, p. 28.
[12] "Melville the Poet", pp. 184-98.
[13] "A Note on the Hamlet of Thomas Wolfe", in *Selected Essays*, p. 183.
[14] "Elizabeth Madox Roberts", p. 38.
[15] "William Faulkner", in *Selected Essays*, p. 73.

minutes. "And God got down on hands and knees/ To peer and cackle and commend/ His own sadistic idiocies".[16] And he admires and wonders at the human virtue to be found "past confusion and wrath", beyond "the stew and stink" of history.[17] Finding his father's old Greek grammar, the poet says: "Amid History's vice and velleity, that poor book burns/ Like fox-fire in the black swamp of the world's error." [18]

Two of Warren's best short stories effectively dramatize this aspect of his philosophy of history. The brutal, senseless killing of Seth Sykes, one of Bardstown's "heroes", by a Federal soldier in "The Circus in the Attic" indicates the random violence and horror of history, a horror that the good citizens and their official historians had forgotten. No one wished to recall the grimness of fact. They had done with history what Bolton had done with his arrowheads, which, "long since washed clean of whatever hot blood had stained them, lay in orderly rows on sagging shelves with the album of stamps . . ." (p. 54). The young boy in "Blackberry Winter" is initiated into the evil and horror involved in the life process which is part of history. This aspect of the boy's education is suggested by the plight of the poverty-stricken Milt Alley, who after the ravages of the flood and the cold will be even less able to feed his large family, and by the filth washed out by the flood from under Dellie's immaculately clean house. But he has more to learn than this. He must understand the process of change and diminution involved in one's own part of history; that is he must learn the nature of time, which, in his prelapsarian innocence, is a fixed climate in which it never occurs to him that his mother would ever be dead or that his life would change (p. 68). To follow the tramp, who comes from "the grownup world of time",[19] is to accept time and change as an aspect of history. Although he does not regard the story as completely autobiographical, Warren has stated that he hopes that he would have

---

16   *Promises*, p. 38.
17   *Ibid.*, p. 52.
18   *You, Emperors, and Others, Poems 1957-1960* (New York, 1960), p. 29.
19   "How a Story Was Born", p. 36.

been able to follow the tramp as the boy in the story did, to have the courage to emerge into history from the innocence of childhood.[20] Time, change, and evil are irreducible aspects of the blind ruck of history; the essence of maturity is to learn to live with them and to superimpose order on their chaos.

It seems that in his first two novels Warren was working toward his theory of the nature of history which he fully dramatized in *All the King's Men*. After the development of the theory in this novel Warren then embodied the theme more subtly in the later novels; he has come to imply it rather than to state it. His philosophy of history has not changed; he has, however, become more fully aware of its implications. The ethical center of *Night Rider* is the admirable Captain Todd, a man with a deep certainty of self. Warren compares him to a great boulder in the violent, flooded stream of history. Todd looks to himself and not to history for value. "Captain Todd could be confident because he knew things and events were blind. Blind as a bat" (p. 44). Perse Munn, unlike Todd, is swept away by the stream of history and can find no inner certainty, for "he was like a man who tries to find in the flux and confusion of data some point of reference" but is unable to do so (p. 251). He becomes caught up in the coiling blankness of the forces generated by the conflict between the growers and the tobacco companies. Even the fanatical Sweetwater of *At Heaven's Gate* realizes that a man must do more than live on the level of history in order to be human; he grimly holds on to the values he has derived, perhaps too easily, from his struggle with the world.

Because it is narrated by a student of history, *All the King's Men* develops and reveals a great deal about Warren's view of the amoral rapacity of history. Because he has studied the past, Jack knows its evil: "A student of history does not care what he digs out of the ash pile, the midden, the sublunary dung heap, which is the human past" (p. 167). His "theory of historical costs" affirms the evil and suffering involved in history. "All change costs something. You have to write off the costs against the gain"

[20]   *Ibid.*

(p. 417). Jack's second theory, "the moral neutrality of history" is the clearest statement of his idea that history itself has no inherent values. "Process as process is neither morally good nor morally bad" (p. 418). Jack also comes to realize and accept man's responsibility to make sense out of history, and he is aware of the contrast between the brute forces of history and human values.

The westward flight, the escape into the past, and the Great Sleep represent ways of evading the responsibility of learning values from history; they are merely ways to sink in "the motionless ooze of History" (p. 288). At the end, however, Jack is ready to go into the "convulsion of the world", into history and "the awful responsibility of Time" (p. 464). That is, he is ready to try to make order out of the chaos that is history.

In his next two novels Warren implies and suggests his philosophy of history rather than explaining it as overtly as he did in *All the King's Men*. Both Warren and Jeremiah Beaumont in *World Enough and Time* see man pitted against the blank forces of "world" and "time" which make up history. Both view the human problem as the attempt to carve human, moral values from the formless mass of historical reality. The narrator suggests that Jeremiah prepared his drama in an attempt to affirm his humanity. "And it may be that a man cannot live unless he prepares a drama, at least cannot live as a human being against the ruck of the world" (p. 5). He wrote his diary as an attempt to see what sense he could make of the history he had lived through, to win something from the "moil and clutter" (p. 376) of his personal history and the "blind, massive drift" (p. 285) of historical events and forces. The plot bears out Warren's concept of history as random violence. Jerry's fight for "justice" at the election does no good, for his candidate is still defeated. It is also cruelly ironic that Jerry struck down Fort before he could divulge his plans for reconciliation of the Old Court and the New. This, Warren says, is history – anonymous forces that in their random savagery may cruelly destroy human values.

In *Band of Angels* Warren uses three events to typify his idea of what history is. The first event is the African massacre which

Hamish Bond has witnessed. Hamish tells Manty of his slave trading days; not having enough slaves, he persuaded a native king to let him lead an expedition to capture more. The result was an epic slaughter with the native women brutally hacking to death all the people they could find. What is so horrible here is the savage randomness of the slaughter; it has no reason, no justification. It is, in other words, like the forces of history. The second event, the New Orleans riots, typifies the chaos, confusion, and irrationality of history. All the suffering and violence which they include serves no purpose. Any ultimate meaning occurs only in the minds of the characters. Manty describes how they started: a policeman arrested a nameless street brat. "In the crazy irrationality of all, in that moment under the blazing noon of Louisiana summer, it was a Negro who fired at the policeman for arresting the white boy and thereby protecting him. It is crazy enough to be true. Or almost" (p. 307). The third event is the historical one of the Civil War, its causes and its consequences. On learning that the first man killed at Harper's Ferry was a free Negro, Manty realizes the cruel irony of history. "Suddenly everything that had ever happened in the world, all history, seemed nothing but a savage comedy" (p. 209). The war itself is presented as nothing but crazy confusion in the background of the story. After the bloody cost of the war the Negro was, if anything, worse off than before, for the banks were putting them back into slavery more cruel than what they had known before. The price of Negro freedom had been blood, but the buyer had been cheated, Tobias decides (p. 245). He learns that it is up to him and other men to make "all the butchery" mean something (p. 265). In *The Cave* Jasper goes into the ground to escape the responsibility of making sense of life and history; Mrs. Harrick wishes to deny the evil and horror of the past, the "sufferings and terror under the stone" (p. 375); and Jack, dying of cancer, tries to deny change and mortality. Brother Sumpter, in learning of the evil in his son and the horror of his own desires, has lost everything he values; yet he maintains his humane, Christian ideals against all the destructive forces of the historical process through which he has lived. Jefferson in *Brother to Dragons* also faces the horror of history typified by the senseless murder of a slave. Warren tells him "For in the great bookkeeping/ Of History, what ledger has balanced yet?/ And every entry is a scraw of blood." And finally Jefferson concludes, "If there is glory, the burden, then, is ours/ If there is virtue, the burden, then, is ours" (p. 211).

2

Nature is one of the forces of history with which Warren has dealt in some detail, concerning himself especially with man's place in it and his relation to it. Nature, to Warren, is destructive of the human because it is savagely innocent. As Delmore Schwartz puts it, to Warren nature is "an inexhaustible threat to the human condition".[21] For nature is chaotic, with no human, moral values inherent in it. Warren interprets Robert Frost's "Stopping by Woods on a Snowy Evening" to mean that man must resist the pull into nature; the woods are beautiful and compelling, but the only values are to be found in man, not nature.[22] Furthermore, this idea of nature underlies Warren's criticism and distrust of science. Since science can deal only with physical problems, it is purely materialistic; it is the study of nature. The values derived from it – success, progress, optimism – are, thus, not the human values which man must fashion. The world which Hemingway depicts in his novels is "the God-abandoned one, the Nature-as-all from Nineteenth Century science".[23] Similarly, Dreiser's philosophy is nineteenth-century materialism, "the vision of the God-abandoned and sanction-stripped world of natural process".[24] To live by science is to forfeit all that distinguishes man from the beasts.

To dramatize this concept of nature Warren frequently has one of the main characters go from civilization into the swamps or

---

[21] Delmore Schwartz, "The Dragon of Guilt", *New Republic*, CXXIX (September 14, 1953), p. 18.
[22] "The Themes of Robert Frost", in *Selected Essays*, p. 124.
[23] "Ernest Hemingway", in *Selected Essays*, p. 101.
[24] "An American Tragedy", p. 3.

wilderness. Like the westward journey and the great sleep, this sinking into nature represents an attempt to evade the responsibility of trying to obtain human values from history; it is a surrender to the illogical drift of the forces of the world. The clearest criticism of romantic naturalism, the myth of primitive innocence, occurs in *World Enough and Time*. Escaping hanging, Jeremiah and Rachel flee civilization and enter the wilderness along the Mississippi where they find anything but an idyllic Eden. Since this episode has no basis in historical sources, Warren included it primarily to present his theme. In the domain of La Grand' Bosse, Jeremiah is overcome by "the brute torpor and mire of the place" and finds there a "black peace" (p. 436). In the cane brakes nothing matters; murder – Bosse replies to Jeremiah, who is trying to justify the murder he committed, "Rien, ce n'est rien," – incest, disease, terrible suffering all are meaningless to these savages who have renounced their humanity. After observing what this life has done to himself and the others, Jeremiah comes to realize the error of seeking peace in nature and calls it his third error, denying the idea to embrace the world as all – "to seek communion only in the blank cup of nature and innocence there", for "that innocence is what man cannot endure and be man . . ." (p. 459). The dark, mosquito and cottonmouth infested jungles of the Louisiana bayous in *Band of Angels* afford a hideout for Rau-Ru and his band of marauding outlaws. To this wilderness comes Manty, led by Jimmee, who on the way senselessly clubs a man who was giving him directions. On a dark night in this waste land Rau-Ru, reverting to the lack of values of his savage heritage, hangs Bond, his former master, who had treated him like a son.

While man as a mortal animal is a part of nature, part of the historical process, as Warren believes, at the same time he is above it. Because of the dual nature of man, who is both in and of nature but at the same time above it, his experience, which history records, is tragic. Man must accept the limitations forced upon him by his place in nature while developing the qualities that differentiate him from the non-human world. Tragedy comes from the fact that man, being above nature, must have the dream, the ideal, but, being a part of nature, his dream will be defeated or limited by history. This belief is at the heart of the Fugitives' *I'll Take My Stand*: man must accept his middle place without sinking into mere naturalism or attempting to achieve perfection; it is the same belief that underlies the myth of Daedalus and Icarus. This view of man, according to John Crowe Ransom in *God Without Thunder*, is the source of the tragic spirit; man can never be completely at home in the world because of the precarious balance he must try to maintain but which he nearly always fails to maintain. Warren stated in "Knowledge and the Image of Man" that "man needs courage and clarity of mind to envisage the tragic pathos of life, and once he learns that the tragic experience is universal and a corollary of man's place in nature, he may return to communion with man and nature".[25] The adequate definition of terror, Warren says in interpreting his poem "Terror", is "that proper sense of the human lot, the sense of limitation and the sense of the necessity for responsible action within that limitation".[26] This is the religious sense, the sense that the Fugitive-Agrarians believed one got from humble submission to a stern Old Testament God, the sense that is best fostered by the agrarian life. Even horribly cruel and evil acts may be but perversions of the attempt to rise above these natural limitations. In *Brother to Dragons* Warren realizes at last that Lil's act was merely creation gone astray. And Warren agrees with Conrad that Brown's brutal massacre in *Lord Jim* represents a distortion but a necessary affirmation of his humanity, the human need for moral vindication.[27]

This discrepancy between human desires and their fulfillment is the chief source of the tragic conflict in Warren's main characters. The plots of Warren's narratives that end in tragedy or defeat can be summarized in these terms: a character attempting to break out of the historical process, to define himself as distinct from nature, sets his goals too high, defines them wrongly, or

---

[25] "Knowledge and the Image of Man", p. 187.
[26] "Notes", *Modern Poetry, American and British*, eds. Kimon Friar and John Malcolm Brinin (New York, 1951), p. 543.
[27] "Knowledge and the Image of Man", p. 189.

uses the means of the world to achieve them, and in the process he destroys himself and others. This pattern recurs in *John Brown, Night Rider, World Enough and Time, Brother to Dragons,* and Willie Stark's story in *All the King's Men.* In the novels that end relatively happily the character, instructed by his failure, learns to accept the limitations imposed upon him by history without denying human values. *Band of Angels, The Cave, Wilderness* and *Flood* exhibit this pattern. In the frequent exempla, the simple agrarians and devout Christians afford a glimpse of those, who, through struggle, have arrived at a balance of the two aspects of man's nature. This dual nature of existence also quite frequently underlies Warren's irony. Jeremiah and Rachel after preparing for their suicides with high rhetoric and noble posturing are denied their idealization of themselves when the laudanum they took acts as an emetic. "So after the fine speeches and the tragic stance, the grand exit was muffed." But, Warren explains, this is what the audience, the face of the world, wants, for it never believes in "the fine speeches and the tragic stance" (p. 402). Man can aspire to the stars, but nature and history are such that he is quite likely to trip in a dung heap.

3

Man as well as history, Warren believes, has a dark and evil side, for his nature is depraved. Warren sees man as both good and bad, a coiling, confused darkness of motives which no one can completely understand. This enormous complexity of motives and hidden desires is one reason why we can never fully understand history, which consists as much of the actions of men as of non-human forces. Then, too, Warren believes that man must understand and accept his own individual evil nature before he can formulate values from history and his own past without merely flattering his own black and hidden needs. The nature of man's self consequently limits his ability to make sense of the past, both its human and non-human aspects, and self-understanding is a prerequisite of a right relationship to history. And since man's acts are to Warren the most important part of history, his views on the nature of the self are directly relevant to a study of his philosophy of history. To Warren man is precariously "balanced in his humanity between the black inward abyss of himself and the black outward abyss of nature" and the other forces of history.[28] Evil remains an inextracable part of the constitution of the self, and man must come to terms with this uncomfortable fact. Original Sin – to use the theological term Warren is fond of – is the sin of pride, the failure to accept human limitations, the sin Milton's Eve committed in her desire to be a "Goddess among Gods". No matter how altruistic and sincere man's motives, they are tainted with his depravity. In *All the King's Men* the Scholarly Attorney's tract, to which Jack gave limited assent, explains how this all came about:

Separatenes is identity and the only way for God to create, truly create, man was to make him separate from God Himself, and to be separate from God is to be sinful. The creation of evil is therefore the index of God's glory and His power. That had to be so that the creation of good might be the index of man's glory and power. But by God's help. By His help and in his wisdom.   (pp. 462-63)

To Warren as to Conrad, "Man is a savage animal driven by a black ego." [29] Indeed, one of the values of fiction according to Warren is that in it we see ourselves. "In our deprived selves we must confront the saintly *and* the wicked and either confrontation may be humbling and strengthening." [30] History too, with its record of human sin and brutality, confirms man's depravity and can help him come to terms with his sinful nature. As John Strugnell says of Warren's use of history: "The retelling of history is our attempt to break through to a new understanding of human ambition and human error." [31] Perhaps Warren uses history in part to confront man with his evil nature; he has often chosen stories of almost overwhelming horror as in *Brother to Dragons*, *At Heaven's Gate*, and "The Ballad of Billie Potts" to make the point that we are all brother to dragons.

[28]   "Conrad and *Nostromo*", p. 55.
[29]   *Ibid.*, p. 47.
[30]   "Why Do We Read Fiction?", p. 83.
[31]   Strugnell, pp. 101-02.

Especially in his novels has Warren presented history in such a way as to confirm the evil and ambiguity in all of man's acts and motives. In his first three novels Warren uses the recurrent image of coiling inner darkness to suggest man's nature. Perse Munn never achieves self-knowledge; hence he does not know why he takes perverse pleasure in making May suffer, why he relished destroying her innocent pleasure in her garden which she always planted but never cared for. Willie Proudfit tells him: "They's a hoggishness in man and a hog blindness" (p. 410), but Munn is so deficient in self-knowledge that he never learns the lesson of the exemplum. Ashby in *At Heaven's Gate* contemplates himself and the part of history he has lived through and finds that man is a depraved creature: "There ain't nothing in him but meanness and a hog hollerness and emptiness for the world's slop" (p. 36). A part of the self-knowledge that Jack Burden gains is the realization of his and every man's sinful nature. The Cass Mastern papers help in this education, since to Cass shared guilt and the shared horrors of history prepare the way for acceptance and love. "It is not hard to love men for the things they endure . . ." (p. 199). They endure not only the blank forces of nature but also, and this is what Cass finds so hard to bear, the blackness within the self.

Jeremiah Beaumont, before his education by suffering, lacks the self-knowledge that would affirm man's darker side. He understands too late that behind even his best intentions black, selfish motives lie hidden. A romantic individualist, Jerry trusts to his own heart for direction and council because he has not confronted the ambivalence, ambiguity, and evil in his own motives. Warren tells us, however, that Jerry's obligation to kill Fort sprang from the depth of his being, his "midnight pulse" (p. 115), "the darkness of self" (p. 171). At the end he realizes that his hope for inward innocence was a false one, that he had not done anything for love, conviction, or justice, but for a black inner need. As Jefferson learns in *Brother to Dragons*, human innocence and perfectibility are false hopes, for each man wanders in the darkness of self and of history: "Each man lost, in some blind lobby, hall, enclave/ Crank, cul-de-sac, couloir, or corridor

of Time/ Of Time or self: And in that dark no thread . . ." (p. 7).
Warren chose Housman's lines, "When shall I be dead and
rid/ Of the wrong my father did", as a motto for *Band of Angels*
to suggest man's sinful nature and the necessity of accepting this
fact. Manty painfully and slowly learns that the self is unpre-
dictable, and capable of almost any sin, and that as Warren says
in *Brother to Dragons* "Every act is Janus faced and double"
(pp. 51-2). She came to believe that Hamish had bought her out
of kindness, and he too tries to believe in the goodness of his
motives. The truth is, however, that his real motive was jealousy;
he had wanted to show up the young dandy. Miss Idell, like the
"old grandpa" in "Original Sin: A Short Story", represents, at
times, the sin and evil of the past, or Original Sin. Manty can
never escape her or the thought of her. It was with the sluttish
Miss Idell that her father had died and for whom he had gone in
debt, and the debt caused Manty to be sold into slavery. It is
Miss Idell who constantly threatens to divulge the secret of
Manty's Negro blood, and it is Miss Idell who vulgarly asks her
about her sex life. Only after accepting the ambiguity and evil in
all people and the idea that her father had sinned against her
from worthy motives can she find any peace.

The characters in *The Cave* are also guilty of evading their
sinful natures. Before the entrance to the cave each one who
achieves redemption confronts his darkly ambiguous self. When
Mrs. Harrick torments Jack by asking him why he did not want
his son to live, she realizes how much evil she is capable of.
Brother Sumpter confesses that he had wanted Jack's unborn son
to die and that he had indirectly caused Jasper's death by refusing
to confront the wickedness in his own son. All three realize and
accept their sad, frail humanity. In Warren's world the first step
toward any sort of redemption is to accept the evil in one's self
and in others.

4

Warren believes, then, that because of Original Sin, the sin of
pride, the sin of self, man's motives always bear the taint of his

evil nature. Hence man often turns to history for selfish reasons. We should study history in part for "a fuller understanding of ourselves, and our common humanity",[32] to see what good man with his sinful nature can achieve in the face of blind history. But knowledge of the self and its black needs is a prerequisite if one is to see history as more than a gratification or a projection of his own darkly ambiguous nature. Going to history without self-knowledge makes the past a mere projection of the evil self. We must, Warren says, look for meaning in history that is "more than an illicit gratification of our secret needs and desires".[33] The historical event of the Civil War especially has been interpreted by historians and others to flatter or excuse themselves and their region. The South, Warren claims in *The Legacy of the Civil War*, has used history as an excuse, and the Northerner "being human tends to rewrite history to suit his own deep needs".[34] He rejects the facts that do not fit into the self-deceiving myth he is creating, for "when one is happy in forgetfulness, facts get forgotten".[35] The North sees itself as gallantly and nobly freeing the slaves, forgetting that the Republicans were ready to protect slavery, that the Emancipation Proclamation abolished slavery only in the South, and that racism was all too prevalent in the North. "It is forgotten, in fact, that history is history."[36] The problem which Warren discusses here is a continuation of the problem which Tobias Sears recognized at the end of the Civil War. He saw the Negro being exploited by his "liberators" and he saw the little and pitiful justice which emerged from the grinding process of history being undone in the headlong rush for material success. The reason for this betrayal goes back to a lack of self-knowledge, a failure to recognize the evil side of all motives and actions. As Tobias says, "Oh, Manty, we [the North] undertook to do good in the world, but we had not purged our own soul" (p. 294).

---

[32] *Legacy*, p. 102.
[33] "Edmund Wilson's Civil War", p. 158.
[34] *Legacy*, p. 59.
[35] *Ibid.*
[36] *Ibid.*, pp. 62-63.

Man, then, cannot rightly understand history if he has not purged his soul, confronted his depravity, and made an honest attempt to see history as something more than a gratification of his own hidden needs. As the poet says in "Pursuit", "But history held to your breath clouds like a mirror." [37] And Warren attacks this exploitation of the past in *Brother to Dragons*:

> We know we all need grace,
> And pity, too, and charity is the index,
> Of strength, and the worship of strength is but the index
> Of weakness, but, by God that's still no reason
> To regard all history as a private alibi factory
> And all God's gleaming world as a ward for
>   occupational therapy   (p. 112)

This is also the main theme of "The Circus in the Attic". Leonard Casper is undoubtedly right in his interpretation: History is a circus which each mind carves to suit its own half-seen needs. Since few men know their own motives or those of others, history all too often is the erection of self-satisfying monuments.[38] The U. D. C., "the defenders of ancient pieties and the repositories of ignorance of history", erected a monument to Seth Sykes and Cassius Perkins, who, according to the inscription, died to keep off the invader (p. 5). So well does this flatter the egos of the citizens of Bardsville that they shut their minds to the historical reality: Cassius was drunk and got on the wrong horse trying to escape when the Yankees shot him, and Seth, who cared for neither side, was killed defending his corn. Old Jake Velie knows part of the truth, but the town "would not have believed him or his truth, for people always believe what truth they have to believe to go on being the way they are" (p. 8). Facts of the past, which are hard to come by anyway, get forgotten if forgetting flatters the ego.

The selfish use of the past is an important, recurring theme in Warren's novels. Jack Burden is tough-minded enough as a historian not to fall into this trap; he refuses to interpret either

---

[37]   *Selected Poems, 1923-1943* (New York, 1944), p. 22.
[38]   Leonard Casper, "Robert Penn Warren: Method and Canon", *Diliman Review*, II (July, 1954), p. 281.

the Cass Mastern story or, later, the little piece of history that is his past merely to suit his own needs. But Adam has romantic notions of history which grow out of his lack of self-knowledge. Refusing to confront the blackness within, he cannot accept the evil in the past; he invents a heroic past that is, as Jack knows, unhistorical. In *The Cave* this problem is applied to the interpretation of an individual's personal past by himself and others, and here the results are also tragic. The other characters had interpreted Jack Harrick's personal history to fill their own inner needs. In their minds he became the legendary hillbilly of the ring-tailed roarer stories. "Yeah, Old Jack, he was a heller. He was ring-tail. Hard working between times and made that anvil sing, but when he tuk over the ridge, he was shore Hell's own unquenchable boy-chap. Yeah, a pearl-handle in his hip pocket – .38 on a .44 frame – and one button of his fly unbuttoned to save time and didn't give a durn which he might git aggervated to use first, pistol or pecker" (p. 14). But the old Jack dying of cancer realizes the vicious falseness of this interpretation of himself and his past. "He was a dream dreamed up from the weakness of people. Since people were weak, they dreamed up a dream out of their need for violence, for strength, for freedom" (p. 389). Since the dream flattered his own needs, he had spent his life trying to live up to it. The legend denied self-knowledge to Jack, gave Monty overwhelming feelings of inadequacy, and sent Jasper into the cave to escape people's expecting him to live up to the false myth. Jack finally realizes that the ignorance, weakness, and evil in his own nature have led him to accept this false idea of his past.

5

History is at best amoral and at worst destructive and evil; in itself it offers no redemption to man. And man, guilty of Original Sin, possesses a nature that is, at best, a confused solution of good and bad and, at worst, capable of any monstrosity of evil. But man, Warren believes, is not completely determined by the blind forces of history and the dark forces within. He has free will, the capacity to make moral choices, to choose salvation or damnation; and even though his choice may make little or no difference physically, it will morally. Warren's doctrine of free will, as James Ruoff has said, endows man with a moral choice but gives him no power over the consequences.[39] This belief underlies Warren's statement in his discussion of Faulkner that the South was and is cursed by slavery even if slavery was a historical necessity.[40] Man is morally reponsible even if not always historically or physically responsible. Accepting this freedom of choice enables man to differentiate himself from the brute forces of history and nature. As Warren says in "Knowledge and the Image of Man", man's freedom of choice makes him more than a sum of his history and different from what history does to him.[41] Yet many critics such as H. M. Campbell, have misread Warren and have seen him as a believer in determinism.[42] Part of the reason for this error is that Warren exhaustively analyzes causes; he is interested in the reasons for human action to be found in history – political and economic forces, for example. But a belief in causality does not imply that man is a mere automaton lacking free will. Because he regards man as a free moral agent, he has rejected the psychological theory of behaviorism, which Jack Burden calls "the Great Twitch", a theory which reduces man to a helpless puppet at the mercy of internal and external forces, a puppet with no capacity for choice and consequently with no moral identity. Warren argues that "behaviorism does not provide a workable basis for literature",[43] that this view of man robs one of a belief in "the dignity and interest of humanity".[44] Behaviorism is the way science views man, and it cannot tell the whole truth about him.

[39]   James Ruoff, "Humpty Dumpty and *All the King's Men*: A Note on Robert Penn Warren's Teleology", *Twentieth Century Literature*, III (October, 1957), p. 130.
[40]   "William Faulkner", p. 75.
[41]   "Knowledge and the Image of Man", p. 187.
[42]   Harry Modean Campbell, "Warren as Philosopher in *World Enough and Time*", in *Southern Renascence*, p. 234.
[43]   "Not Local Color", p. 159.
[44]   "Literature as a Symptom", p. 267.

The doctrine of free will is basic to Warren's reading of history. In "How Texas Won Her Freedom" he directly confronts this problem of fate and free will in regard to Sam Houston. He asks whether Houston stumbled into his greatness, whether he merely rode the wave of history, or whether he planned that victory and created his destiny. As Warren sees it, both history and the individual will were causes. "He was an actor in the deepest sense – the sense that makes a man see himself in history. Even in the moment of action such a man sees the act as a story, fulfilled in the gesture the actor makes. The poor blundering human being, trapped in life's confusions, is always staring at that grander self-image, outside of Time, which even in the moment of despair he must discern." [45] Houston had a plan, and his victory was not merely a result of fate. If this is true, history or fate cannot properly be used as an excuse for failure. At the end of *John Brown* the sick and disillusioned Brown awaiting execution feels himself to be a victim of fate. "It was as if, for the first time, John Brown was thinking of himself as a mere victim, and not as an active agent who willed the deed and its accomplishment." [46] Warren does not agree, for the tenor of the book emphasizes Brown's guilt. Warren does not treat Brown fairly, but he does see him as one who laid a strong hand strongly on life and who had a hand in his destiny. Warren explores this problem more generally in *The Legacy of the Civil War*. By "the Great Alibi" the Southerner blames all his problems, from pellagra and hookworm to laziness and blood lust on history. And he is apt to see the race problem as "the doom defined by history". "Since the situation is given by history, the Southerner therefore is guiltless; is, in fact, an innocent victim of a cosmic conspiracy." "He is trapped in history." [47] But this attitude is, Warren says, a mere escape mechanism to avoid living in "the agony of will". At the end Warren asks "Can we, in fact, learn only that we are victims of nature and of history? Or can we learn that we can make, or

[45] "How Texas Won Her Freedom", *Holiday*, XXIII (March, 1958), p. 73.
[46] *John Brown*, p. 376.
[47] *Legacy*, pp. 55-56.

at least have a hand in the making of, our future?" [48] From what has gone before his answer is obvious. Sam Houston tried to impose his will on history and succeeded; John Brown tried and failed, but both had the dream, the vision outside the ruck of history; both lived in the "anguish of option" while striving in "the hot day and glare of contingency" (p. 111).

All of the novels offer the drama of the individual who, although caught up in the forces of history, in most cases opposes these forces with his will, his moral vision. Though Perse Munn feels trapped in the non-human forces of history and nature, he does have free will. His problem is that he fails to exercise the moral vigor needed to oppose the blind, massive drift of events which in part cause his actions. He does not force his human faculties to try to shape his destiny, and he feels that accidents, "which were his history", determine him (p. 103). Munn merely drifts, surrendering to inevitability, existing in a spiritual and moral torpor. He sees his future already like a memory; this absolves him of responsibility, he believes, for there is "no will in the act of memory, for it is complete and is in one time out of time, he thought; for as he moved down the road, thinking of that other night, he felt removed, even now, from the present experience, as though it were in memory" (p. 191). Dr. Mac-Donald finds the answer to the problem of fate and free will in a deterministic behaviorism. A man, he believes, merely does what is in him; the "thing in him comes out" regardless of his will. "One way or another, that's what a man does. What's in him" (p. 355).

Similarly in *At Heaven's Gate* it is the wills of men as well as historical events that lead to violence and evil. Duckfoot realizes this and will not accept Jerry's repeated excuses that important things came up to keep him from their study sessions. "I shore-God do think it's miraculous how brute event can conform to the secret will of man" (p. 81). The dramatic versions of *All the King's Men* show the central fact about Willie's story even more clearly than does the novel; in these versions of the tragedy Willie

[48] *Legacy*, p. 102.

is caught in the maze he has contrived for himself, contrived out of his own freedom of choice. In the novel Jack is fully aware of the grandeur of Willie's opposing his will to the historical process. The life history of people like Willie, Jack says, is "not, as for you and me, sons of luck, a process of becoming what luck makes us" (pp. 67-68). As in a Greek tragedy, the grinding machine of history wins in the end, but this does not detract from the greatness of Willie's effort, a testimony to the moral superiority of the human to the anonymous forces of history. Later, Jack reaches Warren's conclusion that man has free will in the midst of forces he cannot control. Adam and Willie, he believes, were doomed to destroy each other because both were incomplete. "They were doomed, but they lived in the agony of will" (p. 330). And looking back on the history he has experienced and read about, Jack rejects the Great Twitch, a theory that robs man of all nobility because it teaches that nothing is anybody's fault for "things are always as they are" (p. 330). He had seen too many people live and die to believe in anything that could not give man the dignity of a freedom of choice.

Victimized by self-pity Manty occasionally sees herself as merely an expression of history. ". . . you do not live your life, but somehow your life lives you, and you are, therefore, only what History does to you" (p. 134). Hamish, too, denies freedom in order to justify his slave running, an action he knows to be evil. "And I said, I didn't make this world and make 'em drink blood and didn't make myself and I can't help what I am doing. They drove me to it" (p. 189). But Manty learns by contemplation of her personal history and that of those whose lives had impinged upon hers that fatalism and determinism are merely attempts to evade responsibility in order to surrender to the tide of history.

Isaac Sumpter in *The Cave* is the only major character in the novel who remains steadfast in self-ignorance, self-deception, and self-pity. In order to deceive himself into a belief in his own innocence, he blames everything on history, on the trap of the world which conspired to cause him to sin. With this sophistical reasoning he deludes himself into a belief in his purity. History is at fault, not himself. "For he had planned nothing. That thought began to grow in him. It was all, in a way, an accident" (p. 281). His father, who goes into the cave in order to atone for his son's sin, tells him that Jasper had been too badly stuck to have been saved. Physically, then, Isaac could not have saved Jasper, but morally, Warren implies, he is as guilty as if he had killed him with his own hand. Blind, amoral events caused Jasper's death, but morally it is Isaac's fault for failing to live in the agony of will as his father and the Harricks do. And they salvage something from the horror of the historical process through which they have lived.

World Enough and Time is perhaps Warren's fullest presentation of the relationship between the nature of man and the forces of history – the theme of fate and free will. Yet several critics have misunderstood Warren's presentation of the theme in this novel. Here both philosophy and method cause difficulty. William Frank complains that there is a conflict between theme – the idea of free will – and the plot which, with such events as the triggering of the murder by the handbill, makes Jeremiah seem a pitiful puppet at the mercy of external influences.[49] Frank fails to perceive that to Warren Jeremiah had a moral choice even had he been completely physically determined, which, of course, he is not. As Warren says, "Jeremiah Beaumont was a chip on the tide of things, a tide shot through by sudden rips and twisted currents. But if Jeremiah Beaumont was a chip on the tide, he was a thinking and suffering chip . . ." (p. 283). And this passage illustrates the main difficulty with Harry Modean Campbell's contention that in *World Enough and Time* Warren is a determinist.[50] Mr. Campbell does not see the ambiguity which is Warren's method, a method he uses to support his belief in the enormous complexity of the past and the impossibility of knowing it completely. Jerry, like many of Warren's characters, falls into the error of fatalism. "He felt that the future was beyond plan, it already existed, he would discover it step by step as he moved toward some flame, some point of light, beyond the murk and

[49] Joseph Frank, "Romanticism and Reality in Robert Penn Warren", *Hudson Review*, IV (Summer, 1951), p. 257.
[50] Campbell, p. 229.

mist of things" (p. 62). Then he falls into the error of behaviorism. He felt that all man's life was "but the twisting and contortion of a cat hung up strangling in a string for sport of boys" (p. 388). But in the end he rejects both determinism and behaviorism for responsibility and the freedom of the will even though man must live amid conditions that are likely to destroy both him and his dream.

The blind ruck of history, then, can offer man only raw material to oppose and shape by an act of his will into meaningful human values. Warren has many portraits of people who have given over to the chaos of history, who have sunk into history. To do so is to surrender the purely human to the purely inhuman and to become a monster with no morals. This is precisely what Isaac becomes by trusting to the "logic" of history: "You really couldn't plan. You had to trust to the logic of things to work out. He made his mind a blank" (p. 284). He becomes as brutal and as amoral as the historical process he has surrendered to. Professor Havard has said that the real villains in Warren are "the prideful amoralists", those who have embraced the corruption of the world and have become complete materialists.[51] These are the Bogan Murdocks to whom power and money are everything and the Tiny Duffys, whom Willie keeps around to remind him of that aspect of his own character. The enigmatic Wilkie Barron epitomizes this group. It was he who instigated the tragedy, and it was he who saved Jeremiah from hanging only to have him decapitated later. Jerry decides that Wilkie is but "the mask of the world" and as such neither good nor bad, neither to be loved or hated (p. 456). His actions seem as patternless and capricious as the chaos of history, to which he completely surrenders. "But the Wilkies of the world never have to plan. They need only to be themselves, to be Wilkie, and the world plans for them" (p. 462).

Other characters in Warren's novels by falling into the error of living by history turn naturally to a characteristic of history – senseless violence, while others become brutally indifferent. The

[51]   William C. Havard, "The Burden of the Literary Mind: Some Meditations on Robert Penn Warren as a Historian", *South Atlantic Quarterly*, LXII (Autumn, 1963), p. 521.

violence of his characters reflects the chaotic, random violence of history. Charles R. Anderson states Warren's belief: "Man must live in the world of violence by whatever principles of order he can formulate and believe in. The man who makes up personal rules as expediency dictates or abstract ideas based on imperfect knowledge of the world falls into violence, moral or physical, almost as surely as the materialist who denies the validity of morals in a naturalistic universe." [52] Perse Munn, unable to formulate any moral principles from the confusion of his life, is buffeted by the forces of history and the forces of the self. The novel records his increasing use of force – his night riding, the fight in the bar, the murder of Bunk, the raid on the warehouses, and the killing of the militia men. And all have less and less meaning, less and less principle behind them until they seem as random and irresponsible as history. As Warren says in his interpretation of "Terror", to become adjusted to the forces of history is to fall into senseless violence. The historian who reports the forces of the past and the actions of men and who remains withdrawn, detached, and indifferent, is like the materialist, guilty of surrendering to the neutrality of history. Jack Burden, for a time, tried to be a disinterested researcher looking for the historical facts. "A student of history does not care what he digs out of the ash pile, the midden, the sublunary dung heap, which is the human past" (p. 167). Sinking into the "comforting, subliminal ooze on the sea floor of History" (p. 327), he tries at first to evade the responsibility of making moral sense of history; he embraces its meaninglessness, and this indifference leads to tragedy.

6

What makes history, as Warren conceives of it, hold even more terror for man is that even though historical events are in themselves blind, all people and events which make up history are complexly bound together in a cosmic net like a spider web. Nothing exists in a vacuum; everything impinges on everything else.

[52] Anderson, p. 224.

Warren sees time too as a web. Past, present, and future are inextricably bound together and respond to one another. Any moment of time contains within it not only the past but also the future. This theory gives point to his concern with the past. *The Legacy of the Civil War*, for example, discusses the far-reaching consequences of the conflict and its manifestations today so that Americans can more intelligently plan for the future. And in *Segregation* Warren looks to the past to discover the reasons why Americans are confronted with this turmoil today. Likewise the individual is interrelated not only with others with whom he exists in history, but he exists as a continuum of interrelated selves. The entire past and all the individual's past selves are always present, and there can be no future unless one shoulders the burden of the past. Warren frequently uses the metaphor of the individual's relation with his father or his family to depict this idea. This view of history owes something to the historical sense of the Fugitives to whom the past was a continuing reality and never really dead. But Warren has greatly extended this idea so that his view in some respects resembles Coleridge's "sacramental vision" or the theme of "the one life", which he discusses in his essay on "The Rhyme of the Ancient Mariner". Touching the web of life by killing an albatross has greater and more far-reaching tragic consequences than anyone could have predicted. And in Warren as in Coleridge the web usually results in tragedy for man.

Warren's concept of the interrelatedness of all things in history does not mean that there is an objective moral order to the universe. The ultimate moral meaning of the cosmic web depends upon man, not history. And man must remain ignorant of the consequences of even his most simple acts; hence his proper attitude is one of humility. Further, just to exist without acting is to touch the web. The theme of the victor-victim, the tyranny of innocence, indicates that to Warren innocence is impossible as well as undesirable. A corollary of this web theory is that nothing is ever lost; the reverberations of the web never cease, and man can never know the end of anything. But the fact that all is never for naught can be little consolation to man, for the results may be exactly opposite to his intentions. History can give us only limited perspective on the action of the web, but since the past is always present, the historian's job is important. He must bring the past and the present together so that from them we can frame the future. Every man must be, in a sense, something of a historian, for to achieve self-knowledge one must first come to terms with his heritage and his personal past.

Warren's cosmic web theory can be seen in his admiration for authors who give a lively sense of the presence of the past, those who see the present as an outgrowth of the past in such a way that the past is never really dead. The strength of Faulkner, for example, lies, in part, in his concern with "the interpenetration of past and present",[53] seen too in his distinctive use of time: "Time spreads and is the important thing, the terrible thing. A tremendous flux is there, things flowing away in all directions. Moments not quite ready to be shaped are already there, waiting and we feel their presence." [54] Joseph Conrad has this ability to a remarkable extent. Conrad's statement about Mrs. Gould, which Warren quotes in his essay on *Nostromo*, perfectly sums up his own idea: "It had come into her mind that for life to be large and full, it must contain the care of the past and of the future in every passing moment of the present." [55] Warren in his histories also often suggests the far-reaching repercussions of even the most seemingly trivial events. Mass production, he says in *The Legacy of the Civil War*, came about as part of the Northern war effort, and mass production led to the ready-made clothing industry as an offshoot of the manufacture of large numbers of blue uniforms, "and would not this standardization of fashion, after the sartorial whim, confusion, fantasy and individualism of an earlier time, have some effect on man's relation to man?" [56]

In his first two novels Warren appears to be working toward the cosmic web theory, and he does not seem to be fully aware of the several corollaries he later drew. *Night Rider* exhibits this

---

[53]   "The Redemption of Temple Drake", *New York Times Book Review* (September 30, 1951), p. 31.
[54]   *The Paris Review Interviews*, p. 202.
[55]   "Conrad and *Nostromo*", p. 36.
[56]   *Legacy*, p. 10.

theory only in rudimentary form. To search for an absoluteness in time, as Perse Munn does, is to deny the endless reverberations of any act. Munn wants all of the problems of his life brought together at one place and in one time so that all would be over once and for all. Captain Todd, however, knows that nothing in man's life is ever final. Munn only dimly and vaguely grasps the idea that no act exists in one time only and that there are no endings in history. As he rides down the same road he had travelled a year earlier he thinks: "It is the same road, he thought, and I am the same man and I am doing the same thing, but it is a different time and it is a different thing, or is it a different thing, only a different time? – for then I rode here to find the knife, and my riding here now is part of that same act, completing itself, fulfilling a single thought, the same gesture or an act of the will" (p. 181). But he uses this idea to justify himself, thinking that in memory there is no will; hence he is now guiltless. Later, on killing Bunk he obtains release and fulfillment since he feels that this moment was "a moment without affiliations with the past or the future. He tried to sink into that moment, trying to escape from time by surrendering most completely to time" (p. 202). Warren's lesson is that all time is in each moment; one cannot, therefore, deny the past or the future consequences of the present moment.

With *At Heaven's Gate* Warren has advanced his theory only slightly. Sue is the main character who acts or tries to act as if the present moment was all there was. She shut her mind "to history and the future as to the most trivial irrelevancies" to "maintain and define the moment" (p. 313). And Ashby Wyndham meditates upon the awful irony of life, an irony that indicates the complexity and the crazy interrelatedness of all things. Ashby preached salvation to Pearl, a prostitute, and she repented, but ironically as a result of her salvation she killed a policeman who tried to stop them from preaching on the street corner. As Ashby said, "Oh God she laid off one sin for salvation and salvation taken her to another sin. Oh Lord your will has run lak the fox and sly. The pore man's mind snuffs after it lak a hound dog. But the scent is done lost and the ways of its goin"

(p. 328). Duckfoot Blake at the end rather surprisingly and un-
convincingly loses his cynical aloofness on experiencing a moment
of truth in which he learns that since the past is never dead, nothing is ever over and hence everything matters.

> Duckfoot Blake knew that everything mattered. He knew that every-
> thing he had ever done or said or thought mattered. He knew that all
> those years which had been full of his goings and comings and his
> loneliness and his pride and his pitiful pleasures mattered. He knew it,
> at last, and all the years he had lived were there all at once in him
> and around him, and that was horrible. . . . He knew that it mattered,
> but he did not know how it mattered, or why, as he stood there with
> the long, unpowerful arm uplifted, and felt sick and exalted with his
> knowledge.   (pp. 372-73)

Warren, himself, at this stage of his career seems not to have
fully formulated his theory, and Duckfoot's proclamation seems
an afterthought, for neither plot nor statement has prepared for
it. But it is a development of the theory presented in his first
novel, where the idea that everything matters is absent.

This philosophy of history appears most fully in *All the King's
Men* along with a great deal more philosophical justification and
explanation. Warren explains its operation and explores its several
ramifications fully for the first time. The Cass Mastern story
dramatizes this theory, and it provides the basic metaphor to
explain it. Cass accepts the fact that all the betrayal, suffering,
and tragedy had come from his "single act of sin and perfidy, as
the boughs from the bole and the leaves from the bough. Or to
figure the matter differently, it was as though the vibration set up
in the whole fabric of the world by my act had spread infinitely
and with ever increasing power and no man could know the end"
(p. 189). Cass is able to frame a moral value from the reverberations of the web that Warren had not dealt with before. "I do not
question the Justice of God, that others have suffered for my sin,
for it may be that only by the suffering of the innocent does God
affirm that men are brothers, and brothers in His Holy Name"
(p. 199). After studying the papers Cass left behind, Jack describes what life had taught Cass:

> He learned that the world is like an enormous spider web and if you

touch it, however lightly, at any point, the vibration ripples to the remotest perimeter and the drowsy spider feels the tingle and is drowsy no more but springs out to fling the gossamer coils about you who have touched the web and then inject the black, numbing poison under your hide. It does not matter whether or not you meant to brush the web of things. Your happy foot of your gay wing may have brushed it ever so lightly, but what happens always happens and there is the spider bearded black and with his great faceted eyes glittering like mirrors in the sun, or like God's eye, and the fangs dripping. (p. 200)

Jack finds that the web operates in his own life just as it had in Cass Mastern's. Looking out at the crowd cheering to support Willie in the impeachment trial, Jack knows that all has been arranged behind the scenes. He feels like God "brooding on History" because he thinks he knows how everything will turn out. The crowd to him "looked like History, because I knew the end of the event of which they were a part or thought I knew the end" (p. 161). He had, however, seen only the direct results of the impeachment, not the far-reaching consequences of the forces that had been unleashed. Later, he also learns that all time is one time, that the past and future participate in the present. With Anne in the present he realizes how time is never over; he sees "that the moment tonight was just an extension of the moment long back, on the picnic, that this moment had been in that moment all the time" (p. 293). Hence, ". . . nothing is lost, nothing is ever lost". "And all times are one time, and all those dead in the past never lived before our definition gives them life, and out of the shadow their eyes implore us" (p. 242). "But if anything is certain, it is that no story is ever over, for the story which we think is over is only a chapter in a story which will never be over . . ." (p. 378). It is as Warren describes time metaphorically in his poem, "In Italian they call the Bird *Civetta*": "And Time is crumpled like paper/ Crushed in my hand." [57]

After so clearly presenting the web theory of history in *All The King's Men*, Warren turned in his next novels to exploring it in several of its major ramifications. Indeed, he even parodied the theory in a short story, "The Confession of Brother Grimes",

[57]   *You, Emperors, and Others*, p. 42.

published the year after *All the King's Men*. Sue, the daughter of Brother Grimes, married the wild and reckless Archie Munn, who, soon afterwards, drunk and speeding, ran into a wagon and killed Sue and the Negro driver. Afterwards Archie repented. "Brother Grimes said it had all happened just to save Archie's soul and bring him to his senses and that now he could lean on Archie, and that Sue Grimes and Mrs. Grimes would be glad to have it that way. Either he had forgotten the nigger or he wasn't so sure how the nigger would feel about it" (p. 173). Finally, however, Brother Grimes admits that the real cause of the tragedy was his own vanity: he had been using black hair dye for twenty years.

A major theme in *World Enough and Time* is the tragic irony of history and the dilemmas it offers man. And Jerry recognizes this. He reasons that should he die in killing Fort, Rachel would be left unprotected, but should he stay with her his obligation to kill Fort would remain unfulfilled (p. 211). No matter where he turns, he is damned. It is also ironical that at his trial, although he is guilty, he is convicted on lies. So complex and interrelated are all the neutral events and forces of history that lies can be true and the truth can be a lie. The chief irony of the novel involves the cosmic web theory. Both Jeremiah and Warren in the end ask, "Was all for naught?" (p. 465). The answer seems to be that nothing has been changed by Jeremiah's agony and aspiration, for Warren points out that there is still little justice in Kentucky. The ripples of Jerry's life seem to have died away. Warren's point is that man cannot know the effects for good or evil of this bit of history. Any effects for good come from the instruction Jerry's story offers to individual man, for man not history must make sense. As Dr. Burnham says, "Nothing human was ever to be lost, though burdened with error" (pp. 220, 221).

The chief manifestation of the irony of history, the complex and ambiguous net of history in *Band of Angels* is the victor and victim theme. Warren had in *Brother to Dragons* developed this same theme. George wreaks "his merciless frailty" on Lilburn, and Warren says this means that "we're all each other's victim" (p. 140). Manty's self-pitying innocence has tragic consequences, for she invites the sweet injustice. Her helpless innocence leads

Rau-Ru to hit Charles to protect her, and this act makes him a hunted outlaw. To exist is to touch the web. Manty sets in motion forces that she cannot comprehend. Rau-Ru tells her all is her fault, for "You're just the way you are" (p. 327). Unable to accept the savage nature of her innocence, she constantly looks for reasons for her suffering. But in so doing she has some rudimentary understanding of the tangled nature of life. She thinks perhaps she is in slavery because she had unwittingly told on Old Shaddy, another victim of her innocence. But she feels that her suffering is unjust, not realizing that man's ideas of justice are not inherent in history. Later, meditating upon the great influence on her of such disparate people as unknown New York bankers, Washington politicians, and John Brown, she asks, "Oh who is whose victim?" (p. 135). The answer is, of course, that we all exist in history, and, hence, we are all each other's victims. Illustrating her statement, "For when is the reality of a moment to be defined? In act or consequence? And in what consequence?" (p. 339), Manty begins Chapter Eight with an excellent discussion of the net of history, the way one meaningless event leads to another in a snowballing effect, except that the snowball follows a predictable pattern; events do not. A little girl admired Farragut's braid while he was a member of the Northern forces occupying New Orleans. The girl's mother spat in his face; this caused General Butler's order that Southern women must treat Federal soldiers with respect; this order led to Manty's experience with the insolent Northern soldiers who demanded respect; Tobias Sears came to her aid, and thus she met her future husband. If the little girl had not been attracted to Farragut's colorful braid, Manty would have had a very different history.

In *The Cave* almost every event and action merely continues an event or action from the past. Nick's sleeping with Dorothy Cutlick was only "the unbroken continuum in which other things could be said to happen". It began years before when her father had tried to rape her. "This was simply the extension of what had begun to happen years ago . . ." (p. 59). To illustrate the participation of all times in one time Warren uses the image of a natural process filmed and run off "at a speed to compress all time" (p.

63). And here too is the awful terror of prayer fulfilled, for "who can withstand the horror of that vision of prayer fulfilled?" (p. 91). That is, the web is far too illogical and complex for the poor mind of man to know what it asks for. As Old Jebb in "Blackberry Winter" says, "A man doan know what to pray for, and him mortal" (p. 87). And in *Flood* the characters respond more to the past than to the events of the present.

7

If history is a cosmic net, if all times are one time, if the future as well as the past exists in the present, then the individual self exists as a continuum of selves. Just as the future cannot be radically different from the past, new innocence is impossible. One must frame the future self by an understanding and acceptance of all the past selves, and this idea has the corollary that one must accept one's father, family, and heritage. To reject these is to reject the past and one's past self, and without these there can be no future. The concept of time as a flow, as in "The Ballad of Billie Potts" is wrong and dangerous in that it makes one think that new beginnings are possible. In Warren's works, then, one finds a large number of characters who reject the past in one way or another and who attempt to be reborn, to obtain innocence by rejecting their past selves and their heritage. The recurring theme of loveless and passionless seduction dramatizes this rejection. Sara Darter in "Circus in the Attic" coldly seduces Bolton on the red plush sofa under the portrait of her dead father while her aunt walks about upstairs. The next day she leaves Bardstown for Nashville without taking a single memento of the past with her. Sue in *At Heaven's Gate* indicates her hatred of her father by seducing Jerry, uncomfortable and apprehensive, on the downstairs sofa while her family is in the house. And in *World Enough and Time* Rachel expresses her intense hatred of her mother by giving herself to Jerry while the sick old lady wanders about the cold house. In each case sex represents rebellion, a way of expressing hatred and contempt for one's family and hence indirectly for one's self.

Sex is only one of several ways in which characters reject the past. Because the past holds no importance to him, Perse Munn in *Night Rider* fails to see any continuity in his actions. He searches for happiness "as a thing in itself, an entity separate from the past activities of his life" (p. 160). Since he has denied his past and his past selves, he cannot understand or even plan for the future. "His mind did not really confront the idea of the future." "He did not have the seed of the future in himself, the live germ. It had shriveled up and died" (p. 385). Willie Proudfit returns to his source, his origins, to accept the burden of his heritage and his own personal past. But Munn fails to profit from Proudfit's example.

Father-rejection is the prevailing narrative and thematic pattern of *At Heaven's Gate,* and Warren repeats this theme with repetitious regularity. Most of the characters in one way or another flee their heritage, rejecting their past and their past selves. Ashby sells his ancestral farm, thus rejecting his agrarian past, and goes to work for the exploiters. Realizing his sin, he makes his whole life an atonement. Jerry Calhoun likewise rejects his agrarian past and his noble but clumsy father, of whom he is ashamed, to become an executive for Murdock. He does not realize as did Jefferson that "The failures of our fathers are the failures we shall make" (p. 28). He tries to be totally different. Walking in the woods where he used to hunt, he thinks: "Yes, he said, he had used to come here a lot, a long time back. But it did not seem possible. He thought of himself walking alone through these woods. But it did not seem possible" (p. 127). He exists not as a whole but as a series of unrelated selves. He returns home in the end but not in acceptance. Rather, the past draws him back, proving that it is always present, not to be denied. Sweetwater becomes a Marxist labor organizer in direct opposition to his father, a conservative, genteel Episcopal rector, who lives in dreams of the lost cause. Slim, unable to accept his mundane father, who is a washing machine salesman, invents a fantastically romantic self and past for himself. Father-rejection in each case leads to a lack of self-knowledge, to confusion, and to violence.

All the King's Men also develops this theme but less obviously.
Willie either ignored the past almost entirely or used it to political
advantage. He visits his father, whom he treats with an appalling
lack of courtesy, merely to have his picture taken for the papers,
to prepare the documents for history, Jack says. His ties with the
past and his heritage are phony. The main feature that distinguishes this novel from the earlier ones is the presence of significantly more hope of reconciliation. Jack had rejected his sup-
posed father because he could not accept his weakness, and his
mother for her lack of love. Learning that Irwin is his father and
that his mother was capable of deep human involvement, he
accepts them and his past. He tells Anne that "if you could not
accept the past and its burden there was no future, for without
one there cannot be the other, and how if you could accept the
past you might hope for the future, for only out of the past can
you make the future" (p. 460).

Both Jeremiah and Rachel in *World Enough and Time* deny
continuity, Rachel by her implacable hatred and rejection of her
mother and Jerry by thinking that if he killed Fort "the past
would be dead" (p. 213). And these attitudes combine to help
bring about their tragedy. Learning of her Negro blood and what
she thinks is her father's betrayal, Amantha Starr in *Band of
Angels* can accept neither. Her life becomes a resolute attempt to
put the past behind her. On marrying Tobias she feels that he has
released her from her bondage to her personal history. "Free
from everything in the world, all the past, all my own self, free
to create my new self." "What had the past to do with me? Nothing, I told myself, and believed it" (p. 234). But, like Jack, she
regains her past by accepting her father and the ultimate goodness
of his motives and this sets her free to plan for the future. Hamish
Bond is in bondage to the past because he has denied it by taking
a new name – Alec Hinks is his real one – and inventing a new
self. The two separate identities and his split personality – the
brutal slave trader and the generous rich man who has kindness
like a disease – point out his fragmentation. *The Cave* explores
all these themes but not repetitiously. Isaac Sumpter not only
rejects his father by leaving, but also cruelly taunts the old man

who had sacrificed himself in order to save his son. Nick Papo-
doupolous, Jack Harrick, and Mr. Bingham all confront the
same problem. They cannot see how what they are now is dependent on what they once were. How, Jack wonders, did the little
boy he once was turn into an old man dying of cancer. As Mr.
Bingham asks, "How could such things be in the same life?"
(p. 398). This is a basic question in Warren's novels. How does
one moment of time contain within it all moments?

8

There is a close relationship between image, structure, and theme
in all of Warren's novels. Recurrent images, for example, suggest
that in the blank forces of history it is man who must create
ideals and values. The many descriptions of a small area of
human warmth and order surrounded by vast stretches of waste
and desolation or of a small bit of light surrounded by vast darkness suggest that man and his values are dangerously situated
amid the forces of history. At the conclusion of "The Unvexed
Isles" Professor Dalrymple realizes the insubstantiality of his life,
and Warren ends the story with a description of a precarious
island of light amid violent darkness. "While the wind sweeping
down the great valley of the Mississippi beat the town, beat the
house, and hurled the sparse lost flakes through the upper
reaches of darkness, he sat in the ring of steady light from the
bronze lamp on his desk" (p. 203). Perse Munn is, throughout
the novel, forever outside any light or warmth. Travelling through
the bare fields in the snow Munn notices the contrasting brightness
and warmth of the senator's house, but he himself is outside in
the cold. He frequently stares into the "blue blankness" of the
sky (p. 442), and the only light and warmth he achieves is ironically the flash of his pistol as he fires blindly into the dark. As
the images suggest, he has created no human values out of history. While Sadie tells him of her part in the tragedy of history
which they have both lived through, Jack looks out from the
sanatorium window to the bayou "coiled under the moss depending from the line of tattered cypresses on the farther bank,

the algae-mottled water heavy with the hint and odor of swamp, jungle, and darkness, along the edge of the clipped lawn" (p. 436). Man here seems to be fighting a losing battle against the forces of nature which threaten to obliterate his poor achievements. Rachel's garden, which is mentioned frequently in *World Enough and Time*, stands in lonely solitude in the emptiness of the vast landscape. "Then she looked away over the fields to the woods and thought how small the garden was in the wideness of the land . . ." (p. 53). And it is only for a short time that Jeremiah finds in Rachel's lighted library a center of brightness amid "the violence and mire and dullness of the world" (p. 98). Manty's nightmare, recurring throughout *Band of Angels*, is of loss of human identity in a wasteland of desert. "It was the feeling of that old nightmare of mine, of being in the middle of a desert and the horizon fleeing away in all directions" (p. 163).

Warren uses several other devices besides images to reflect his philosophy of history. His characteristic method of proliferation of detail, of completeness of presentation ties in with his cosmic web theory. If any detail may be connected with any other detail in mysterious and illogical ways and thus have far-reaching consequences beyond its intrinsic importance, how can one decide which facts are important enough for inclusion and which are not? Then, too, the use of many facts and details indicates the complex density of historical reality and the enormous difficulty of man's task of making moral sense of the flux of history. Warren's use of ambiguity and irony, similarly, suggests the complexity of history and the impossibility of arriving at any final answers about the past. To reflect historical truth a novel must sometimes be ambiguous. Warren in *Night Rider*, for example, asks why the men led by Captain Todd defended the ford against two companies of Yankee soldiers even though all was lost. The answer is ambiguous, for Warren provides several explanations in the form of questions. In *World Enough and Time* Warren consistently uses the method of ambiguity to speculate on causes and motives. Since irony, he believes, is often inherent in man's contact with the forces of history, it becomes one of his favorite devices. Good intentions ironically, and cruelly or tragically so, often bring evil results. In his attempt to obtain justice for the tobacco farmers, Perse Munn becomes an almost inhuman moral wreck. Willie's noble idea of building a hospital to benefit all and of keeping it free of graft brings on tragedy and installs Tiny as governor. And finally, there is the irony of history which is the hardest for man to bear – that all seems to have been for naught; man's efforts and suffering seem to have yielded nothing. The narrator of *World Enough and Time* informs the reader that in spite of Jerry's noble search for justice, in spite of the tumult of the Old Court versus the New, in spite of the search for justice by many of the characters, there is today in Kentucky and in all the land no more justice than in the eighteen-twenties. And despite the human effort and the suffering involved in trying to wrest something enduring from life, Fiddlersbrug, in *Flood,* is soon to be obliterated by the TVA lake.

Warren's method of ordering his novels and of presenting chunks of experience reflects the idea that each moment of the present contains the past and the future. He never uses a straightforward chronological arrangement, but rather structures his novels to show the presence of the past, to gain a perspective on the future, to illustrate the chaotic and complex flux of history, and to show the way in which any action may set up a chain reaction that can reach out indefinitely and have consequences far beyond man's ability to foresee. Warren in his first novel moves backward and forward in time to show how one time can influence all time. He frequently explains Munn's present feelings by comparing them with his feelings as a boy. When Munn learns that his life has no center, Warren explains his feelings by the way he reacted as a child when he found that the beautiful, motionless world of the stereopticon was not real but just a flat, lifeless card. Then, too, Warren presents an action and only much later does he fill in the background. Chapter Ten, for instance, begins, after Lucille has already become Munn's mistress, with his waiting for her to come to him. Only later does Warren present the sequence of events leading to this result, by such statements as "But the hinges worked silently now, not like the first time" (pp. 236-237). Chaos in structure in this novel reflects the chaos in the mind of Munn and others who are caught in the turmoil of history of which they can make little sense. Chapter Eight begins in the middle of a serious meeting of the association at Wilson's Cafe. Only very slowly does the reader discover what the meeting is about, and until he does, the events seem a meaningless flux of unrelated items.

The narrative line of *At Heaven's Gate* opens *in medias res* with Jerry at the height of his career. From this point Warren works both ways, explaining the present and the future by returning to the past, while gradually advancing the plot. The large number of characters and their separate stories add further complexity to the narrative line partly in order to reflect the confusions of history. The rather surprising way in which the two narratives, which had seemed entirely separate, converge at the end of the novel affirms structurally the cosmic web theory – the far-reaching influences of any act and the strange way in which lives touch other lives. Flashbacks here give a sense of the never-ending past. But frequently they are not logically convincing. Warren states that Jerry ordinarily never thought of his past, yet in order to fill in his personal history and heritage, he has him think back to his boyhood in an extremely long flashback while he sits with the important guests at Bogan Murdock's house. And within this flashback concerning Jerry's early life on his father's farm Warren glances into the future to the time when Jerry is helping his father financially (p. 49).

All the King's Men also begins in the middle with Jack using long flashbacks as he slowly advances the narrative in an extremely complex pattern. Early in the novel, Jack, telling in 1939 of the trip to Mason City in 1936, flashes back to the morning in 1922 when he met Willie at Slade's place. While telling this he jumps ahead to a conversation with Willie about their first meeting, a conversation later than the time from which he originally began the flashback (pp. 16-18). As he frequently does, in *All the King's Men* Warren often passes up suspense by telling the outcome before he dramatizes the story. His purpose is to give a sense of all time present at once. Jack presents the Cass Mastern Story in this way. And immediately after Willie was shot Jack states: "The Boss did not die there in the lobby under the dome. In fact he lived quite a while and died on a clean, white, antiseptic bed, with all the benefits of science" (p. 421). Casting *World Enough and Time* in the form of a history provides Warren with excellent opportunities to indicate his ideas on time. Warren as a historian can convincingly fill in the background and ancestry of the characters, and he can plausibly jump ahead to the future even beyond the end of the action involving the historical characters. For example, he introduces Skrogg, dramatizes his past and ancestry, tells of his future up to his death, then finally returns to the moment when he first met Jeremiah. This method implies that the drama Skrogg plays out with Jeremiah is dependent upon the past and is a determiner of his future (p. 86). Warren, as a historian over a century removed in time, adds a modern perspective to Jeremiah's story. On discussing duelling, for example, he states that although in our complacency we think it silly, we are like them after all, for even in modern war we must carry our idealizations with us when we face death (p. 118).

Amantha Starr, in narrating the story of her life, although she follows more of a chronological order than does Jack, also jumps about in time. Occasionally she goes forward to a time in the very distant future. Telling of the New Orleans' riots she suddenly jumps far ahead – some eighteen or twenty years – to the time when she read about the riots in the *Report of the Select Committee*, while sewing on a dress for her teen-aged daughter, who, at the time of the riots had not been born. Again Warren is willing to forego suspense for structural confirmation of the idea of the present holding the future within it. Warren also arranges the events of Manty's life so that they often seem to be re-enactments of previous events in order to show how one moment prolongs itself to infinity. Charles returns to Pointe-du-Loupe and sits in the same chair as he had done sixteen months earlier. Manty thinks, "the whole episode began to assume the quality of a recollection with strange distortions, a recollection that somehow fulfilled the event recollected" (p. 153). In *The Cave* Warren goes backward and forward in time, using flashbacks within flashbacks and leaps into the future. He also uses one moment of time, one action, to integrate the novel and the characters. On discovering that Jasper is trapped in the cave, the panic-stricken Jo-Lea runs for help. Warren introduces each character as he sees Jo-Lea, fills in his background, returns to the moment in the present and then moves on to the way in which another character lived this moment. Then, at the end, all the lives of all the characters converge in time and space in the clearing before the mouth of the cave. Such characters as Bradwell Tolliver and Yasha Jones of *Flood*, engaged in trying to make sense of their life and experience, think back into their past at every opportunity. Without telling who she is, Warren has Brad think of episodes in his life with Lettice. This method shows the presence of the past while at the same time it illustrates the chaos of Brad's mind. In his novels, Robert Penn Warren thus affirms his philosophy of history by literary devices and by structure. Images suggest that human values are won and maintained with great difficulty amid the wasteland of history. The devices of ambiguity and irony attest to the complexity of history as a blind process; and his methods of presenting the narrative line illustrate his idea that any one time contains all the past and all the future.

The essence of Robert Penn Warren's concept of history is that it is a blind, impersonal flux of events and actions that in their innocence are destructive of the essentially human qualities. History is the raw material from which man must fashion, by an exercise of his will, human values and ideas; in so doing he must accept the evil and tragedy inherent in man's contact with history without sinking into it. That is, "History is blind, but man is not." But nothing in history exists in isolation; all people and things impinge, or can impinge, upon all other people and things. And this makes existence even more treacherous to man, for it defines his responsibility as absolute and infinite. Man necessarily touches the web of history, and he can never know the full results of anything. Because written history can suggest to man only some, but by no means all, of the ramifications of actions in the past, in this sense it can be humbling. Warren's ideas on history are skillfully used in structuring the novels, the genre in which they are best and most fully dramatized.

IV

MAN IN HISTORY: TRADITION AND MYTH

No subjects have engaged Warren and the other Fugitives more than have tradition and myth. In Warren's case the reason for this concern derives directly from his concepts of the nature of man and of the nature of history. Man, guilty of Original Sin, is a complex mixture of good and bad. Left to his own devices with no guides for conduct, he will invariably fall into sin and error. He therefore needs codes to follow, and tradition gives him prescriptions for behavior that have the wisdom of the ages behind them. But man also needs a center to his life, something to believe in outside his own self. Myth not only provides man with a system of belief, it also justifies, emotionally and intellectually, the traditional codes of conduct. Beyond this need for myth, however, is Warren's belief that the nature of history necessitates a myth, for myth is what accommodates the blank, destructive forces of history to man's human values and his psychology. The human, moral sense which each man must make out of history is embodied in myth, and in this way each man is a myth-maker as he carves the formless material of history to suit, not his own selfish needs, but the values that separate him from the beasts. And there is in Warren also the suggestion that, in the last analysis, the horror of the historical process makes illusions needful. That is, man's mind cannot take too much reality, and even if myths are not objectively verifiable, they are still imperative. The "truth" of a myth inheres in its embodiment of human values. Warren, then, goes to history to gather raw material for the study of valid traditional codes of behavior and to find material to shape into myths to undergird these values. And his philosophy

of history, derived from his study of the past, and his concept of
the nature of the creative process have led him to the belief that
an artist has no greater purpose than the creation of myth.

1. TRADITION

Tradition consists of the rules of conduct that frail men in the
past have carved from the ruck of history and have found valuable in guiding their behavior. Since man cannot live according to
history and is unable to trust even himself, he must guide himself with tradition based on human values. Tradition is the codifi-
cation of man's attempts to achieve human values. These rules
are, of course, never absolute and unchangeable, for they were
achieved by man, not handed down from God. Yet the individual,
Warren believes, must think long and hard before acting outside
these sanctions. As he says in *John Brown*, one "must live in an
imperfect world and should try to do what one can with the imperfect institutions devised by other imperfect men. . . ." [1] Hence,
the study of history assumes great importance to Warren, because
from it we can see what values have proved efficacious in the
past. Warren, as a historian, has been concerned with what traditional values can be salvaged for the modern world from the
ruck of history and the disintegrating forces of the present. His
idea of time as well as his historical sense calls for a respect for
tradition since this concept emphasizes the continuity of the past
and the present; to follow tradition is to assert the presence of the
past.

Warren's concern with tradition is also closely related to his
interest in regionalism since these rules, he believes, grow out of
a community and embody its values; they depend upon a sense
of place and of history. This feeling of belonging to a community
is of value to the individual because it gives him identity by
relating him meaningfully to the past and to other people. Regionalism also is a healthy movement in literature if the writer
"understands his regionalism in terms of the history of his re-

[1] *John Brown*, pp. 317-18.

gion".[2] The writer in a tradition does not separate his themes from a consideration of time and place. "For the writer in a tradition . . . time and place are one thing." "The writer in a tradition realizes that these two considerations cannot be separated unless the meaning of both is destroyed." [3] His regionalism is thus directly related to his concern with tradition. He writes about the South partly because the South has been slower in overthrowing the traditional values. The South, he states in *Segregation*, still has "piety" – a desire to hold on to the values of the past.[4] And as C. Vann Woodward suggests, the Southern heritage is perhaps more in line with the common lot of man than the ideas of opulence and success of the North, for the South is the only part of the nation that has known military defeat.[5] Throughout his career Warren has defended Southern traditions. He insisted quite literally in *John Brown* and "The Briar Patch" on an agrarian socio-economic order and the segregation of the races. Today he still defends Southern traditions, but he has reinterpreted them much more generally. He no longer insists on an agrarian society nor does he believe one possible, but he does advocate the values – individuality, piety, humility – that this system fostered. Although he sees the South's treatment of the Negro as morally wrong, he admires the values that cause the Southerner to resist pressures toward conformity and abstractionism. His development, then, has been away from the defense of the specific embodiment of the Southern tradition towards a defense of the more general values inherent in it, values that must be translated into new terms.

There are important reasons why Warren feels that a tradition is necessary for man's psychological, moral, and spiritual well-being. First, man's depraved nature makes it necessary, for with no guides to follow, man becomes a prey to the tainted, unconscious motives of the self as well as the blind forces of history and nature. Tradition supplies man with time-honored principles,

---

[2]   "Poor White", *Nation*, CLIV (February 28, 1942), p. 261.
[3]   "Not Local Color", p. 154.
[4]   *Segregation*, p. 52.
[5]   Woodward, p. 25.

more ample and human than any that he could devise alone. Second, since to Warren tradition is social it gives the individual a sense of belonging to a community and a sense of continuity, of connection with his heritage. This problem of community is especially acute today, Warren believes, for modern traditionless society has lost its "sense of community and of human ties". "Man, in fact, seemed to be living in a No-Society – in even an Anti-Society – an agglomeration of No-Persons whose relations in satisfying certain appetites, fundamentally denied certain human needs. The greatest need it denied was the sense of identity – only to be had by a sense of meaningful relation to other men and to nature." [6] The Fugitives, Warren stated at the Fugitives' Reunion, were trying to form a notion of democracy that would make a community of people possible in an attempt to remedy this loss of a sense of community and the resultant loss of the individual's feeling of identity.[7] He defines Clyde's tragedy in *An American Tragedy* as the American one – that of namelessness – "the story of an individual without identity, whose responsible self has been absorbed by the great machine of modern industrial secularized society".[8] In other words, the self needs society for wholeness and the urban group offers no hope for community in any true sense.

Third, man needs a tradition for self-fulfillment and self-understanding. By giving one an immediate awareness of the fundamental principles by which one may act in any given situation, tradition provides "moral certainty of self", wholeness, an inner balance, self-control, independence of character, and discretion. These virtues are to be found in those in whom the old values remained active, men like Alexander Hamilton Stephens, Robert E. Lee, and U. S. Grant,[9] all of whom by adherence to a worthy code were enabled to rise above "the mechanical process" of life.[10] A traditional code of behavior helps the individual to

[6] "The Veins of Irony", p. 12.
[7] *The Fugitive's Reunion*, p. 215.
[8] "An American Tragedy", p. 14.
[9] "Edmund Wilson's Civil War", p. 54.
[10] "William Faulkner", p. 73.

realize his highest potentialities as a man. And, finally, tradition is necessary, Warren maintains, in order for the artist to realize his highest potentialities. His task is much easier if he has a usable tradition from which to work because then he can build upon what others have achieved. The artist today has few ideas in common with his audience; unlike the artists of older cultures he must invent his deepest assumptions before proceeding to his art.[11] The writers of the past had half their thinking done for them and thus did not have to search for ideas to embody in their art. Their cultural traditions provided such writers as Hawthorne, Melville, and Dickinson with ample themes. In contrast to them is the traditionless Sherwood Anderson, who did not understand the world or himself, and Edwin Arlington Robinson, who had "no larger terms in which experience can be translated and rendered comprehensible".[12] But even though the modern writer is doomed not to have ideas and assumptions in common with his readers, he should still attempt to build upon the achievements of writers of the past. The best of the English poets "have tried to make a fruitful assimilation into their own poetic method of the poetry of the past. They have not been eclectic, but they have been concerned with discovering the grounds upon which the poetry of the past could become immediately available for them as poets." American poets, on the other hand, because they have characteristically rejected the examples of their predecessors, have written poetry that tends to be fragmentary with no central impulse.[13] Warren is most likely to approve of writers who have not been extremely experimental, writers like Rolfe Humphries, who, he believes, achieved poetic excellence by devoting himself humbly and honestly to the poetic tradition of English poetry.[14] Excellence in literature as in life is, thus, best fostered by an intelligent respect for tradition.

[11] "Literature as a Symptom", p. 266.
[12] "Hawthorne, Anderson, and Frost", *New Republic*, LIV (May 16, 1928), p. 400.
[13] "The Present State of Poetry: In the United States", *Kenyon Review*, I (Fall, 1939), pp. 386-98.
[14] "Principle and Poet", *Nation*, CLIV (April 11, 1942), p. 439.

Because of the importance he attaches to tradition and man's need for it, Warren has been greatly concerned with the effects of a lack of tradition, effects that, he believes, one can observe everywhere in the modern world. In his discussion of Hemingway he notices above all else how Hemingway's characters search for a center but find nothing but despair; they try to find their way over a terrain for which the maps have been lost.[15] Likewise the Snopeses in Faulkner have no positive values. Hence, they are exploiters, pure pragmatists.[16] Man without traditional sanctions is left, then, with no idea of how to act and no way to understand and control himself. In poetry and fiction Warren has presented vivid pictures of man's need of traditional sanctions for his conduct, for a map to help guide him over the treacherous terrain of history, and he has dealt with the effect on the individual and society when there is no tradition or when the individual has rejected tradition to live by his own self-determined ideas of right and wrong. Along with the anonymity and lack of community – time is "no-place" and "no face" – Billie as modern man in "The Ballad of Billie Potts" has lost all sense of tradition and community; "Therefore you tried to remember when you had lost whatever it was you had lost,/ But it was a long time back." [17] The dirty foul-mouthed tramp in "Blackberry Winter" with his out-of-place city clothes, who has no roots or tradition, constitutes a striking contrast to the boy's father secure in his traditional agrarian code of conduct.

John Brown, with whom Warren dealt in his first book, is the prototype of his characters who choose to reject tradition to live by self-determined values; and in his first novel he portrays one who has absolutely no commitments to any tradition. Because he held himself to be superior to any tradition or any of society's institutions, Brown rejected them all. Like Emerson and the transcendentalists and many of the abolitionists, he felt he was privy to God and thus had no need of the frail virtues achieved

15   "Ernest Hemingway", p. 81.
16   "William Faulkner", p. 63.
17   *Selected Poems*, pp. 10-12.

by frail man in the past. With such ideas it was only logical, Warren maintains, for him to follow no law and even try to overthrow the national government. *Night Rider* more clearly than any of Warren's other works portrays a man with no tradition. That man, Perse Munn, has no center to his life, no self-understanding or self-certainty and hence no self-control. John Brown looked for a center within himself. Munn, like modern man in his other-directed society, turns outward. He first looks to the association for a worthy purpose to act upon as a substitute for tradition. Submerging himself in the association with its limited and purely practical aims, he loses all sense of traditional sanctions to conduct and all sense of responsibility to his neighbors. Next, again like modern man, he looks for a center in other people, first, the crowd, then Senator Tolliver, and finally Lucille Christian. But these referents, like the association, betray him. Senator Tolliver, despite his outward appearance, devotes himself to selfish pragmatism, and Lucille is as empty and cold as Munn himself. Unlike Captain Todd he has no "enveloping confidence" (p. 43), no inner certainty, no sense of community or human responsibility. Because he has no tradition and hence no self-knowledge, his acts lack moral purpose. He seeks fulfillment in senseless violence; he feels, for example, that to kill Senator Tolliver would fill his own inner emptiness. But action and violence without the referent of a tradition are as aimless as Perse's random shots with which the novel ends.

At Heaven's Gate becomes a massive image of modern traditionless man adrift in an urban situation. Warren seems to say that there is little hope for man who has rejected all traditions that afford any basis of hope. Jerry leaves, both physically and mentally, his father's farm and the agrarian values associated with it. Sweetwater rejects his father's traditional religion for Marxism. And even Ashby sells his family farm to the exploiters and goes to work for them. The outward results are restless boredom and compulsive violence. The inner results are a lack of self-understanding, the inability to believe in the reality of the self, and moral confusion. Sue's cry, "Oh, what am I?" (p. 307), is the cry of those who are liberated from the moral restraints of the past.

At Heaven's Gate is Warren's harsh condemnation of modern urban society.

All the King's Men, likewise, illustrates the effect of a lack of tradition on modern man. Willie Stark has rejected hereditary values and conventional morality for utility. Law to Warren is a part of the traditions of society; it consists of rules that have been found valuable over the years. To Willie, however, the law is merely something to use for his own self-determined ends.

Hell, the law is like the pants you bought last year for a growing boy, but it's always this year and the seams are popped and the shankbones to the breeze. The law is always too short and too tight for growing humankind. The best you can do is do something and then make up some law to fit and by the time that law gets on the books you have done something different. (p. 147)

Willie pictures himself as superior to tradition, but without principles his actions lead nowhere. Jack, too, is alienated from his heritage. As a result he is rootless and lacks any real purpose – a trait that Anne clearly sees. Jack, on looking out a train window, sees a woman throw out a pan of water; he feels like crying because he thinks that at least she has a home, a purpose, and hence reality (p. 81). But eventually even Willie seeks some connection with the values of the past through Jack, Anne, and Adam. So Jack, through his interest in history and his acceptance of his personal past and his family, finally attains a worthy tradition. Likewise, in *Flood*, Bradwell's compulsive drinking, Lettice's nymphomania, and their restless devotion to communism, psychoanalysis, and art result from their failure to find a worthwhile tradition and the failure of an urban society to provide a sense of community and place as did the small town of Fiddlersburg.

The dire consequences of the lack of a tradition are not peculiar to twentieth-century man. As Warren makes clear in *World Enough and Time* and *Band of Angels*, those in the nineteenth century also suffered from this problem. Although the traditions are there for him to follow, Jeremiah, possessing the romantic delusion of self-sufficiency, ignores them to follow the inclinations of his own heart. Jeremiah's circumvention of the law to search for his own justice is a denial of tradition. At first he is attracted to the legal profession, but when he finds that the law is imperfect, he rejects it entirely: "How had he ever thought that the law answered the deep cry of the heart?" (p. 57). He feels free to go outside the law for the justice which his heart sanctions and even outside such extra-legal but traditional actions as duelling. By having Jeremiah reach his resolve to kill Fort before he has even met Rachel, Warren makes it quite clear that he is not a lover defending the honor of his beloved. Rather he is one who feels free to use any means at his disposal because he feels his aim is just. Then, too, he sins against tradition by trying to exist apart from society. He isolates himself from the human community just as he cuts himself off from tradition. His act has no larger frame of reference, and it is incomprehensible to society. In another example of isolation, Manty in *Band of Angels* belongs with neither the Negroes or the whites. Warren uses this fact to suggest man's alienation from his heritage and his lack of a human community – his rootlessness. Trying to define herself by the various men in her life – Hamish, Rau-Ru, Tobias – she tries to live parasitically on the truth that others seem to have found. But she cannot even understand those who act according to traditional codes. Why, she asks, had Mumford pulled down the federal flag and thus gotten himself hanged? "Oh, what were those colored rags men put on sticks and made music under and died following in the smoke?" (p. 221).

Although Warren seems to favor the past, he does not merely peevishly complain that the past is nicer than the present. Rather he wishes to criticize the present by means of the past in order to bring the traditional values into the modern world. To Warren, "The drama of the past that corrects us is the drama of our struggle to be human, of our struggle to define the values of our forebears in the face of their difficulties." [18] Like the admirable Southern idealists whom he praises in *Segregation*, Warren also dreams "of preserving the traditional American values of individuality and localism against the anonymity, irresponsibility, and materialism of the power state, against the philosophy of the

---

[18]   *The Fugitives' Reunion*, p. 214.

ad-man, the morality of the Kinsey report, and the gospel of the bitch-goddess".[19] This is, Warren asserts, "the Age of Conformism".[20] And he has analyzed in detail the forces in the modern world which he believes have destroyed traditional values. First among the forces which he indicts are the socio-economic ones of industrialism, big business and finance capitalism, urbanization, mobility, the mass communication media, and the power state. "Society with the rise of industrialism, finance capitalism, and the great power state, seemed to be losing its old sanctions; the sense of community and of human ties was being replaced by anonymous forces; communion seemed to be lost in the noise of communication by mass media; the historical sense disappeared into a cynical, or supine acceptance of the incoherent present." [21] Not only do these modern socio-economic forces destroy the old way of life, they also foster attitudes that are detrimental to the continuance of traditional values. With industry and business has come an emphasis on practical success – a worship of the bitch-goddess – in which utility is the measure of excellence. This attitude causes man to recognize only physical problems, and its philosophy of logical positivism denies the validity of metaphysics and the value of aesthetics. And along with psychiatry, it robs man of a sense of sin by recognizing no spiritual and moral problems, only problems in adjustment. But the opposing philosophy of romanticism is also dangerous, for it teaches the individual to look not to society's traditions and the codes of the past for sanction but rather to one's own tainted heart.

To survey Warren's work is to see him constantly adding to the long list of modern institutions, forces, and ideas which destroy the positive values of man's past. "The Patented Gate and the Mean Hamburger" deals with the destruction of the old agrarian order by the city and by finance capitalism. Since the subject of *Brother to Dragons* is a horrible, senseless, and brutal murder drawn from the annals of history, Warren had to use

[19]   *Segregation*, p. 55.
[20]   "A Lesson Read in American Books", *New York Times Book Review* (December 11, 1955), p. 33.
[21]   "The Veins of Irony", pp. 10-11.

caution not to make the past seem worse than the present. Hence, Warren and even Jefferson comment that Lil's crime was no worse than many later ones which did not have even a perverted traditional code behind them. Jefferson documents various evils more far-reaching than Lil's crime, evils derived from industrialism and capitalism: "And Haymarket and Detroit, and Henry's goons", and the Harvard scholar "who made/ Good learning pimp for brokers". George's screams typify all this horror (p. 137). And Warren professes a dislike for the signs of modern "progress". Smithland was once beauitful but is no longer, for "gas pumps are a rash that's worse than measles" (p. 206).

Finance capitalism is the chief villain in his first novel. The huge tobacco companies of *Night Rider* could hardly be seen in a worse light by Upton Sinclair or John Dos Passos. They are completely lacking in human values. Warren makes it perfectly clear that the great majority of social turmoil, unrest, and human suffering comes directly from the greedy practices of the companies in banding together to deny the farmer a fair price for his crop. *At Heaven's Gate* continues Warren's indictment of capitalism and big business, both of which threaten the older more stable way of life of the people of the South. Warren here adds industrialism and urbanism to his catalogue of disruptive forces. Bogan Murdock, a machine-like creature with no human ties or humane values, a pure materialist trying to control nature and people by economic power, serves as Warren's symbol of the new that is replacing the old. He is a spokesman for the New South doctrine of Henry Grady with its fine phrases of progress, development, awakening, all of which mean to Warren the rejection of traditional Southern values associated with agrarianism as a way of life. Murdock says that in China "the modern world ... the world of industry and finance and science – our world – is face to face with an old world" (p. 221). He cannot see that his world is face to face with an older, nobler world right in Tennessee. Not only does he exploit the people for money, but he does it to cater to his pleasure. He and his friends force Jerry's father and the other small farmers off their land in order to build the Happy Valley Hunt Club where executives could ride to the hounds.

Bogan and those like him create a dehumanized, competitive, urban society in which man is confused and lost. Jerry Calhoun represents modern man adrift in the city. He is confused and disoriented. And he is exactly like all the other young men at Meyers and Murdock and the other brokerage firms. All these bright young men dress alike, talk alike, and even think alike. Their world is far different from men like Mr. Calhoun, for they are sure of everything. Jerry, for example, enjoyed studying business and finance texts. "It was so clean and sure . . . a guarantee that the world was secure, was a pattern which you could grasp and live by" (p. 77). The effects of the victory of Bogan Murdock's forces are clearly demonstrated in the story of Ashby Wyndham, one of the poor hill people exploited by the capitalists. Deserting the family farm for the alluring promise of wages from the Massey Mountain Company, he even sells his land to them. The new way of life proves not to be as attractive as it seemed and most of his money goes right back to the company store where the workers must trade. And finally when the timber gives out, Ashby and the others are simply fired with no warning. The company and its directors lack human kindness or any sense of responsibility to the land or the people. The victory of industry and capitalism over subsistence agriculture proves as destructive to Ashby as it has to Jerry.

In his next novel Warren adds the pragmatism of the power state to his list of destructive forces. As Jack maintains, the power state is founded upon the philosophy of Machiavelli, which Warren lists in his "Knowledge and the Image of Man" as distorting the heritages of western culture.[22] "A man may forget the death of the father, but never the loss of the patrimony, the cold-face Florentine, who is the founding father of our modern world, said, and he said a mouthful" (p. 417). A world in which workableness is the sole justification for action has no place for a heritage that recognizes a distinct difference between right and wrong and which emphasizes the spiritual and the moral as much

22 "Knowledge and the Image of Man", p. 182.

as the practical. Willie's utilitarianism justifies him, he feels, in ignoring the traditional values of his heritage. Similarly tradition cannot survive in a society whose most cherished ideals are based on money. Warren traces the beginning of the money-mad culture to the period right after the Civil War. Here is where America went wrong, he believes. During Reconstruction and the administrations of Grant and Coolidge the Yankee exploiters came in "and the Yankee dollar and Confederate dumbness collaborated to heal the wounds of four years of fratricidal strife and all was merry as a marriage bell". But then the pines gave out, and the "big boys" were gone leaving the land to wash away and the natives to sink into poverty (p. 5). Warren goes on to attack another force that has been unleashed by science and which is destructive of some of the traditional values he holds most important. Psychiatry is blameworthy for its attempt to rid man of a sense of sin and of guilt. The pre-frontal lobotomy which Adam performs is designed to make the individual perfectly adjusted to his environment and to free him from feeling humility and guilt. Sadie Burke retires to a sanatorium "to drown in the eyes of a psychiatrist" (p. 432) in order to rid herself of her unbearable sense of sin and responsibility. In failing to be concerned with moral and spiritual problems, modern medicine aligns itself with the destroyers of tradition.

In *World Enough and Time*, Jeremiah's attempt to follow the inclinations of his own heart abandons him to the dark, evil forces of the self and results in tragedy. But the world of today is even worse off. Warren constantly shifts to the present to compare the modern world to the world of Jeremiah Beauchamp. In each case the earlier period is presented in a better light. Warren achieves historical irony, as T. S. Eliot often does, by a juxtaposition of a banal present which has lost all standards of value against a past which, despite its folly, is undeniably noble. Warren frequently contrasts the old Kentucky and the new with its signs of "progress", of commercialization, industrialism, and capitalism, of rampant materialism. The novel closes with a long and witty catalog of the great strides Kentucky has made in the years since Jeremiah lived, a progress measured by modern standards of money, bigness, quantity, and conformity, not by measures Jerry, Fort, Burnham, and most of the others would have used. The state University now has 8,000 students and a championship basketball team; the parimutuels do a $40,000,000 business; "the Negro is emancipated and can vote and if he is smart he can even get paid for voting (just like white folks), and anyway he is free and can die of tuberculosis in a Louisville slum if he wants to and nobody will stop him (for it is his legal right and is damned near the only right the white folks will let him have)." Moreover, "things are improving as all statistics show and civilization is making strides, and we can look forward to a great future for our state (if we can accept the challenge, if we carry on our great tradition, if we pass on the torch)" (pp. 464-65). This is what has replaced first the Indian idea that Kentucky was a holy land and then the striving for justice and nobility of people such as Jeremiah, Fort, Hawgood, and Madison. "But when the white man came the gods fled, either into the upper air or deeper into the dark earth. So there was no voice here to speak and tell the white man what justice is" (p. 465). The gods, it seems, have fled not only "the dark and bloody ground" but also all of the modern world.

Warren's fullest criticism of the forces that immediately before and after the Civil War accelerated the replacement of traditional values with the materialistic worship of financial success of the Gilded Age occurs in *Band of Angels*. The novel is thickly peopled with characters who worship at the shrine of "the bitch-goddess". Tobias' father, for example, a New England industrialist, follower of Emerson and supporter of John Brown, was a conservative business man opposed to child labor laws or any other legislation that would deny his class the right to exploit the people and the land and to get rich. And the bright young Harvard and Amherst men in St. Louis after the war are no better than the dishonest Mr. Muller, despite the fact that they speak not of making money but of "an interesting possibility" and "the duty of expansion" (p. 340). This rampant materialism produces a civilization inferior to that of the past. Manty compares the young Seth to the old-fashioned reformers who acted from a conviction of right and not the expectation of making money. "They were, in brief, old-fashioned reformers, a breed gone out of our country now with the tide of success and money-madness with Mr. Astor and Mr. Vanderbilt running things, with railroads across the continent, and people filling up the plains and extracting rich ores from every mountain, and only those who have failed in the scramble are now given to reform and criticism, or are willing to speak well of the time past" (p. 340). After the war Tobias wrote *The Great Betrayal*, and Warren's summary of it presents his own views on the forces destructive of the old values. Big business, Tobias wrote, betrayed the ideals for which the war had been fought and now in the Gilded Age there has been a sad decline from the nobility of the past.

... and now in a land that had once produced statesmen, prophets, explorers, scientists, poets and seers, we found politicians who were gate keepers for pelf, judges who were janizaries for the National Debt, courts that were a Swiss Guard for credit, prophets who were prophets for six per cent, scientists who were subsidized tinkers, teachers who were catalogers of libraries and philosophers who would justify all.

Hence the union is now "a league with dollars and a covenant with death" (p. 343). For these views Tobias' father disinherited him because he was "unaware of the obligations which wealth entails" (p. 348).

Mass communication, especially television, Warren believes, has helped to spread the gospel of an urban, industrialized, de-humanized, materialistic, stereotyped civilization to all parts of the country and hence to speed up the destruction of the values that a tradition has through the years encouraged. *The Cave* is his fullest criticism of the mass media. His treatment of the folksy TV announcer is bitterly satirical. Wes Williams had a good face, "and if the tailoring on the good shoulders was perhaps excessive-ly good, it was casual; and the face was a face that loved the land we live in and loved you, the face of the American boy coming home, home to Mom, home to the old swimming hole where that delicious mud got between the toes, home to apple pie, home to a man-to-man talk with the soda-jerk he used to go to school with . . ." (p. 247). With no thought of the suffering he causes others, he cruelly exploits the tragedy for national television, turning it into standardized sentimentality. The grief is not at all sacred to him. Not only does our TV culture lead to standardization and conformity, it produces a society that cannot provide worthy dreams, aspirations, and ideals for its members. It produces, on a much larger scale, the same sort of false values Hollywood movies foster. Nick the Greek, for instance, is a sympathetic if slightly slow-witted character. Like Jay Gatsby, however, he has only the dreams of his society to inspire him. He has two unworthy ideals given to him by his culture. Jean Harlow represents to him the epitome of womanhood, the height of all he values. This fixation on platinum blondes results in an immature adjustment to sex and to married life. His only other dream is that of a Cadillac, which to him symbolizes affluence and success. In our conformist culture the ideals represented by Jean Harlow and Cadillacs have replaced more worthy, traditional ideals of the past.

Man thus needs a tradition to guide him; but what sort of a tradition? What must it include? Warren has made his answers to these questions very clear. First, he believes in the moral worth of the agrarian tradition because it helps man to realize his human limitations, causes him to recognize evil and to face it, and shows him the inscrutability of God. Secondly, any tradition to which Warren would assent would recognize human worth and value while keeping in mind man's depraved nature. He would insist, too, upon the value of the aesthetic and the humanistic. In other words, his values derive from two main sources: the Southern agrarian tradition and Christian orthodoxy. In his works, consequently, there are two main groups of characters whom he admires for their rather strict adherence to traditions: the Southern gentleman with a life close to the soil and the orthodox Christians. Often these two traditions are combined in one character. Charles R. Anderson defines the Southern gentleman of tradition as "a man of principles founded upon knowledge of the ethos of his civilization so that his actions have a frame of reference more ample and human than any rationale of conduct arbitrarily de·

vised".[23] These men are like those Warren mentions in "Infant Boy at Midcentury":

> And in even such steu and stink as Tacitus
> Once wrote of, his generals, gourmets, pimps, poltroons,
> He found persons of private virtue, the old-fashioned
>   stout ones
> Who would bow the head to no blast; and we know that
>   such are yet with us.[24]

Captain Todd of *Night Rider* embodies most of the qualities of Warren's aristocratic Southern gentleman. He has moral certainty and self-knowledge, for his code combines a respect for law with a love of the land; unlike Munn, he knows instinctively what is right or wrong for himself. He upholds respect for human worth and the right of each individual to define himself in his own way, and thus he cannot in conscience force others to join the association even though he believes its ideals are right. Yet, when it is absolutely necessary, when more is at stake than money, he can join in violent action as he did as a heroic leader in the Civil War and as a Klan member during Reconstruction. Because of his tradition he is sustained always by a deep conviction and confidence. Similarly old Mr. Barron in *World Enough and Time* exhibits these qualities which the agrarian system encouraged. And he was sustained all his life by simple, hard labor. He "had done what men do and had done it well. He had worked, loved, fought, kept his word, given charity, cleared land, raised children, paid his debts, been just to his servants, prayed to his God, read his Bible, and feared no man" (p. 123).

Christianity also provides a worthy tradition for some of Warren's characters. In most cases they are characters that are either strange, ignorant, or for some other reason out of the main stream of life. Rarely does Warren relate them directly to the central part of the life of his novels. These characters have made a meaningful adjustment to life, but Warren seems to indicate that, although the values of Christianity are still valid, its theology

---

23 Anderson, p. 224.
24 *Promises*, p. 52.

cannot literally be insisted upon today. Willie Proudfit represents orthodox Christianity as well as the agrarian tradition in *Night Rider*. After his epic sojourn in the West, where he slaughtered buffalo, he returns to the simple labor of his fathers and to the stern religion which counsels humble submission to the inscrutable will of God.

Ashby Wyndham, the poor, ignorant hill man, stands as a corrective example to the traditionless characters who populate the city in *At Heaven's Gate*. And here, unlike in *Night Rider*, his example does have an effect. He is the means of Porsum's redemption, the reason he is able to see his own evil and to stand up to Bogan. Ashby's religion, which he spreads as he goes from city to city on a quest for the brother he has injured, emphasizes the recognition of evil in the universe and in man, who cannot be good except in the "light of God's eye" (p. 119); man's responsibility; the necessity of suffering; and the impossibility of understanding the ways of God. Cass Mastern comes to believe in Ashby's type of religion, but his experiences cause him to stress the brotherhood of man, human dignity beyond the heart's evil, and the need for love. Jack Burden also gives limited assent to the Scholarly Attorney's religion with its emphasis on identity and salvation by means of evil. But Cass Mastern is from the past, and the strange Scholarly Attorney, who devotes himself to the care of the injured circus performer who makes angels out of masticated bread, seems just as removed from the main stream of modern life. Traditional religion survives also in the modern world of Johntown, Tennessee, in the person of Brother Sumpter. Religion provides him with an adequate code with which to live today, just as it had provided Willie Proudfit, Cass Mastern, and the others with a valid response to their earlier, simpler time. Sumpter's religion and the example of his life stand as correctives to his son's worship of success, Jack Harrick's selfishness and pride, the commercialized conformity of modern TV culture, and Mr. Bingham's world of money. His code, a survival of the traditional values of the past into the present, gives him the physical courage to go into the cave where others were afraid to go; and he has the moral courage to go against his conscience in lying to save his son, and the ability to face up to the evil in his own heart and the treachery of his son. The values of the Christian tradition represent, in this case, a valid code of conduct around which to order one's life.

Yet Warren is no blind worshipper of tradition and has no delusions concerning its value. Despite its great importance to man, Warren believes that for most people, who must live in the modern world of contingencies, the old traditions unmodified are unable to offer a valid code of behavior. The old beliefs must be reinterpreted for and by the modern world. He has stated that our modern problem is "that of finding in our time and in our new terms a way to recover and reinterpret the 'Founder's dream' ".[25] He does not desire "a world in which circumstances and values are frozen".[26] And he believes that the old traditions are too simple and primitive for today, for modern man has "inherited the responsibility to define his role more broadly in a more complicated world".[27] Warren too has characters like Faulkner's Sartorises, who are "wrapped in the myth's languor",[28] who because of a rigid adherence to a tradition are unable to act. Mrs. Lovehart in "The Circus in the Attic", for example, traps Bolton in the false codes of the aristocracy. Telling him he must never be common, she will not allow him to take up tickets at the movie or to perform any self-fulfilling work. Similarly, Mrs. Jordan in *World Enough and Time* continually insults Cassius Fort because she feels he is below her socially. Rachel takes him as a lover in order to outrage her mother. The sin of Judge Irwin and Governor Stanton was their inability or unwillingness to go outside their idealized Southern codes or to reinterpret them in order to bring about urgently needed social change and economic reform. Jack realizes that it is they who made Willie Stark possible and even necessary. They, not Willy, are the villains.

What Warren desires, then, is neither a blind adherence to tradition nor a complete denial of it. His real heroes are those

25   *Legacy*, p. 49.
26   *Segregation*, p. 55.
27   *Modern Poetry*, p. 543.
28   *Selected Poems*, p. 33.

who, instructed by the past, take these values and interpret them to fit new and changing conditions. Abraham Lincoln to Warren epitomizes this approach. Lincoln was a "pragmatist with a vision", one who, without being a slave to the past carries its values into the modern situation.[29] Unlike the simpler followers of the traditions of agrarianism and Christianity, these Lincoln-like characters appear not in the exempla but in the main stories, for Warren uses them to show the relevance of traditional values to the world of action and to the modern world. These are not strange people or people who have retired from life, but rather they are in the midst of the struggle.

His first two novels have no such characters; it is as if he believed that the admirable values of a Captain Todd and an Ashby Wyndham are possible only in the older, simpler social orders, and he cannot see how the values of agrarianism and Christianity relate to a later time. In *All the King's Men*, however, Hugh Miller, with "clean hands and a pure heart", is a man of principles and of action. Just as Jack interprets the lesson of the Cass Mastern story to fit his own experience in contemporary society, Hugh Miller translates the lessons of the past into the language of the present. Because he cannot condone or ignore the rampant corruption of the Stark regime, he resigns. Yet in so doing he is not, like Adam, merely ignoring evil. Jack says that Miller is going to get back into politics, and when he does he will use the law to aid the people – progress within a framework of tradition. Cassius Fort in *World Enough and Time* takes into account the time-honored values of tradition while dealing creatively with modern problems. It was he who had devised a reconciliation between the forces of the Old Court, to whom law was an absolute to be followed exactly, and of the New Court, to whom law was a servant of man's needs to be modified at will. He knew the values of both tradition and change. Blanding Cottshill, the lawyer-farmer of *Flood*, attempts to bring the values of the past into the modern situation. And this is exactly Warren's own

[29]   *Legacy*, p. 23.

position, a position he clearly states in his own social writings such as *Segregation* and *The Legacy of the Civil War*.

2. MYTH

Because man is basically evil, he needs definite ideas of conduct; because history is treacherous, he needs a myth. Since history has no meaning inherent in it, man must himself make sense of it, and the sense he makes of it is part of the myth. Hence, history is "the big myth we live". This sense, this partial myth, may be an illusion, but this is not to say it is, therefore, false. Furthermore, myths are needed to help filter out some of the horror of history so that man can live in the historical process without going mad – hence the theme of the true lie, true, that is, to human values rather than the objective facts of the historical process. Warren has also engaged in a criticism of false historical myths in order to pave the way for a valid one. Finally myths and their related rituals are valuable in satisfying certain basic human needs.

It would be a mistake to think that Warren conceives of myths merely as lies or stories men tell to console themselves when they realize the horror of the last secret. On the simplest level he uses myth to mean merely the moral value each person should impose upon history, and the meaning each person attaches to history; but he also uses it to mean a dramatized or poeticized embodiment of particular moral values. Although myths take into consideration the spiritual and the supernatural in their attempt to account for nature in full, they are not superstitions but attempts to relate the self to the universe. Everett Carter states that to Warren myth is "a pattern of belief involving emotion, imagination, and intellect, which provides the uncriticized assumptions by which men conduct their moral lives".[30] But, ideally, a myth is social; it is the pattern by which an entire society makes sense of its universe. And since myths are, like poetry, concrete, the ideas and values they embody are immediately available to the individual. Here is Warren's definition:

[30] Everett Carter, "The 'Little Myth' of Robert Penn Warren", *Modern Fiction Studies* (Spring, 1960), p. 3.

A myth is a fiction, a construct which expresses a truth and affirms a value. It is not an illustration of doctrine. It differs from allegory in that its components, not to be equated with anything else, function in their own right. It is the dynamic truth, the dynamic value. The philosophy of a given myth may be defined, but the definition is no more the myth itself than the statement of the theme of the poem is the poem; in each instance the value becomes static and may be discussed but not felt, the conviction of experience is forfeited. In other words, myth represents a primary exercise of sensibility in which thought and feeling are one: it is a total communication.[31]

He concludes this definition with, "The myth then defines the myth-makers world, his position in it, his destiny, and his appropriate attitude." [32] When the artist attempts to create myth, as Conrad did in *Nostromo*, he creates "a great, multiphase symbol to render his total vision of the world, his sense of individual destiny, his sense of man's place in nature, his sense of history and society".[33] Warren has been more concerned with historical myths – made from the common history of a people to embody their values – than with religious myths – myths that explain man's relation to God and to the universe. Religious myths, Warren believes, can help provide a purposeful adaptation to life, but he has never committed himself to any one theological system as he has to a particular concept of history.

Warren's definitions of myth proclaim his belief in the need for them and the great importance he attaches to them. Man needs myths, first, because they link the past and present since the material from which they are formed is history and the values they should embody derive from the past. Myths help give man a historical sense, a feeling for his heritage. But the most important reason man needs a myth is to cure what Warren calls the special disease of our time, the dissociation of sensibility, the splitting of intellect and feeling, the fragmentation of the several aspects of man's complex nature.[34] Man, Warren believes, has a moral and spiritual nature as well as a purely physical one. Since

[31] "John Crowe Ransom", p. 96.
[32] *Ibid.*, p. 97.
[33] "Conrad and *Nostromo*", p. 48.
[34] "John Crowe Ransom", p. 97.

myth is total communication, it takes man's whole nature into account. One of the main reasons, according to Warren, for the decline of literary and in particular poetic excellence is the modern lack of common myths. The artist, then, also needs myths for maximum effectiveness. Donald Davidson, who shares this belief, stated that the Fugitives struggled to unite the form of their poetry with the myth which they thought ought to belong to it, and, according to Davidson, Allen Tate believes that the "form requires the myth" – that is, "the images and symbols, the total economy of the poem, require the support of a tradition based upon a generally diffused belief".[35] The writers of the past were fortunate in that they had a ready-made myth which they could bend to their esthetic purpose, from which they could draw symbols and allusions.[36] Today modern science offers no mythology; the poet must find his own as Yeats did. But, like Yeats, the modern poet runs the risk of being incomprehensible to his audience. Further, any exposition of the poet's mythology is irrelevant to his poetry because "a poem must carry its own philosophical and mythological baggage".[37] Because the poet lacks a mythology capable of being embodied in poetry, modern poetry, like modern man, is fragmentary.[38]

Just as the forces of industrialism, capitalism, and urbanization have been at work destroying tradition, science, the basis of these forces, the rationale for them, has abolished or limited the myths on which the older traditional codes were based. In Warren's view science is a false myth which

provides a form of knowledge concerned not with the concrete but with the abstract: not with quality, but with quantity. It professes to fit its items into a system, but any one item, in its richness of being, may defy the system until Doomsday. Science provides only one type of chart for the experience of man in the world; in so far as this becomes the basis of education, that is, the basis of interpretation for

---

[35] Donald Davidson, "The Thankless Muse and her Fugitive Writers", in *Southern Writers in the Modern World* (Athens, Georgia, 1958), p. 29.
[36] "Hawthorne, Anderson, and Frost", p. 400.
[37] "James Stephens Again", *Poetry*, XL (July, 1932), pp. 231-32.
[38] "The Present State of Poetry", p. 398.

other charts, a violence is done to human sensibility, which likewise has an appreciative concern with persons, objects, and events of this world, a concern called, in its formal aspect, art.[39]

That is, unlike a valid myth, science fractionalizes and compartmentalizes man. But what is worse, the false myth of science has led to an overemphasis on the rational, the logical, the physical and a concomitant slighting of the imaginative, the religious, the supernatural, the mysterious, and the aesthetic. Science too has destroyed the old belief in sin and guilt and replaced it with an explanation of the soul in terms of adjustment to the physical world. "Terror", for instance, attacks the idea that science will solve all our problems by helping us to adjust. And our popular conception of science has destroyed the old idea of an inscrutable, stern God and replaced it with the idea that man can conquer nature and that this is all the individual needs for a successful, happy life.[40] Because science has narrowed the area of possible faith, modern man cannot see beyond the easy, rational answer; unlike Macbeth we see not the ghost but only the empty chair.[41]

The poet in *Promises* tells his daughter: "You will live your own life, and contrive/ The language of your own heart, but let that conversation/ In the last analysis, be always of whatever truth you would live." [42] Modern man must, thus, create his own myth. He must not, however, ignore the grimness of historical fact. Complications, complexities, and facts cannot be denied, for the making of myth is difficult as well as risky. It is risky because it involves the possibility of attaching moral significance to history prematurely and because of the danger of being wrong and hence appearing foolish or hypocritical.[43] It is difficult because one must use all the resources of historical research – as Warren does in *The Legacy of the Civil War* – to enable one to understand fully the history from which the myth is made. Besides the myth the individual must make from history, there is

---

[39]   "John Crowe Ransom", p. 98.
[40]   *Modern Poetry*, p. 543.
[41]   *Selected Poems*, p. 20.
[42]   *Promises*, p. 13
[43]   "Edmund Wilson's Civil War", p. 158.

the myth he must make of his self. He must make sense of the self and place the self within his myth of history. Abraham Lincoln performed worthily both of these myth-making responsibilities. He made a myth of history in that he imposed a certain moral view on the national history and destiny. He also predicted his role in the social myth he created. These myths were noble in that they embodied humane values; but even Lincoln's myth was not completely adequate, for he could not know of the uncoiling powers of big technology and big business that were gathering on the horizon.[44] Warren does not think that the average person should undertake as ambitious a myth-making venture as did Lincoln, but each of us must do the same thing on a lesser scale, and each of us runs the same risks.

Warren's characters engage in a quest for a myth. Jefferson in *Brother to Dragons* created a myth of the perfectibility and the ultimate goodness of man. His myth, however, is inadequate, as Warren shows him, because it is contrary to the facts of history and of human experience; but the worst indictment of it is that of Merriwether Lewis, who shows that it has disastrous consequences when one tries to center one's life around it. It fails to promote the right human values, and this is the ultimate test of the "truth" of any myth to Warren. Unlike most of the other characters in *At Heaven's Gate*, Sweetwater realizes that man needs a myth. Rejecting his father's Christianity, he embraces Marxism and defines himself by it. "Everybody stands for something", he believes, "and till you know what you stand for you ain't anything" (p. 307). The trouble with his myth is that it is too precariously built to accommodate human values and not flexible enough to withstand new knowledge. He triggers the murder of Sue by refusing to marry her because his myth has no place for marriage. "Perhaps his wall wasn't built right. Perhaps you ought to build what you believed in so you could take out a lot of bricks or stones and it would stand up. But he had built the only way he knew" (p. 314). Here, too, Warren deals with the creation of a myth of the self. Slim and Bogan are both myths

[44] *Ibid.*

dreamed up by themselves in the desire to escape into a fabulous self-conception, and their myths have no desirable relevance to the outside world. Slim invents a fantastic story of his family and his past in which his mother is a prostitute, and his father a nameless sea-captain, and he himself a romantic Byronesque character. Bogan lacks substance and reality since he too in forming his myth of self wishes to escape unpleasant facts. As Duckfoot says, Bogan is not real, only a dream he thought up (p. 373).

Seymour Gross has said that *All the King's Men* is about "Man's attempt to formulate a moral perspective on the brute facts of good and evil in a world in which the traditional guides to moral conduct have been obscured by various disruptive forces".[45] That is, its subject is the making of myth. This statement could be applied to all of Warren's novels. After rejecting the various answers offered by modern society, Jack comes to ground his world view in a reinterpreted Christian mythology combining the Scholarly Attorney's Manicheanism and Cass Mastern's Christian orthodoxy, tempered with his own scepticism. Jeremiah in *World Enough and Time*, however, creates a romantic myth, a drama, of himself. He returns from murdering Fort with Rachel's sash on a switch like a knight returning from combat. This action contrasts sharply with the ugly reality of his stabbing Fort. Manty's problem is that she never achieves a myth, only moments of truth which do not endure. These are fragments of myth. "Everybody, even the most confused of us, must have such moments of vision, glimpses of a beautiful possibility of life. But the truth must be that you can't live by the moment of vision. You have to be the vision, not see it" (p. 264). Since myth is an enduring vision that involves the whole person, an adequate myth would make her part of the vision. And as most of the characters of *Flood* know or learn, "*Everybody ought to have something.*"[46] Without a belief, that is, history is almost unendurable.

[45] Seymour Gross, "The Achievement of Robert Penn Warren", *College English*, XIX (May, 1958), p. 363.
[46] *Flood: A Romance of Our Time* (New York, 1964), p. 100. All references in the text are to this edition.

The creative writer is the one on whom the responsibility to create myths lies most heavily, for, Warren believes, it is he who must create society's myths. In the creation of myth the poet fulfills his social responsibility – a much greater responsibility than the correction of any specific social evil. To Warren poetry is "the little myth we make", but it should also contribute to our big myths. This is the basis for his belief in the tremendous importance of poetry or any creative, imaginative literature and the basis of his equation of religion and art. The creative artist is no mere entertainer; his aims should be far more serious than this. And, although Warren wishes to divorce literature from purely practical utility, he emphasizes the relation of literature to ethics and insists upon an ethical center to a work of art. Thus his purpose in his essay on "The Rhyme of the Ancient Mariner" is to show Coleridge's serious moral concern, to show that the poem is more than romantic escapism. Today, in Warren's view, many writers no longer view themselves as important in embodying worthy values in myths, but rather they serve, all too often, limited ends. "Literature looks out – it records a world. Literature looks in – it records a man. Or we might say, it *creates* a world, and creates a man." [47] The world it creates is the myth. And this is the way the artist engages in the life of the community; he creates myths which should quicken "our comprehension of general human nature and of a particular heritage".[48] With this view of the artist as myth-maker Warren is naturally impatient with such writers as Stribling, Fast, and Sinclair who would lessen the almost religious importance he attaches to literature, and with those who do not take their role seriously enough. In Warren's view William Faulkner, best of American writers, has fulfilled the writer's social responsibility, for he has created a myth out of the material of Southern history, a myth of human nature that is not locally bounded. The myth he has created is a repository of worthy, traditional, humane values. The poetic imagination, Warren maintains, is the myth-making faculty; it

---

[47] "The Veins of Irony", p. 12.
[48] *A Southern Harvest: Short Stories by Southern Writers*, ed. R. P. Warren (Boston, 1937), p. XVI.

provides the best access to religious, supernatural knowledge. The imagination is the active, shaping, creative, value-producing function of mind, as he defines it in his essay on Coleridge. One's reason can lead him to see the necessity of myth, but only the imagination can create values from history or go further and embody these little myths in a larger myth and hence make them available to more people. The imagination also establishes the relation between man and nature, and it puts man in tune with the universe and with others.[49] The nature of history makes this impossible for man using only the unaided intellect.

Literature and myth are quite similar, and the aim of literature is to rise to the status of myth. Both are total communication able to convey values and other important truths. Fiction and poetry like myth are grounded in the concrete, and hence they are the best realized communication. Because their issues appeal to the emotions as well as to the intellect, their values are immediately available to the individual and relevant to all of man's nature.[50] If myth results in belief that is capable of promoting action, then art, like myth, makes experience and history meaningful and reconciles us with reality; art is, in fact, a "myth of order".[51] As Warren said in his essay on Robert Frost, true art is a magnified dream of the literal world as it has achieved meaning.[52] "If poetry does anything for us, it reconciles by its symbolical reading of experience (for by its very nature it is in itself a myth of the unity of being), the self-divisive internecine malices which arise at the superficial level of which we conduct most of our life." [53] He means that, like myth, poetry helps us to bear the horrors of history and of life better; it is the best way to comprehend naked reality. Literature also makes historical facts more available by clothing them in flesh and blood, hence making them capable of being felt as well as merely understood. As is said in *Brother to Dragons*, we know the names, facts, and figures of the history,

[49]   "A Poem of Pure Imagination", p. 275.
[50]   "John Crowe Ransom", p. 98.
[51]   "Why Do We Read Fiction?", p. 84.
[52]   "The Themes of Robert Frost", p. 135.
[53]   "A Poem of Pure Imagination", p. 274.

"but what is any knowledge/ Without the intrinsic mediation of the heart?" (p. 212).

Literature conveys its knowledge and values through form, by which Warren means the organic participation and interplay of ideas within the total economy, the total structure of the work. Form is, of course, uncommunicable except as itself. Form, he states in "Knowledge and the Image of Man", is the result of the imagination's contact with the world; it springs from "the deep engagement of spirit with the world". It reconciles man with chaotic reality by giving "the image of experience being brought to order and harmony". "The rhythm is, as it were, a myth of order, or fulfillment, an affirmation that our being may move in its totality toward meaning." Like myth, literary form attaches meaning and significance to history, with the purpose of preparing one to act and to enter the world of society. It "prepares for the moment of action, of creation, in our world of contingency. The might is there for the moment when the soul lifts her head." [54] Since, therefore, myth is extremely important to the individual and the artist and their society, and since, because of the similarity between imaginative literature and myth, it is the artist's highest social responsibility to help create myths, Warren has joined the other Fugitives in calling for the creation of a myth, an epic for modern America. At their reunion at Vanderbilt in 1956 the Fugitives urged the creation of a native myth and discussed at length why, despite all their promise and their concern with myth, none of their group had produced one.

Warren regards many of the myths which men have created as wrong and dangerous. He has criticized unhistorical myths that ignore the facts of the past and dangerous ones that ignore the human values he emphasizes, or those created to pander to selfish human needs. He feels that the Civil War in particular has been used by people who have created from it self-satisfying myths that ignore both facts and complexity. From the beginning of his career Warren has been trying to free the Civil War of the false myths that cling to it. *John Brown: The Making of a Martyr*

---

[54] "Knowledge and the Image of Man", p. 192.

attacks the abolitionist sentiment that has contributed to our present lack of understanding of this event. His idea was to discredit Brown and consequently destroy the myth that Emerson, Thoreau, and other abolitionists had created from Brown and his exploits, exploits that Warren considered nothing better than illegal marauding. The myth of John Brown had been created, Warren argues, by ignoring the facts of the past, by uncritically taking Brown at his word, and by using the past to prove one's pet ideas.

In most of his novels Warren portrays a character who has fashioned a false historical myth from the Civil War and in this way dramatizes his criticism. May's aunt Lucy Burnham in *Night Rider* created a personal myth around her father, General Sam Burnham, who had been a politically appointed officer in the war. As Lucy became poorer and poorer she began to invent fabulous honors for her father, and his few, pitiful exploits grew increasingly great as she "began to push back into an ever more magnificent and fantastic history" (p. 226). Retreating into her myth, she withdrew from past and present reality. The treachery and materialism of another character, Senator Tolliver, can be traced in part to his father's fanatical devotion to the Southern cause; he had given himself unsparingly and religiously to the Southern myth, and in so doing let his lands and money waste away. The Civil War in *Night Rider* is, then, still dangerous long after the last shot has been fired.

Immediately after the war Tobias Sears of *Band of Angels* creates in poetry a sentimentalized version of the Civil War that even the bright young men who devote their energies to getting rich admire, for it makes them feel that they have been part of the glory of an ideal fulfilled. Manty describes these poems that are like so many of the period. "Yes, the hero of those poems, whatever his various names and avatars, spoke always from the grave beside many a sad pine grove, by many a moonlit water, spoke in accents of sober dedication veined by melancholy sweetness" (p. 341). Even this early the war was becoming a refuge, a city of the soul, a false historical myth. One of the main points in *The Legacy of the Civil War* is that we must not accept myths that turn the Civil War, or any war, into melodrama. Wars are bloody tragedies, and myths must not ignore this fact. And as he had done less fairly in *John Brown*, Warren again attacks the unhistorical idea which flatters the North that the war was a noble, righteous crusade for liberty and right. Neither side, he explains, had a corner on truth or virtue, and each was sadly human in its mixture of worthy and unworthy motives and deeds. There is no historical justification for the North's feeling of moral superiority nor indeed for our national feeling of righteousness, our "moral narcissism".[55]

But here Warren attacks the Southern myths as well. Nothing, he argues, could be further from the Confederate ideal (as exemplified by such men as Robert E. Lee and Alexander Hamilton Stephens) than the howling mob of racists at Tuscaloosa, Little Rock, and New Orleans. Such riots are, rather, "an obscene parody of the meaning" of their history.[56] These false myths have resulted not in illumination and human truth but in delusion. If "without historical realism and self-criticism, we look back on the war, we are merely compounding the old inherited delusions which our weakness craves". But if we were to achieve Warren's aim of seeing the war accurately, we might "find ourselves nakedly alone with the problems of our time and with ourselves".[57] Warren's destruction of these false myths of the Civil War is not a dwelling on the past, but a preparation for the future, the preparation, perhaps, for a new myth.

Like myth, illusions, or "true lies", in Warren's meaning, do not necessitate a forfeiting of the right to knowledge. Christianity and the glory of God do not demand a restriction of knowledge, and Warren has no sympathy for the concept of the mystic worth of ignorance.[58] It is always wrong to ignore facts or suppress evidence in forming ideas, concepts, and values. But the nature of history – blank and threatening – and the nature of man – weak and faltering – make desirable a filter for truth. Those who

[55] *Legacy*, p. 71.
[56] *Ibid.*, p. 57.
[57] *Ibid.*, p. 76.
[58] "Knowledge and the Image of Man", p. 184.

face the truth directly at all times are quite likely to become permanently embittered as does the grim Matilda Tolliver, who never smiled, or perpetually sad like Cassius Fort, who in unguarded moments could be seen wearing a suffering, hurt-animal expression because he had faced " the blankness of the last secret". Further, these themes in no way indicate that Warren himself has turned his back on problems in order to protect frail dreams, as W. M. Frohock accuses him of doing.[59] It is rather that Warren is pessimistic to the degree that he feels life is possible only because we do not have to face realities too often, for man cannot take too much truth and remain sane. Warren argues, further, that virtue and values are necessary even if they are not objectively verifiable in the chaos of history.

The true lie is the unavoidable contradiction between the nature of man and history and man's values which he must create. That is, it is the glory of man to desire some ideal good which in the blind neutrality of history may have no real existence. History can affirm man's feeble attempts to live up to these noble ideals, but can give no proof that they actually exist. Man must have something to live by, some referent, even at the cost of forfeiting complete objective truth or at the cost of being betrayed by the referent as in Jeremiah Beaumont's case. Warren regards the themes of the true lie and the value of illusions as important in the works of Joseph Conrad. Values in Conrad are necessary illusions and are the mark of human achievement. They are infinitely precious and are man's only truth.[60] Man, lost in the overwhelming scene of nature and history needs illusions. Decoud, for example, cannot attain faith, but he, like Warren, does gain the knowledge of "the pragmatic efficacy of faith", despite the fact that he thinks it is an illusion.[61] This theme is well described in Warren's poem "Infant Boy at Midcentury":

> Yes, the new age will need the old lies, as our own one did;
> For death is ten thousand nights – sure, it's only the process

[59] W. M. Frohock, "Mr. Warren's Albatross", in *The Novel of Violence in America*, 2nd ed. (Dallas, 1957), p. 105.
[60] "Conrad and *Nostromo*", p. 45.
[61] *Ibid.*, p. 38.

Of accommodating flesh to idea, but there's natural distress
In learning to face Truth's glare-glory, from which our eyes
   are long bid [62]

Lucy and Jack in *All the King's Men* find illusions needful. Lucy
must cling to her belief in the essential greatness of Willie, despite
all she knows about him, in order to justify her life in the horror
of the historical process she has lived through. Jack, too, must
believe in Willie's greatness or admit that his own life had no
meaning. But, further, Lucy, who has suffered and endured
through the years as Willie's wife, in order to maintain her balance and sanity desperately holds on to a belief that the baby she
adopted had been fathered by Tom despite knowing that her son
was merely one among a great many men who had had relations
with the mother. Part of Jack's education involves learning the
value of lies. As a disinterested, tough-minded historian he had
earlier relished uncovering the truth no matter what the human
consequences. The truths he uncovered destroyed Adam and
Willie; thus, he learns that while the truth can set one free, it can
also kill, and one should, therefore, be true to human values even
if this sometimes necessitates being false to the facts of history.
In a scene echoing the conclusion of Conrad's *The Heart of
Darkness*, Jack when he tells his mother that Judge Irwin had
been in no trouble, shields her from the full horror of reality by a
lie. The truth, he knows now, consists of human values, not brute
facts. Even art itself is to Yasha Jones in *Flood* a true lie. "Yes,
reality was the uncapturable. That was why we need illusion.
Truth through lie, he thought" (p. 50).

    Closely related to tradition and myth in Warren's works is the
recurrent theme of ritual, a theme that despite its prevalence has
not been adequately commented upon. Proper ritual is the outward sign of acting in accord with a tradition; it is the traditional
and instinctive way of responding to certain situations. Ideally,
ritual action has some sort of mythological justification and explanation. As part of the sacramental vision, and hence worship,
it indicates humble submission to a higher power and to the

---

[62] *Promises*, p. 51.

traditional ways of doing things. It is an action that relates one to
the human community and to history. It is valuable also in that it
fulfills a human need for action, particularly at crucial times in
one's life. Ritual, Warren states, is "an enactment that numenous-
ly embodies the relation of self to its setting in nature, in the
human community, and in time".[63] Edith, young Tom's wife in
"Prime Leaf", is attuned to traditional codes of behavior. As she
brings her father-in-law a lamp she proudly tells him that young
Tom, returning to time-honored ways of conduct, has decided to
get out of the association which has resorted to force. Her action is
ritualistic. "With the burden of the lamp she moved slowly;
there was a certain gravity, like that of a ritual, in her step and
bearing as she crossed the room to Mr. Hardin" (pp. 258-59). In
All the King's Men, Anne, on returning with Jack to her childhood home, feels the need of a ritual, which seems to indicate her
acceptance of the past that makes her whole and not "rags and
patches". She resembles a priest at an altar as she kneels amid
"the sepulchral sheeting and the out-of-time silence" "before the
cold blackness of the wide fireplace to put pine cones and bits of
light-wood beneath the logs there". She says to Jack, who is about
to light the fire, "No, let me do it. It's my house, you know, and
I ought to light the fire when I come back like this. You know, a
ritual" (p. 219).

Despite the fact that traditions and their supporting myths have
been limited or destroyed, the human need for a ritual, an act
more meaningful because it appeals to more human faculties than
do ordinary actions, remains. The ritual alone even without the
belief has at least some value in satisfying human needs. This
need leads people to empty rituals, actions with no reference to
any meaning or justification outside themselves, or to empty actions in the hope that the ritual will bring the belief. Many of
Warren's characters misuse rituals in an attempt to avert their
minds from some unpleasantness, in a blind desire to escape guilt
and responsibility. Professor Dalrymple in "The Unvexed Isles"
has made a hollow ritual out of his life in such events as his

⁶³ "Elizabeth Madox Roberts", p. 21.

Sunday afternoon parties. "Sacramentally, the whiskey sloshed into the glass." And when he learns that his wife and a former student have been kissing while he was preparing the drinks, he avoids confronting himself with this unpleasant fact by lingering ritualistically over serving the drinks and putting down the tray (p. 201). Perse Munn is able to forget the horrible importance of his murdering Bunk by ritualistically focusing his eyes on one spot. The ritual becomes more important than the shooting. Ritual, Warren implies here, should serve human values, not help one forget them. Other characters use ritual almost reflexively in an unconscious desire to hold on to some belief, some meaning. After being sold into slavery Manty cannot pray because of her lack of faith, so she unconsciously says the multiplication tables. "I had got halfway through the three's before I realized what I was doing. But if you can't pray, I suppose you have to hang on to something" (p. 93). Ritual can also be used as an expiation of guilt in a desire to atone for evil done. After Rachel had a miscarriage, she became quite ill. Jeremiah's caring for her became a ritual. "It was a ritual of tenderness, but more, a ritual of expiation. For he felt guilty for all" (p. 205). Ritual, then, even when not meaningfully related to a tradition or a myth, meets a human need and hence, Warren believes, can frequently be misused.

Warren's over-all purpose in his literary career seems directed toward the creation of a native myth from the materials of American history. Not only does he regard the making of myth as the artist's highest function, he also has actively engaged in the criticism of historical myths he regards as false and dangerous. He, further, uses a great many mythic elements in his works. His narrative patterns frequently follow the mythic patterns. As Frohock has shown, his hero assumes the suffering of a group, becomes a criminal, incurs condemnation, and sometimes dies.[64] The repeated pattern of flight and return is similar to the many myths of the prodigal son. And, as Robert Slack has pointed out, in *All the King's Men* Warren uses the familiar Telemachus theme in relation to Jack, who is the dispossessed young man.

[64] Frohock, p. 90.

searching for a spiritual father and striving to re-establish a lost relation with his home, community, and the world.[65] John Bradbury has shown that the symbolic pattern of *World Enough and Time* is oriented about the primitivistic shedding of blood and the ritual's idealization in romantic tragedy.[66] *The Cave* repeats the mythological theme of the blood ritual. Giselle believes that Nick's blood can somehow replace hers. "She felt that, as it were, his blood might mystically replace whatever blood she had lost, or might lose; that blood-taken-in might, by a mystic homeopathy, cure the disease of blood-going-out" (p. 47). Warren also makes the Biblical myth of Abraham and Isaac central to his theme and his narrative pattern in this novel. He not only has organized his novels on the familiar mythical patterns, he has also frequently chosen stories that are already partly mythologized, events that have become legendary. The historical materials he used to create "The Ballad of Billie Potts" and *Brother to Dragons* had become frontier legends of old Kentucky. The Beauchamp-Sharp affair had, as early as the eighteen-twenties, become folklore, and there had been numerous folk tales and ballads based upon it. Warren himself recognizes the tendency toward myth in his own works. *Brother to Dragons*, he stated, deals with the same themes as his other works but in a more mythical form.[67] Warren has also been extremely interested in attempts by other writers to create a native American historical myth. Hart Crane's *The Bridge*, Stephen Vincent Benét's *John Brown's Body*, and Donald Davidson's *The Tall Men*, he feels are the three major efforts to create "the native myth"; but although he admires the attempts, he finds none of these completely satisfactory.[68]

Many critics, perhaps prematurely, have stated that Warren has already produced the myth that he has obviously been aiming at. His novels, according to Michel Mohrt, are "modern myths,

[65]   Robert C. Slack, "The Telemachus Theme", in *All the King's Men: A Symposium*, ed. A. Fred Sochatoff et al. (Pittsburgh, 1957), p. 29.
[66]   John M. Bradbury, *The Fugitives: A Critical Account* (Chapel Hill, 1958), p. 212.
[67]   *The Paris Review Interviews*, p. 185.
[68]   "A Note on Three Southern Poets", *Poetry*, XL (May, 1932), p. 108.

parallel to those of Greece, which Robert Penn Warren has made
spring out of American soil and history".[69] To Irving Kristol,
Brother to Dragons is an epic poem,[70] and to Elizabeth Janeway
World Enough and Time is saga and even myth.[71] F. C. Flint
thinks that Warren has come closer than any of the other Fugitives
to creating a national myth.[72] Whether or not Warren has at this
stage of his career created a myth is, of course, debatable. But
because he believes that man needs a tradition bolstered by a
myth and that history requires a myth to accommodate it to
human values and the human mind, Warren has been concerned
with these problems throughout his career. In order to fulfill
what he thinks is the writer's proper social responsibility he must
try to create a native historical myth or at least contribute to the
creation of one. *Wilderness* is his most significant attempt.

[69]   Michel Mohrt, "Robert Penn Warren and the Myth of the Outlaw",
Yale French Studies, No. 10 (1953), p. 75.
[70]   Irving Kristol, "American Ghosts", *Encounter*, III (July, 1954), p. 74.
[71]   Elizabeth Janeway, "Man in Conflict, Mind in Torment", *New York
Times Book Review* (June 25, 1950), p. 22.
[72]   F. Cudworth Flint, "Five Poets", *Southern Review*, I (Winter, 1936),
p. 674.

V

WILDERNESS: THE "LITTLE MYTH"

What our society needs most, Warren believes, is a historical myth and an artist to shape it from our native history, for only the creative imagination, he maintains, can achieve this high goal. Why, one wonders, with his enormous talent and energy and his great learning has Warren not attempted to fulfill what he considers to be the artist's proper social function? Three major attempts, *John Brown's Body* by Stephen Vincent Benét, *The Bridge* by Hart Crane, and *The Tall Men* by Donald Davidson, have not been socially effective or artistically successful. It cannot be seriously argued that Warren has as yet created a native historical myth or that he has even made a whole-hearted attempt. But in *Wilderness,* as in some of the best of his other novels, he tries to do the same thing as myths do – to make serious issues and worthy values immediately and completely available to his audience by imaginatively dramatizing them in a compelling story drawn from native history. And here he uses, as background and as subject, the Civil War, the event he feels is the most important one in American history, not only because of its far-reaching consequences, but also because it is the only common history that lives in the American imagination. For these reasons he believes that the Civil War is the best candidate for an American myth. It would seem that in *Wilderness: A Tale of the Civil War* Warren is paving the way for the creation of a myth from the Civil War. That is, by making it more available to more people and by throwing over it an aura of myth he can prepare for its more complete embodiment in the future.

Regardless of the question of myth, however, *Wilderness* is noteworthy for other reasons. It represents at this stage of his career the culmination of the trend in Warren of a decreasing dependence upon the proliferation of facts, details, and examples as a technique toward a more highly selective and symbolic method and a correspondingly greater concern with meaning and philosophy. Although this trend is observable to some extent in his other novels, *Wilderness* is so great a change that it is rather startling. It is as different from his other novels as Melville's *Benito Cereno* is different from *Moby Dick*. *Wilderness* is, however, merely different from his other novels; it is by no means unique. Here Warren has pruned his novel of all excess details, but – and this is a great tribute to his skill as an artist and as a historian – he has not sacrificed the illusion, the feel of life or the vital re-creation of a historical moment, characteristics that are among the chief triumphs of his novels. Further, in three hundred and ten pages he has effectively dramatized his most important themes. And he does not need to rely on the device of the exemplum, unabsorbed philosophizing, prolongation of the story beyond its dramatically required ending, the introduction of a host of characters not fully assimilated, or melodramatic or sentimental actions and events. He has, thus, achieved his aim of producing a unified, organic work of art. Yet another reason for a close study of *Wilderness* is that since it deals with the Civil War, an event about which Warren has written a great deal, it provides the best opportunity to observe Warren's historical imagination and his philosophy of history as they come into contact with a specific historical event.

Critics, however, for the most part have not agreed with this evaluation. *Wilderness* received relatively few reviews, and many of these were decidedly unfavorable and unsympathetic. The reviewer for *Time*, for example, concludes that in *Wilderness* Warren has used his remarkable skill as a novelist "with carelessness and cynicism".[1] Several object to the pruned and compact method Warren uses here more than in his other novels. John Strugnell finds a weakness of "plot and observation",[2] and

[1] *Time*, LXVIII (November 17, 1961), p. 61.
[2] Strugnell, p. 101.

Charles Samuels objects to the paucity of details.[3] Several object
to the character of Adam, finding him a totally unbelievable
puppet, a mere symbol.[4] To George McMichael the novel is weak
structurally and philosophically, a pretentious failure, with symbols giving it a mere sham elegance.[5] James Magmer finds too
little faith in the novel and accuses Warren of having abandoned
all hope for man.[6] Charles Samuels, on the other hand, finds too
much faith, accusing Warren of abdicating reason in a gratuitous
leap of faith.[7] A close study of the structure and themes of the
novel reveals that the few critics who thought the novel a significant success perhaps approach closer to the truth. Samuel Hynes
finds in *Wilderness* a vivid and accurate re-creation of a piece of
America's past; he is undoubtedly right in judging the author to
be a meticulous historian as well as a brilliant fictionist.[8] And,
finally, J. N. Hartt states that if viewed correctly and in its own
terms the novel is as good as *All the King's Men*.[9] An investiga-
tion of Warren's dramatic embodiment of his historical themes in
this novel indicates that Mr. Hartt's judgment is not an exaggera-
tion.

1

The reasons for Warren's persistent concern with the Civil War
and the reasons he chose it as subject and background in *Wilderness* go far deeper than a mere intellectual interest in this great
event, and are certainly deeper and more organic than the desire
to gain readers by riding the crest of the popularity of the Civil
War during its centennial. They are closely related to his ideas on

[3]   Charles Thomas Samuels, "In the Wilderness", *Critique*, V (Fall, 1962),
p. 46.
[4]   "Loss of Illusion", *London Times Literary Supplement* (June 1, 1962),
p. 385.
[5]   George McMichael, *San Francisco Chronicle* (January 7, 1962), p. 17.
[6]   James Magmer, *Catholic World*, CXCIV (January, 1962), p. 215.
[7]   Samuels, p. 57.
[8]   Samuel Hynes, "Quest for the Meaning of Freedom". *New York Times
Book Review* (November 19, 1961), p. 58.
[9]   J. N. Hartt, "The Return of Moral Passion", *Yale Review*, LI (December, 1961), p. 304.

myth. Like the material from which myths are made, the war has personal relevance to a large part of the American population, many of whom, like Warren, had relatives who fought in this conflict. "I had two grandfathers at Shiloh, that morning of April 6, 1862, young men with the other young men in gray uniforms stepping toward the lethal spring thickets of dogwood and redbud, to the sound of bird song." [10] It seems almost that Warren was there, for unlike Adam, who cannot truly feel the events at Rastatt in which his father participated, Warren has entered into "the pathos of that far time and place".[11] Because of their personal involvement in it the Civil War has much the same relevance to Warren and many other Americans as had the Trojan War to Homer and the Greeks. The Civil War is thus our only "felt history" – "history lived in the national imagination". It is therefore already partly mythologized since it appeals to more than just the intellectual side of man; it is more total and complete in its appeal than any other American history. To the American imagination the Civil War is "the great single event of our history"; to the American mind it IS American history.[12] In World War II, Warren explains, we looked not to the Revolution or World War I for our inspiration but to the Civil War which lives in our minds and appeals to our hearts. Society's myths nearly always center on their most important history, the one historical event from which a people can trace their development as a nation and in which they can see the beginning of issues, attitudes, and political and social forces that reach into their present. To Warren the Civil War, which he calls "that mystic cloud from which emerged our modernity",[13] perfectly fits this requirement. Warren believes the war is the fountainhead of our power and prestige, the source of our modernity, and the beginning of modern America.[14] And it is important because in it "appear in violent and tragic form the issues which are central in our

10 *Segregation*, p. 5.
11 *Wilderness: A Tale of the Civil War* (New York, 1961), p. 121. All references in the text are to this edition.
12 *Legacy*, pp. 3-4.
13 *Ibid.*, p. 49.
14 *Ibid.*, p. 76.

modernity".[15] For one thing, the Civil War made unionism a fact, and Warren speculates that this idea can give us our most significant sense of identity and may be our best and most inclusive hope for our future and that of mankind.[16]

Beyond these reasons, however, the Civil War has much to offer the myth-maker because of its richness of meaning, its tragic depth; it is, he says, "massively symbolic in its inexhaustible and sibylline significance" because it is "an image of life" with many kinds of meanings inherent in it. By studying and anatomizing this portentous richness we may, he says, be better able to understand ourselves; it can give us a clue to our nature and destiny.[17] It was a CIVIL war, the prototype of all war, for the self-division of a country is the mirror of the deep conflicts in life and in the individual.[18] The study of the Civil War, then, is a way to national self-understanding, a way to realize "our common humanity", and this, as myth should, helps prepare us so that we can better face the future.[19] The nature of history and the nature of man as Warren sees them make man's place in the universe a tragic one. The Civil War confirms this view; it is tragedy in that it is a story of crimes of monstrous inhumanity and terrible suffering, a "common tragic entrapment". It confirms the tragic ironies with which we must live in history.[20] But it is tragedy in the classical sense also; it is "the image in action of the deepest questions of man's fate and man's attitude toward his fate".[21] The war dramatizes our humanity just as tragedies do.

And, furthermore, the people who engaged in this historical event provide worthy heroes for myth; they are the sort of people around whom legends are woven. The Civil War, Warren states, provides a great gallery of men, noble yet human, "caught out of time as in a frieze, in stances so profoundly touching or powerfully mythic that they move us in a way no mere consideration of

[15]   "The Present State of Poetry", p. 388.
[16]   *Legacy*, pp. 5-7.
[17]   *Ibid.*, p. 81.
[18]   *Ibid.*, pp. 83-84.
[19]   *Ibid.*, p. 100.
[20]   *Ibid.*, p. 106.
[21]   *Ibid.*, p. 103.

'historical importance' ever could". "That was our Homeric period, and the figures loom up only a little less than gods, but even so, we recognize the lineaments and passions of men, and by that recognition of common kinship share in their grandeur." [22] They draw our imagination because like us their aims and commitments are divided and unclear in the complexity of life. Those who fought in the war were caught in a collision of blind forces which they understood imperfectly or not at all. In other words, they are like us, and we can thus identify with them.

But these heroes also attract us by their difference from us, he maintains. They were, first, committed to a cause; honor and duty to the self, to society, and to God meant something to them. They had moral awareness in contrast to our conformity. Even "the corrosive of historical realism" [23] cannot disenthrall us; these people of the Civil War cannot be debunked by historical scholarship, Warren believes. Their actions draw us "to the glory of the human effort to win meaning from the complex and confused motives of men and the blind ruck of events". And despite their failings, blindness, and vice they affirm the possibility of the dignity of life – a tragic dignity.[24] Unlike modern man, these men had a sense of community, a sense of locality with shared sentiments, and this helped them achieve identity. This sense of community and identity is perhaps the chief value to be derived from myth in Warren's estimation. In our restless mobility and conformity we look back nostalgically "on the romantic image of some right and natural relation of man to place and man to man, fulfilled in worthy action".[25] Our contemplation of these people can have positive values for us today. One way, Warren advises, for modern man to retain the value of individualism, variety, and integrity is to study the Civil War and those men caught up in it.[26] To observe these people acting in accord with a worthy tradition

22 *Ibid.*, pp. 81-82.
23 *Legacy*, pp. 91-92.
24 *Ibid.*, p. 108.
25 *Ibid.*, pp. 91-92.
26 *Ibid.*, p. 49.

can perhaps inspire us to seek what is valid in the past, and it should teach us humility.

And in the contemplation of the story, some of that grandeur, even in the midst of the confused issues, shadowy chances, and brutal ambivalences of our life and historical moment, may rub off on us.[27]

Thus a positive value of the Civil War is that it provides the basis for a good symbolic myth with an enduring appeal to the imagination. Warren is, of course, not the only American writer to recognize the mythic significance of the Civil War. It has been a subject of almost obsessive interest to American writers, and both Benét and Davidson based their attempts to create an epic upon it. Historians too are aware of its epic qualities. Otto Eisenschiml and Ralph Newman, for example, entitled their collection of eyewitness accounts of the most important battles of the war *The American Iliad: The Epic Story of the Civil War*.

But there are many other indications in *Wilderness* beyond the subject matter and historical background that indicate that Warren, while not trying as obviously and as self-consciously to create the native myth or epic as did Benét and Davidson, was at least trying to give his novel mythic overtones and hence to show its kinship with myth. The narrative form, a much simpler form than Warren has ever before used, follows the archetypal pattern of a quest, a common form of myth, the form of *The Odyssey*, *The Aeneid*, the myths of the golden fleece, and the Holy Grail, and the Oedipus myth. Indeed, *Wilderness* is in many respects quite similar to the Oedipus cycle. Adam like Oedipus has a club foot; Adam like Oedipus has a violent fight on the highway over the right-of-way, and both lose control of themselves; and both in the end find truth and peace in a sacred grove. They even think alike. The frontpiece of *Wilderness* contains the soliloquy from *Henry V* on the responsibility of kings for their subjects. Both Adam and Oedipus feel responsible for the suffering of those around them, and both learn that, in fact, they are responsible; and because of the ensuing guilt each appropriates all

---

[27] *Ibid.*, p. 109.

suffering to himself. In his quest for the meaning of life and for his own identity Adam progresses through various states of mind, trying in his travels, like Telemachus, to establish a right relationship with his father. Choosing this simple, picaresque form, Warren merely has Adam encounter various people and situations which he must understand and account for in formulating his ideals. Each encounter – with the hanged man, Maran Meyerhof, Monmorancy Pugh, and the Rebels in the wilderness, for example – initiates him more fully into life and its meaning. The form then is a sort of parable – R. W. Hertz calls it "a philosophical parable" [28] – with Adam as Everyman seeking meaning in the wilderness of history. Warren has, thus, chosen a simpler and more mythic narrative pattern than he has ever before used. The austere simplicity of the style, more pruned and compact than in the other novels, likewise suggests kinship with myth. Its poetic quality, as in the opening lines, sounds like the chant of a Greek chorus:

If the mountain had not gleamed so white
    If yonder under the peaks, the snaggled line of the fir forest had not been so blue-black, against the white.
    If the sky above that glitter of snow on the Zelzsteinberg had not been heart-breaking with the innocence of new blue. If one puff of cloud, white as whipped cream, had not lounged high in the washed glitter of blue. If the world had not been so absolute in beauty. (p. 3)

And the novel abounds in repetition, alliteration, and rhythm, as in the following passage:

He found himself looking at that thronged road with distant disdain.
    I did not come here to go with them, he thought.
    I came here to find something, he thought. *In Virginia,* he thought.
    And now he was free to go. It did not matter what had made him free, what murky complications or blind accidents of the past. Suddenly, all the past was nothing, and joy flooded his heart.
    He was free, at last, to go. (p. 245)

More than any other aspect of the novel, the characters, because of their mythological connotations and Warren's overt allusions

---

[28] R. N. Hertz, "Spiritual Journey, Philosophical Detours", *New Republic*, CXL (December 18, 1961), p. 23.

to the people, beings, and creatures of legends, connect the novel with myth. Adam is Everyman, but he is also quite literally a wandering Jew, who, like the legendary Wandering Jew, is an outcast of society, his banishment and rejection deriving from his lameness. Granville Hicks also sees him as a Christ figure, because he suffers for the sins of the world and because at the age of thirty he, like Christ, finds truth in the wilderness.[29] Throughout the novel the Negro is presented as the sacrificial victim, the scapegoat in the mythological significance of the term. The powerful scene in the hospital tent shows the Negro as suffering victim. Because he had bravely saved his white lieutenant and in so doing been shot, the Negro private bleeds to death on the hospital table. The lieutenant, repeatedly calling him a "black son-of-a-bitch", cannot bear the thought of owing his life to an inferior or the thought of the responsibility the Negro has thrust upon him by dying in his stead. Almost the first sight that greets Adam in the New World is the horribly mutilated body of a Negro hanging from a lightpost. This Negro suggests both the legendary hanged man and Christ, and Warren overtly draws this connection. Adam prayerfully stares at the Negro's wounds just as he had seen an old man in Bavaria stare at the wounds of an icon of Christ at a wayside shrine. But to his shame and sorrow Adam feels little sympathy and nothing happens in his heart. Maran Goetz Meyerhof is clearly meant to represent the earth mother, the goddess of fertility, Demeter, or Ceres. This is the way Warren first describes her:

She was a large girl, wearing some kind of a long blue dress, yellow hair braided and wrapped around her head, a fat baby propped on one hip, on the other side, an arm dangling to hold a flattish basket, heaped high with purple grapes, and behind her was a tangle of leaves, brightened to gold and translucent green by the last sunlight striking through them. (p. 110)

It is, of course, the time of harvest. The baby, the ripe grapes, even the color of gold are traditionally associated with the fertility goddess, the goddess of the harvest. And while talking with

---

[29] Granville Hicks, "Crusader in a World of Chance", *Saturday Review*, XLIV (November 18, 1961), p. 19.

the men and eating grapes she unself-consciously nurses her fat, healthy baby. "The girl's breast was large and full and extraordinarily white, almost bluish, with a delicate, vinelike tracery of blue veins" (p. 113).

The character and appearance of Jedeen Hawksworth is also rooted in myth. In his moral ambivalence and ambiguity, his bravery and nobility and his greed and meanness he is quite appropriately the centaur – half man, half beast with a nature partaking of both. His lower half was clothed in old work clothes, but his upper half was dressed in an old frock coat, waistcoat, a blue silk stock, and even a gold watch chain. "The lower half of Jedeen Hawksworth, in other words, seemed adapted to the dreary grind of life and the brute work of the world. He was a kind of centaur, a centaur with the animal part drearily plow-broke and spavined, but the upper half affirming some dignity and aspiration, some human hope" (p. 96).

Like a ballad, a legend, or a myth *Wilderness* contains a large number of stylized details and ritualistic actions. Even the names of minor characters are frequently given as generalized, descriptive phrases – the hairy one, the nondescript man, the leaper-over-ferns, the scarecrow – rather than as proper names. The chief purpose of Warren's frequent mentioning of numbers is to give a ballad-like atmosphere to the novel. "The eight maniacal scarecrows burst into the glade" (p. 291). Adam watches one of these scarecrows duel with a Yankee soldier, and he counts their thrusts and parries. "Five times Adam saw this, and five times heard the smart clash, or clink, then the small grind of metal at the instant of disengagement" (p. 297). These events seem to Adam so stylized that they suggest to him "a charade, a dream, a drama" (p. 299). And Warren compares the fight in the glade to the ballet, the most stylized of art forms:

The hairy one had leaped again, over the dead horse and fallen scarecrow, in a great burst of awkward, angular energy that was, somehow, as beautiful as a dance; and with those crazy, cranky leaps over the ferns, one boot on, one boot off, beard whipping in the wind, rags flapping, bayonet glittering in jagged arabesques, tethered boot snatching and jerking at the waist, was gone. At that instant of disappearance into the greenery the head had turned, the mouth had opened, and a quavering of heart-broken sound had come forth. (p. 298)

At times it almost seems as if the characters, especially Adam in his slow methodicalness, are taking part in an elaborate religious ritual; frequently their actions seem as deliberate and stylized as a mass. Adam thinks of Maran as she goes about her chores in her kitchen as a priestess in a ritual. The entire final scene in the clearing in the wilderness is enacted as drama, the epitomization of the religious ritual. With careful meticulousness Adam moves about the glade after all the violence.

He rose and moved with barefoot stealth, across the ferns. He crossed to the other side of the dead horse. He set the boots on the ground, very tidily, near the body of the man. Near enough, he realized, to be within easy reach.

In a numb, quiet way he thought how foolish this was.

He felt ashamed of his foolishness. But with the same stealth, the same control of breath, he withdrew. He crouched on the ground, near where he had been making ready to put on the boots. He peered at the objects among the ferns. (p. 307)

Wilderness, like myth and indeed like most of Warren's novels, contains much speculation on religion and the nature of God and man's relation to Him. Warren here dramatizes his theological speculation through the thoughts and conversations of Adam, whom he convincingly characterizes as a young man naturally given to religious meditation. But in *Wilderness* there is more of the supernatural, the legendary, and the mysterious – important ingredients of myth – than in Warren's other novels. Adam frequently has the feeling of an impending doom, a nemesis. "He shivered in the sunshine. He felt the sweat slide down his armpits. He thought: *If I'm not careful something will happen.* He did not know what it was. But he knew it was terrible" (p. 99). Antigone, Cassandra, Oedipus, and Medea experienced a similar mysterious sense of doom. Images – "kneehigh spook-white weeds" by the roadside (p. 106) and miscellaneous details – both of the Meyerhof barns had "askew cabalistic signs at the gable" (p. 106) – reinforce the atmosphere of mystery.

Superstition is also a theme in *Wilderness*. Jed is a prey to superstitious beliefs. Although he could not bear the company of Adam and Mose, "He had, too, the superstitious conviction that if he lost them his prosperity would vanish, like fairy gold" (p. 117). Warren also includes legends that early grew up around the Civil War. A soldier, trying hard not to believe it, tells Adam: "They say if Ole Lee gets a man's face down here square in his spyglass, that man has lost his odds, his chances is used up. He may git acrost the Rapidan when we moves. But he won't git back" (p. 203). While not trying to create an epic or a myth in the same way as Benét or Davidson, by using such devices as epic catalogs and epic similes Warren does give his subject, a subject he has deemed worthy of being made into a myth, an aura of myth. An examination of his other themes and methods in *Wilderness* shows that this novel comes as close as any of his works to meeting one of his definitions of myth, "a great, multi-phase symbol to render his total vision of the world, his sense of individual destiny, his sense of man's place in nature, his sense of history and society".[30]

2

The first characteristic of myth as Warren sees it is concreteness and an accurate, factual, and detailed development of history. Although *Wilderness* is more selective in the use of documentation than any of the other novels, it does not disappoint in this respect. It is not that Warren has become less specific and more general; it is rather that he has become more selective, and instead of amassing example on top of example he picks the telling detail, the fact heavy with implication. Frederick J. Hoffman has said that Warren's novels are overwritten and luxuriant and "suffer from an embarrassment of riches".[31] If this is true of his earlier novels, it is certainly not true of *Wilderness*, in which almost every detail seems to rise to symbol. Also, more of the action is

[30] "Conrad and *Nostromo*", p. 48.
[31] Frederick J. Hoffman, *The Modern Novel in America, 1900-1950* (Chicago, 1951), p. 200.

internal; there is more introspection. Although he experiences a great deal, Adam does very little, and this makes him seem curiously passive. But what he does and thinks is so exhaustively analyzed that the reader knows Adam as fully as he knows any of Warren's heroes. The greatest drawback to this method of character development is that the reader is perhaps not as deeply involved with or interested in Adam as he is Jack Burden or Brad Tolliver, for instance. Although the novel contains all of Warren's major themes, and Adam follows the same sort of philosophical and spiritual journey as do Jack Burden, Jeremiah Beauchamp, and Amantha Starr, *Wilderness* is less than one-third the length of the novels in which these characters appear. Warren's problem here was the same one he solved with notable success in *Brother to Dragons*, the problem of paring away "the merely circumstantial interest" while keeping "enough for interest".[32] Warren sees the artist's task as "the study of the problem of concretely realizing the theme in projected human experience".[33] Prior to *Wilderness* his method was "to realize" the theme by a proliferation of detail so that there tended at times to be an excess of subject over theme. This can also be said of *Flood*, which like *Band of Angels* and *World Enough and Time* is extensive, abounding in details, characters, and stories. But in *Wilderness* his talent is intensive, "a talent exhaustively aware of the immediate richness and implication of the single scene".[34]

The novel has a detailed richness and a solidity of specification, but these details relate to one another and to the major themes so that they do more than merely document. When Warren does need to convey facts, he is specific but succinct. Earlier he would perhaps have spun out into several pages a description of the ship which brought Adam over and the life on board. Here he uses one sentence: "It was the second morning out of Bremerhaven, on the *Elmyra*, side-wheeler, 1,940 tons gross, English registry, when after the breakfast of bully beef, hardtack, and tepid coffee, the agent in charge rousted them out on deck, all 125 of them"

---

32 "The Way It Was Written", p. 25.
33 "Literature as a Symptom", p. 36.
34 "The Fiction of Caroline Gordon", p. 5.

(p. 18). Not a word or detail, despite the exactness, is wasted. And despite the brevity of the novel, Warren accurately reproduces various dialects such as the talk of the old sailor:

Yes, my sonnywhack, you be squatting yonder by that stanchion, out of harm's way. Chipping on your chain like it was for Eternal Life. You will be of no slightest interest to no human creature. No man will give tuppence nor fishhook for you, my cock. You will be of such general interest as a seaglin at sunset.   (p. 38)

While accurately and vividly describing Adam's home town in Bavaria, Warren is at the same time revealing Adam's attitude toward it, and the monotony and ugliness of his life:

He opened his eyes. He saw the crooked street and the frozen mud of winter thawing gummily where the sun reached it but freezing again where the shadows of houses lengthened over. He saw the arch of the stone bridge over the Zelz, where the thaw-raddled fragments of ice slid by, like sputum on the black water. He saw, beyond the Zelz, the Schloss, gray, ugly, hulking and improvised, the squat twin towers, each surmounted by a dome the shape of an inverted turnip, the lower wall, where moisture from snow, snagged in crenelation, bled darkly down over the gray stone.   (pp. 5-6)

Recurrent imagery and the natural way in which details become symbol illustrate Warren's skillful mastery of the use of facts, his subordination of accurate observation to his artistic intention. The two sets of recurrent images – those associated with living creatures, especially ants, and those associated with caves and darkness – reinforce one another. They suggest the insignificance, the frailty of man lost in the blackness of the self and the darkness of history – the horror of the historical process. The repeated ant imagery suggests the teeming confusion and apparent futility of man's activities, especially in war. "A great boot had, as it were, kicked over the winter camp like an ant hill, and the life was seething desperately forth" (p. 235). In the glade Adam, like Frederick Henry in *A Farewell to Arms*, becomes intensely involved with the struggles of the ants carrying crumbs. He is like God observing man in history, man who works hard but achieves little.

Imagery associated with animals suggests the terror of history and, more specifically, the cruelty of war. Jed, for example, refers to Gettysburg as "the slaughter pen" (p. 135). And the soldiers and Adam refer to the Confederate Army as a huge elephant and Lee as a dangerous beast. "He thought of a dark forest, far to the south, where Lee crouched like a beast, hurt perhaps but full of coldly exalted ferocity and patient in cunning, waiting in the darkness of Virginia like a cave" (p. 135). This imagery associated with caves and darkness recurs throughout the novel, especially in the episode involving Monmorancy Pugh, who had given in to the horror and irony of history. The door of his cabin, Warren says, opened inward "on a blackness like a cave" (p. 247). And later Adam thinks: "It was bright morning outside, he could tell, but this place was more like a cave, a den than a constructed habitation" (p. 253). His wife's eyes stare at Adam "like eyes spying from a thicket" (p. 248). After helping him across the Rapidan, Monmorancy leaves Adam: "He had, without a sound, slipped into darkness" (p. 281). Warren here also effectively uses his characteristic device of the symbolic moment, what he calls "stopped time" or "freeze time". When the "eight maniacal scarecrows" burst into Adam's glade "the ferocity of motion was frozen for his inspection". "Then the instant in which all had been frozen for his inspection exploded around him. It crashed like an enormous glass demijohn hit by a brickbat. It crashed and flashed in all directions" (p. 292).

In *Wilderness*, more than in any other of his novels, Warren more nearly achieves his aim of making naturalistic facts and historical documentation rise naturally and subtly to symbol, of organically relating theme and subject; as in the best of his other novels he never seems to be doing merely one thing at a time. In a powerfully dramatized scene at Simms Purdew's party Warren depicts one of the soldier's "games". Negro volunteers, hands tied behind them, root with their heads in a barrel of flour for dollar bills, while the soldiers beat upon them. For sport Simms Purdew hoists one of the Negroes by the feet until the unfortunate man nearly smothers; tiring of his fun, Simms merely lets the man fall to the floor like a sack of potatoes where he sits whimpering and wheezing:

But his teeth were clenched. He clenched something between his teeth.
     With his right hand the fellow took the thing from between his teeth. It was, clearly, not something you could simply spit out and be done with it. The fellow held it up, still puffing and wheezing. Beneath the streaks of flour the face was grinning. It was a wan, sickly distorted, flour-streaked grin, but a grin.   (p. 187)

This episode concretely reveals an aspect of army camp life, the fact that idle, bored men can easily become cruel men. Since Warren has Adam react to this scene, it also serves to characterize him as well as the participants. But, more significantly, this episode is profoundly symbolic, for the Negro's plight images the way Warren sees man in history. The historical process involves terrible and even senseless suffering for man, but if he, like the Negro, can grasp something of value, he can at least make brutal life a little more endurable. Similarly, the old man painfully but carefully carrying an out-sized Wedgewood soup tureen as he moves out with the army amid violent confusion suggests the same idea of man holding desperately on to something he has found valuable in life. Even geographical features unobtrusively become symbols. The Rapidan is for Adam more than just a twisting river with treacherous fords beyond which the enemy lurks in the dense wilderness. It becomes a symbol of a goal which Adam, like every man, must set for himself and struggle toward. Indeed, although Adam's journey to the wilderness of Virginia is a well documented, believable trip, it becomes also an almost allegorical journey into the darkness of history, the evil of man, and the wickedness of the self, for in the glade or on the way Adam sees the horror of history, the depravity of man, and the evil he himself is capable of – all presented and dramatized quite specifically. And Adam's deformed foot braced by a special boot symbolizes human limitation which Adam like all men must accept and learn to live with.
     Although he always seems real, a man of flesh and blood, Mose, with his ambiguously mixed character, seeming now noble and now utterly depraved, has symbolic significance. He is, Adam must learn, like all men; he is what Adam must come to terms

with and still love man. Adam can easily love the heroic Negro, but to admire and respect Mose as an individual and not just an abstraction is a great deal more difficult. Finally, in *Wilderness* the characters' names are heavy with implication but rarely too obvious and never violate the reader's sense of fact and probability as the names of others of Warren's characters occasionally do. Jack Burden, who shoulders the "burden" of the past, while obvious is believable. But Gummy Larson as a name for a dishonest contractor perhaps strains credulity. The name Adam, Hebrew for man, approaches the obvious, but it is not difficult to imagine his father giving him this name. Rosenzweig – twig of rose – however, is weighty with meaning, and it is a likely name for a Bavarian Jew. It suggests both the good – the rose – and the bad – the thorn – in Adam's physical makeup since he is handsome but crippled, and good and evil in the moral nature of man. Warren, then, does not slight facts and details in *Wilderness*; he uses them sparingly but tellingly and frequently makes them bear a larger weight of implication than in his other novels. In fact, one of Adam's major faults which his experiences correct is that he, like many idealists in Warren's novels, ignores facts in a devotion to the abstraction of human freedom. He learns that in the enormous complexity of history such absolutes are not easily come by – that one cannot care for Mankind without caring first for men and that one cannot formulate truths and ideals until one has mastered the facts.

3

One of the most interesting aspects of this novel for the reader is Warren's embodiment in fiction of some of the facts of the war and his thoughtful consideration of the historical event that has been almost an obsession with him. His other novels abound in reference to the war, in reverberations from it, and even occasionally in brief, direct dramatizations of it, but none can match the detail and fullness of its treatment in *Wilderness*, the only novel in which the war is the central historical situation. In this novel Warren well absorbs the "impurities" of historical facts and speculation; he does not merely load his work with historical facts, episodes, characters, and his ideas on them; rather they arise naturally and organically from the narrative itself. In *Wilderness* theme and subject are well suited to one another. For some participants such as Adam and Hans Meyerhof the war was indeed a struggle for freedom. Thus, the question of human freedom, a major theme of Warren, derives naturally from the historical setting. Further, Warren chose to focus on the Battle of the Wilderness, one of the war's most crucial encounters between Lee and Grant, a battle termed by most historians as the turning point of the war. This battle provided him with an excellent image of his philosophy of history and nature – man struggling with the confused blankness and horror that everywhere confront him in the wasteland of history and nature. Setting and event shade imperceptibly into theme so that all are organically interrelated. A description of the setting by an actual participant indicates why Warren chose this area and this battle for Adam to struggle in to find his truth.

The Wilderness is a densely wooded region of great extent, remarkable on account of its dreary and dismal woods. A dense undergrowth of scraggy pines, dwarfed oaks and laurel bushes has spung up, while in the low points are sluggish streams and dank marshes choked with alders, twined closely with luxuriant tangled and prickly vines, making many places almost inaccessible.[35]

And he continues, "It was a battle fought where maneuvering was impossible, where the lines of battle were invisible to their Commanders, and where the enemy also was invisible." [36] This description could not have provided a better central image for Warren's novel. In the Civil War and in particular in the Battle of the Wilderness Warren has found a nearly perfect subject and setting in which to dramatize his major themes.

In presenting historical events and background in *Wilderness* there are several significant new departures from Warren's usual methods. For the first time to any extent, Warren goes outside the

[35] Otto Eisenschiml and Ralph Newman, *The American Iliad: The Epic Story of the Civil War* (New York, 1947), p. 560.
[36] *Ibid.*, pp. 561-62.

Southern and even outside American history for some of his
background, and he uses a Bavarian Jew as his main character.
In this sense *Wilderness* is less provincial and regional. But his
main purpose is undoubtedly to gain a wider perspective on his
material from American history. In two places he introduces a
bit of German history – the peasant's uprising in Germany in
1848. Both Adam's father and his father surrogate, Hans Meyerhof, fought at Rastatt. We learn that at two P.M. on March 18,
1848, in the Schlossplatz in Berlin, Leopold stood with others
against General von Prittwitz and his Prussian infantry, and that
a year later he and Hans were both at Rastatt when it fell. This
seemingly irrelevant history places the Civil War in the broad
sweep of human history and of time. The Civil War is another
Rastatt, another cause for those who like Adam and his father
wish to fight for freedom, no matter how futile the struggle. And
Adam's uncle points out that Leopold's valor at Rastatt resulted
only in his imprisonment and that there was no more liberty after
the war than before. Warren implies that, although it is another
chapter in the human struggle for justice, the Civil War was
perhaps just as futile. The use of German history serves to give a
historical perspective to the material, a perspective that is needed
because there is here no narrator to go forward in time. In
Wilderness Warren goes further back into the past rather than
forward to the present. He uses Hans Meyerhof, who fought in
both wars, to point up the connection. Warren also keeps the
battles always in the background. Like a character in a Greek
tragedy, Adam hears of the violent action second hand or observes it after it is over. He sees Gettysburg two months after the
battle and hears what happened from a maimed Northern soldier
who withstood the Rebel charge. As J. N. Hartt has said, Warren,
eschewing the panoramic effect and concentrating on the shape
and feel of the war, paints the combat experience on a small
corner of his canvas and fills it out with splendid effect.[37]

In most of his other novels Warren has relied rather heavily
for imaginative stimulation on real events from the past. Even

---

[37]   Hartt, p. 304.

The Cave is modeled on a real historical event, although the characters are, for the most part, original. But in *Wilderness*, although the background history, characters, battles, and social and political history are scrupulously accurate, the central plot and the main characters are not historical. One can speculate that perhaps the germ of the novel owes something to the fact that Leopold Karpeles, the first person of the Jewish faith to be awarded the Congressional Medal of Honor, was wounded in the Battle of the Wilderness, but Adam and his adventures are purely imaginative creations. By having the real historical events in the background, Warren achieves the same feel of historical verisimilitude which novels, such as *Night Rider* and *At Heaven's Gate*, which are based on real events, possess. The historical details in the novel are extremely accurate. Monmorancy Pugh, helping Adam ford the Rapidan, mentions a better ford at Germanna, and later Warren states that Adam crosses the Old Turnpike Road. By such clues one can find on a map almost the exact location of Adam's glade between the opposing armies. The facts of the past are still of the utmost importance to Warren, and from his scrupulous accuracy it is clear that a great moment of history has lived itself through him.

Although they are kept in the background in *Wilderness*, Warren does dramatize battles, campaigns, and strategies and even presents several of the major historical personages. He has imaginatively grasped and assimilated these facts so that the history does not obtrude or detract from Adam's quest. He absorbs the facts into his artistic form so that they are charged with emotional and imaginative significance as well as intellectual meaning. Early in the novel, in order to give the necessary background history and the exact date, Warren has Adam find a fragment of a five-day-old newspaper dated July 10, 1863, in which he reads about Meade's defeat of Lee at Gettysburg and a criticism of Meade for not pressing his advantage. This device, while perhaps a bit artificial, enables Warren to give background information without taking the focus off Adam and without interrupting the narrative movement.

Warren also assimilates into his novel two conflicting accounts

of the behavior of the Plattdeutsch at the Battle of Chancellorsville. Aaron Blaustein blames the Germans for running and losing
the battle in which his son Stephen, who had been with Howard's
Corps, was killed. "It was Stonewall, and those Germans broke"
(p. 75). The official versions in the newspapers also place the
blame on the Germans in order to excuse the Federal leaders, a
charge which causes Hans Meyerhof, a German who fought for
the ideal of freedom, great suffering. He had also been with
Howard's Corps, and his wife tells Adam Hans' version, one that
seems more likely: "The Rebels came out of the woods, and
surprised 'em. That Jackson – he came. Hans said it was the
fault of the generals and those people. It wasn't their own fault
that Hans and those men got surprised, and had to run. But they
tried to fight. That's how he got shot – trying to stop the Rebels"
(pp. 127-8). These two conflicting versions of the same historical
event offer concrete examples of the difficulty of knowing the
past and the manner in which people interpret history to flatter
their own needs; they also give some of the facts of an important
battle of the war.

During the slow, peaceful trip through Pennsylvania only
echoes of the war reach Adam, Jed, and Mose, but this is enough
so that the reader has some idea of its over-all progress. Jed tells
them, "The Yankees are moving in. In Virginny. Looks like Old
Meade is hunting a fight" (p. 107). They leave the Meyerhof
farm when Jed decides that Meade is not going to get his fight.
Warren gives some of the officer's strategy and comments upon
it, not overtly in an authorial intrusion, but through a veteran of
Chancellorsville. He says that Grant is going to take them South:

But I hope to God he has more sense than that General Hooker.
Hooker, he taken us right in the Wilderness, and they hit us in the
woods. Yeah, I was at Chancellorsville, and it was a God-A-Mighty
big elephant. Yesh, if Grant takes us in there it'll be Chancellorsville
all over. All that brush and scrub oak and blight pine and you can't
see yore hand afore your face. Hell, going in them woods after
Ginnal Lee – it is like crawling in a cave at night to wrassle a bear
and it the bear's cave.   (pp. 201-2)

The manner in which Warren presents the Battle of Gettysburg epitomizes one technique he uses in Wilderness to include the facts of history. Arriving at the battlefield two months after the battle, Adam hears part of what happened from Dr. Mordecai Sulgrave and part from a wounded survivor who tells them what happened and how it felt to be there. This conversation adds the personal, emotional, human aspects to what could have been a dull recital of dry facts. Although he had been safely under the bed with his wife on the outside, Dr. Sulgrave in his inflated rhetoric tells part of what had happened. Pickett and Pettigrew, he says, three times charged the hill "with the red flags of treason, battle, and rapine. It was shot and shell. See this very tree under which I repose myself. It is sawed off by Minnie balls. Fifteen, twenty thousand Rebels – they are coming" (p. 142) Sull Hankins, who had lost his arm in the battle, gives a clear and vivid account of Pickett's charge which he had endured and of the remarkable bravery he had witnessed:

They hit right along here. I was behind that wall and I seen 'em coming. When they stopped throwing them cook-stoves I peeked over the wall. They was down in the valley marching at us. Pickett and them Virginians yonder – he pointed his finger weakly to the left – and them North Carolina bastards down here. They was angling up the rise. They marched into the canister. A bastard would get hit and fall, but they'd close up and come on. By God, I'll say this fer 'em, them bastards would close up and come on. They come marching. They held their line. They durn near held it clean." (p. 151)

Warren has even contrived to present a portrait of General Grant, the only historical character described at first hand in the novel:

Then he saw, in the fresh memory more sharply than he had in fact, the figure of the second of the three men riding in front, a smallish, lumpish, bearded man between two goldgleaming warriors, a man who, despite his lumpishness, sat his mount well, a man with a hat pulled low on his brow, no insignia on his coat. The coat was unbuttoned and hung without tidiness. Adam realized that he had seen, under that unbuttoned coat, a gold sash bound over the incipient paunch of middle-age. (pp. 198-9)

Warren has, thus, without intrusion or didacticism, absorbed into his novel a great many of the facts of the past, so that it has, despite its brevity, factual exactness and solidity of specification.

4

In *Wilderness* Warren is also deeply concerned with the meaning of the Civil War and with its causes and consequences. In this novel he has subtly dramatized his reading of this history which he presented overtly in *The Legacy of the Civil War* and in several articles. It is immediately apparent that Warren like Edmund Wilson in *Patriotic Gore* is out to shock our "official versions and received opinions" of the war.[38] Warren has long maintained that the war was no crusade for freedom and that the North by no means had all the right on its side. Ironically, fresh off the boat Adam falls into the midst of the conscription riots caused by the people's unwillingness to fight for "freedom". In his innocence Adam thought the riots were in celebration of having defeated the Rebels. The riot echoes Warren's judgment that the North was racist and solidly segregationist, with even the abolitionists believing in Negro inferiority. The mob scene powerfully dramatizes the hatred and resentment of the North toward the Negroes. Led by a huge, red-haired woman brandishing a butcher knife and shouting, "Shag them niggers! Shag 'em!" they brutally kill terrified Negroes:

A woman leaned over and uttered a shrill, sustained whinnying sound, and plunged her knife into the man's thigh, not terribly deep, and with a ripping motion jerked it downward. Adam could hear the sound of the blade – it was not a big knife, something snatched in haste off the kitchen table – ripping the denim of the man's trousers. The man, staring upward, uttered no sound.   (p. 50)

They then divert their attention to drowning Negroes in the basements where they had taken refuge.

Several times Warren makes the point that racism and prejudice were prevalent in the invading armies. A soldier strenuously objects to Mose watching Mollie the Mutton getting "ten on the bare doup" (p. 204), and at Gettysburg a Northern soldier does not want to drink after Mose. It is ironical that at the scene of one of the largest battles in a war for Negro "freedom" the men

---

[38]   "Edmund Wilson's Civil War", p. 151.

care nothing for Negroes, collectively or individually. In his essay on Faulkner, Warren states that although the South was cursed by slavery and the Civil War was the fulfillment of that doom, the North was little better than a blind instrument of fate.[39] *Wilderness* affirms this, for even Simms Purdew, who had won a medal for gallantry at Antietam, kills because he enjoys it and not for any cause. Even Adam at first has the same blood lust that Warren had accused the abolitionists of in their zeal for freedom. To his Uncle's assertion that God is with the persecuted even when they are persecuted righteously, Adam replies, "I do not believe He weeps when the wicked are persecuted to bring Justice. Nor do I weep for them" (p. 16). The obvious way to dramatize this theme would have been in relation to abolitionists. But Warren eschews the obvious here, for Adam's uncle is speaking not of the Civil War but of the peasants' uprising.

The ideas about the war which Warren dramatizes in *Wilderness* go much deeper than a criticism of the North and its role in the war. As in *The Legacy of the Civil War* he finds the South very much at fault too. The strong crypto-emancipationism in the South led to a sense of guilt, and this guilt combined with fear of slave uprising caused cruelty to the slaves, and it caused the South to become a locked-in society willing to hear no criticism of "the peculiar institution" either from within or without. This refusal to allow for change, Warren maintains, denied the very concept of life and history, "the working of the life process through history".[40] When the South repudiated the critic, the war became almost inevitable. These ideas are presented primarily in the story of Jed's background which vividly depicts the closed society of the South locked in its defense of slavery. After taking the side of a slave against the Master, Jed was tarred, feathered, and run out of town. The reason for the people's cruelty, Aaron Blaustein explains, was that they were worried: "About uprisings. About Abolition. About themselves, too, I suppose" (p. 102). Both North and South, Warren believes, must share the guilt and responsibility for Reconstruction, which com-

---

[39] "William Faulkner", p. 63.
[40] *Legacy*, p. 34.

pounded problems rather than solved them, and today we still have not recovered from these abuses: "But history is irreversible, and we are still picking up the pieces." [41] In the plight of the lazy, drunken Southern unionist, whose daughter is debauched by General Barton, and who is himself corrupted by the Federal officers, Warren has dramatized the fate of the South during Reconstruction when Yankee shrewdness and unscrupulousness combined with Southern lethargy and ignorance to impoverish and plunder the South. The Unionist, whose house had been burned by the Confederates, now lived in his old slave quarters on handouts from the Federal army. Like the South after the war he "moved through the season in his rhythm of elation and nausea, in a world of delusion and fictions and self-justification" (pp. 174-5).

One of the main points concerning the war that Warren makes in *The Legacy of the Civil War* is that during this time and immediately afterward the United States was catapulted from an agrarian-handicraft society to a society based on capitalism and big business. The country went money mad. This was when our materialistic, modern society was born. These themes run throughout *Wilderness*. Aaron Blaustein prospers from the war, telling Adam that "everybody is getting rich now". "Everybody, that is, who isn't getting killed" (p. 75). In forecasting the money that will flow after the war the sutler who tries to get Adam to come to work for him takes it for granted that Adam wants to get rich. "A smart fellow like you and ed-jucated – he kin git rich. This country is gonna be full of money. It is gonna be as full of money as hog meat is of grease. Hell, walk in the right place and money will stick to you like cockleburs. Hell, money is gonna be as common as choly-morbus in dog days, and a sight more pleasant" (p. 243). Jedeen Hawksworth becomes rich selling inferior goods to the armies at inflated prices. As he gets richer he becomes greedier until he is a suspicious miser unable to think of anything beyond making money and more money. His money belt, which he even sleeps in, symbolizes the shamefulness of this attitude. In

[41] "Edmund Wilson's Civil War", p. 158.

Jed's financial dealings – he got permission to set up as a sutler by bribing an army official and by procuring the daughter of the Southern unionist for General Barton – there is a forecast of the crooked money grubbing and financial shenanigans that seemingly held full sway after the war; according to Warren in *The Legacy of the Civil War* it was men like Jed and the other sutler who inherited America after the war and who created the Gilded Age. *Wilderness*, then, not only effectively presents many historical facts of the Civil War in dramatic form; it also includes, skillfully incorporated into the other themes and the narrative, Warren's reading of the meaning and significance of the Civil War.

5

Granville Hicks has said that in *Wilderness* Warren sums up what he has learned about the nature of history and of man, but he does this in imaginative terms offering an experience, not a formula.[42] The shortest of Warren's novels is almost a compendium of his familiar themes, but these themes are dramatized in new, original ways. *Wilderness* offers one of the fullest, clearest and most artistically effective presentations of his theory of the moral neutrality of history. The title itself suggests the nature of history; it is a wilderness in which man must wander, from which man must wrest human values. The final scene is powerfully symbolic. In the midst of the wilderness, the Poison Fields, of which Monmorancy Pugh says, "It is shore-God a place a man can wander and not know" (p. 276), Adam finds his truth in a man-made glade: "The place was a little glade, set around by sizable timber, oak and gum, and a thick tangle of brush. The glade was, clearly, man-made; the scattered stumps, even in their late decay, still showed the mark of the ax" (p. 294). The clearing, like human values carved with difficulty from the ruck of history and always threatened by darkness and disorder, thus admirably symbolizes Warren's philosophy of history.

---

[42] Hicks, p. 19.

The plot, likewise, confirms this reading of history, for everything that happens to Adam seems arbitrary, and on his travels he is initiated into the horror and irony of history. At every encounter with historical reality he is disillusioned. The murdering of the Negroes, the burning of the colored orphans' home, the beating of Mollie, the senseless violence and brutality are all a part of the horror of history. And, what is even worse, man can, ironically, accomplish little. Adam's father died a lingering death from his fight for freedom and there had been nothing achieved from it. Jed's testimony did not save the Negro, who was hanged anyway. Hans Meyerhof and Stephen Blaustein fought and died for freedom but accomplished little. And Adam comes to fight "fur die freiheit", but, by chance, he is rejected.

In order to escape all this terror and confusion Adam occasionally desires to give up and sink into the dangerous blankness of nature where there is peace without the struggle for human identity.

Adam looked off into the woods. The first shadows were beginning to gather. Deeper and deeper the woods recessed, in vault after dimming vault of shade and coolness to that inward point where shade was beginning to coalesce to darkness. Adam, looking into the depth, thought of quietness. He thought of peace. He thought of time moving deeper and dimmer, into coolness and peace.   (p. 109)

But Adam, like the narrator in Frost's "Stopping by Woods on a Snowy Evening" remembers his human commitments. All this teaches Adam a fundamental truth that many of Warren's heroes learn: "*Only in my heart can I make the world hang together*" (p. 169). That is man must first achieve values, then maintain them no matter what history does to him. The ending is similar to the conclusion of "Promises", where, despite the betrayals of the past, the children still stand as images of hope. He came here, Adam thinks, to know if there is a truth in the world. He knows now that all the others – Hans, Stephen, even Simms and Mose, who had "found their truth and died" (p. 299), had not simply come upon it by good fortune; they had made their truth, created it despite history. And Adam himself comes to his truth despite the "temptations, disillusion, fear, the blankness of the world and time, all the betrayals of his dream" (p. 299). The very appearance of the glade suggests just what a difficult task this is: "He swung his gaze around the glade, the trampled ferns, the wrecked wagon, the scattered debris, the dead horse, the woods leaning closer, darkening" (p. 300). And he has an allegorical vision of the cruelty of history in the form of the futile effort of wounded men to escape the forest fire. ". . . wounded men those who were able, would drag, pull, claw, hunch, hump, roll themselves, inch by inch, over the ground in a lethargic parody of flight until the moment of surrender when the summarizing scream of protest would be uttered, but heard by no ear" (p. 309). The truth, then, he must believe, is in the human heart, not the blind ruck of history: "He knew that he would have to try to know that the truth is unbetrayable, and that only the betrayer is ever betrayed, and then only by his own betraying" (p. 310). From this theory of history Adam draws the corollary that Cass Mastern drew and that Warren drew in *Brother to Dragons*. He comes to love man for what he endures; hence the horror of history can, in the end, be beneficent.

Adam develops, finally, the correct philosophy of history and attitude toward it, but several characters see the historical process and man's place in it wrongly. Answering the charge that he had made a good thing out of "perambulatory embalming", Dr. Sulgrave says, "If a man does a good deed and in so doing prospers, does it not prove merely that his faculties are working in harmony and under Divine sanction?" (p. 148). Warren earlier had attacked the North's rationalization that success proved the righteousness of one's cause. The blind ruck of history can prove nothing about a man and the worthiness of his ideals and motives. Confronted with the horrible destructiveness of history, Aaron Blaustein becomes bitter and cynical and worships history rather than God, in whom he can no longer believe. History, he says, is, like God, the "reason for things" (p. 73). History is, to him, "the agony people have to go through so that things will turn out as they would have turned out anyway" (p. 77). Objectively this may be true, but the duty of man is to oppose the blankness of history with his human ideals and values, not worship it.

Monmorancy Pugh instead of worshiping history determines to live on the level of the brute forces of history. He no longer tries to maintain his faith and ideals. Warren indicates this symbolically by describing his house as "more like a cave, a den, than a constructed habitation. Even the objects constructed by human hands scarcely bore the mark of hands upon them; the fabricating hand had, in some dire contempt for the human need that had demanded the object, left only the merest mark of its humanity" (pp. 253-4). Monmorancy's wife explains her husband's philosophy:

He said the Lawd God shore taken a pleasure to joke and prank. He said the Lawd God said thou shalt not kill and then put a fellow in a tight whar he had to kill to keep from killen. He said the Lawd God let a fellow grab holt of a hickory limb hung out over Hell-fahr and then taken a chicken feather and tickled the bottom of his bare feet till he bust out laughen and let go the hickery limb to scratch. (pp 261-2)

Translating this idea into conduct, he decides to scratch wherever it itches, and from then on he sinks to the level of history, killing and stealing whenever he wishes. In *Wilderness* Warren has convincingly explored the theme of the nature of history and man's relation to it in widely different minds – most centrally in Adam, Aaron Blaustein, and Monmorancy Pugh – so that the reader views this part of his philosophy of history in several different perspectives. And here plot, images, symbols, and dramatized overt philosophizing – the total economy of the novel – combine to interweave these ideas organically into the tissue of the work.

6

In order to present fully his philosophical position on history, Warren must also deal with such abstruse topics as the nature of man and the question of fate and free will. None of Warren's novels dramatizes these themes more effectively than does *Wilderness*; they appear as experience, never as unabsorbed speculation. Part of the dramatic tension of the novel derives from the complex, dual nature of man – depraved and guilty yet capable of rising above his evil nature. And, as much as in any of his novels, one feels in *Wilderness* the conflict between these two aspects of man's nature, as Warren explores the tragic implications of this duality. Faced with the blankness of history and the evil of the self, all men yet long for some "glory" – truth, justice, or any such concept – but to achieve this is to suffer, perhaps tragically. Adam's boot symbolizes this idea; he says, the pain of wearing it is the price "of being born into manhood" (p. 17). Because he is somewhere between the beasts and the angels, man must suffer, but, as the quote from Pascal on the frontpiece says, "Toutes ces miseres-la memes preuvent sa grandeur. Ce sont miseres de grand signeur, miseres d'un roi depossede." The tragic conflict between the two aspects of man's nature and between man's ideals and the blankness of history is seen first in Adam. Adam came to America to follow a noble ideal of justice and freedom, and he does with difficulty maintain at least some of his faith. Yet he soon comes to realize the evil in himself. Despite his humanitarian ideals he becomes caught up in the lust for blood during the conscription riots. "He felt a crazy elation. He felt the need to thrust with that knife. He crouched and gripped the haft and knew that he would thrust" (p. 52). Later, in Pennsylvania, Jed's cold appraising eye and Mose's mumbled "sawf and juicy" make Adam unable to deny his evil motives and hence unable to stay with Maran and wait for Hans to die, as deep inside he would like to do. "They had understood his every motive, penetrated every self-deception. Dully, he asked himself if virtue was possible only in the shame of discovery, in the terror of accusation. He asked if there is such a thing as virtue in the last private darkness of the soul" (p. 133). Only after accepting the blackness of the self can he rise above it and know that he, like all men, is capable of good, of formulating and living by worthy, unselfish ideals.

In the other characters, too, Warren gains dramatic tension by contrasting the evil side of their nature with the noble side. From beginning to end the novel provides ample evidence of the depravity of man and of the nobility even the most unlikely men are capable of. The brutal acts of the mob confirm man's evil cruelty, as does the pleasure of the soldiers as they watch the almost ceremonial beating of Mollie. The men stared, "some avid and intense, some with schooled detachment, some with idiotic grin and wet lips". One says as the lash fell, "Diggety-dawg, got meat that time." One of the audience correctly observes that they are all "foul-minded and debased" (pp. 206-7).

But Warren balances this depravity with the noble heroism and dignity of the black soldier who, shot while saving the life of his white lieutenant, bleeds to death on the hospital table. In *Wilderness*, just as Faulkner does in *As I Lay Dying*, Warren sees the dignity and nobility possible in the lowliest, most depraved men. Dr. Sulgrave is one of the most unlikely persons in whom one would expect to find redeeming virtues; he reveals himself to be a cowardly rascal engaged, at the moment, in the grisly pursuit of plundering the bodies of the soldiers buried at Gettysburg. Yet the nondescript man reveals that Sulgrave had risked his life in order to save a sick child by sucking the pus with a tube from the boy's infected throat. In presenting this conflict of good and evil in the character of Jedeen Hawksworth, Warren is purposefully ambiguous. Jed protects Mose by saving him from detection only to taunt him cruelly. He had bravely testified on behalf of the slave, but he drains the act of all nobility by telling Adam that he did it out of hatred and shame for what he terms his father's "ass-kissing" of the rich and powerful Colonel Johnston F. Harris, not from any love of justice or humanitarian concern for the slave. Like all men his motives are ambiguously mixed.

The reader along with Adam learns of the difficult character of Mose. At first Adam believes that Mose saved his life from noble motives. Mose tells him, however, that he did it merely to keep from being detected himself. Only later does Adam learn that this is not the whole truth, for Mose could have more easily and safely cut his throat than pulled him to safety. Like most of the characters in the novel Mose is embarrassed and ashamed of his ill-understood motives that have some unselfishness about them. And even the murder he treacherously commits is "the last justification of manhood" (p. 228), for it is the only way he has left to affirm his humanity, his difference from the beasts. Before killing Jed he took with him his alphabet cards, the symbol to him of a high and worthy goal. "So Mose Talbutt – Mose Crawfurd – on his way to do the deed that all his life had been leading toward, had paused in the dark hut to reach out and take away with him those cards, which, evening after evening, he had pored over, like a child" (p. 231). Adam has now learned what Aaron says is the most difficult lesson – "that other men are men" (p. 67). No matter how depraved or ignorant, all the major characters in *Wilderness* achieve some glory so that there is here a conflict, a tension between the two aspects of man's nature and his compulsion to affirm his humanity in the face of the blankness of nature and history. This conflict can yield tragedy only if the characters have free will and are more than mere victims of the forces of history, nature, and the self. Any determinism here operates in the physical realm of history, not in the moral sphere. Monmorancy Pugh's wife is right in saying "Ain't ever thing in the world a man kin help" (pp. 258-9). But the important things – his own motives, ideals, and some of his actions – he can. Oedipus was foreordained to kill his father, but he was not doomed to kill him in a petty brawl at a crossroad. Adam has the last word on the subject. He thinks, *"We always do what we intend"* (pp. 309-10). Physically, the ruck of history may defeat one's best intentions, but if one is true to them one remains, in a deeper sense, undefeated. Adam decides that he had done only what he had had to do and that, if necessary, he would do it all again. *"But, oh, with a different heart"* (pp. 21-2). And this makes all the difference.

7

Wilderness provides one of Warren's most subtle dramatizations of the second aspect of his philosophy of history, the spider web theory. It is as clearly presented as in *All the King's Men*, and here it emerges entirely in terms of the novel's characters and events, requiring no slowing of the narrative movement. In *Wilderness* Warren dramatizes the connections between all events and all times and the terror that this can hold for man by the repeated "if theme". This is a new and effective method of presenting the spider web theory, for it emphasizes better than Jack Burden's exposition the illogicality of these connections, the fact that they derive from chance not plan. The novel begins with a series of "ifs", propositions that led Adam to decide to go to America. If the mountain had not been so white, the forest so blue-black, the sky so blue, the world so "absolute in beauty", Adam would have stayed in Bavaria (p. 3). At sea a roll of the ocean betrayed Adam's deformity, and the recruiter rejected him for military service. Adam felt that he was the victim of a gigantic conspiracy, in which the whole world participated:

And, in a sense, he was right. If the long sea had not broken its rhythm, and given that mysterious twitch like the twitch of a horse's hide, then Adam Rosenzweig would not have struck that finicking pose and held out his boot for all to admire. If Meinherr Duncan's scalp had not been itching intolerably, from the sunburn, his temper, though generally uncertain, especially after too much grog the night before, might have been better this morning. If Meinherr Duncan, at the First Manassas, had not been clipped in the knee by a Rebel rifle slug, then he might not have been so sensitive about Adam Rosen-zweig's special deformity. If, indeed, Meinherr Sergeant Duncan had not, at the First Manassas, discovered himself to be a coward, having been, in fact, the first man in his company to break and run and then been clipped reprovingly in the back of the knee even as he found his stride, he might have been less sensitive. If, on the instant of his discovery of Adam Rosenzweig's deformity, the ocean had not twitched the second time and set him upon his rear. If somebody had not laughed. If all these things had not happened in their unique pattern, then things might have been all right, after all.   (p. 247)

This is the sort of illogical and confused complexity, what Adam calls the "murky complications" and "blind accidents of the past" (p. 161), that confronts man in history. As Jed says, in the complexity of life man is lost. "You live yore years and time it looks like you never know who to thank. And what for" (p. 74). But the web of history provides man with a slim basis for hope. Even if it can bring damnation, it can still offer the prospect of good coming from evil, and this seems to be the best man can hope for. The only way man can live in the horror of the historical process, Aaron tells Adam, is to remember always that everything is part of everything else. "Whatever comes out of History – out of this anguish even – will come only because everything is part of everything else" (p. 99). At the end Adam, standing in the wilderness surrounded by the debris of the historical events he has participated in, gains as much knowledge, truth, and understanding as man can expect. The cost is great, but he does achieve a measure of salvation.

Since all time participates in each moment and all the past and future converge on the present, the individual must accept the past and take full responsibility for all the consequences of his existence. The past and his past self imperceptibly drift away from Adam: "And the self that had once existed and had had that dream no longer existed. Only the dry, pale shell, like that discarded by a locust, existed now" (p. 121). The need to know the past is why he questions Hans so intently about his father. "But if that man had seen his father he might now know – know in a deeper and fuller way, a way more essentially involving his own being – that his father had actually stood at Rastatt, had fought and suffered. Entering into the pathos of that far time and place, he felt that he might be somehow freed from a burden" (p. 194). The scene between Adam and Mollie the Mutton subtly dramatizes the individual's rejection of the past, of memory. Adam asks her where she was from and was it beautiful there. Her reaction is violent because she feels she is unworthy of her past: " 'You son-of-a-bitch,' she said, her voice shaking with rage. 'You louse-bit son-of-a-bitch of a fool. I was about to give it to ye. For nothing, you fool. I swear it – I swear it by the sweet wounds of Our Lord' " (p. 308). She hits him and blunders off into the woods. Warren has here strongly made his point without the overt philosophizing and direct statement of some of his other novels such as *At Heaven's Gate* and *The Cave*.

In the end, Adam accepts his past and its traditions, and "that place and this place, and that time and this time, flowed together" (p. 133). All times and all places, he knows, are one. At first Adam tries to evade the responsibility that living in history necessarily entails. He rationalizes that it would have been no sin for him to have stayed with Maran, for he was not responsible for Hans' lingering death. "Nothing was his fault" (p. 40). This is the same self-justification that Jed and Monmorancy Pugh indulge in. Adam's coming to America is, in fact, his westward flight, a desire to be "like a leaf in the eddy of a stream, like a mote of dust in the wind" (pp. 224-5), a desire, that is, to evade responsibility. To Warren, however, the king is "bound to answer the particular endings of his soldiers" even if he does not purpose their death. Adam, by means of the vividly dramatized scene in which Mose saved him in the flooded basement, realizes the sin of existence, and this argues moral responsibility beyond knowledge and physical responsibility. "Then he thought that for himself drawn up in the blind lottery of that cellar to the shelf others had not been drawn up." "It was all a blind lottery. Like your life. He lay there and thought of the price of his life. Others had paid the price of his life. Then he told himself that that was not logical. It was completely illogical" (p. 302). And he cannot deny his guilt as he contemplates more "ifs". If he had not come to Virginia, Aaron would not have died and Jed would not have been murdered. If he had not called Mose a black son-of-a-bitch, Mose would not now be a frightened murderer. "So Jed, he decided, had had to die in his place. And then, with that thought, he wondered if every man is, in the end, a sacrifice for every other man" (p. 164). With this idea he accepts full responsibility for his existence and for his acts; and the idea of every man a victim of every other man convinces him of the brotherhood of man.

In *Wilderness* as in many other of the novels Warren effectively indicates the web aspect of his philosophy of history by plot and structure. There are numerous examples of the terrible and cruel irony of history that can result from man's contact with the web. The best intentions can have unintended but evil consequences, so complicated is history. Trying to stop Simms Purdew's cruel treatment of the Negro who is rooting in the flour, Adam becomes enraged when Mose, knowing that Simms would kill him, holds him back, and in his fury Adam twice strikes Mose. In trying to prevent pain, he causes it; he is cruel in his fight against cruelty. Adam finds himself in a dilemma over whether or not to return Monmorancy's carbine. If he does return it, he may be shot and Monmorancy will certainly use it on others. But, on the other hand, if he does not Monmorancy will kill another sentry for his gun. Either choice, then, is certain to have evil consequences.

With Adam as with many of Warren's heroes the least sight, the smallest gesture opens a vista into the past, thus indicating the presence of the past, all time in one time. In the camp in Virginia as Adam stares into the fire he thinks of his father's funeral and the words asking peace for the dead; this thought brings him back into the present to think how the living have no peace. And Adam even while observing another character, sees him in the present moment and as he was as a small boy. Looking at Simms Purdew, whom he detests, he does not see that vile creature: "He was seeing, somehow, the face of a young boy, the boy Simms Purdew must once have been, a boy with sorrel hair, and blue eyes dancing with gaiety, and the boy mouth grinning trustfully among the freckles" (p. 69). In the glade at the end of the novel Adam thinks back over his past to his mother and his conflict with her. This brings the past vividly alive to him, and it serves to fill in his background at a time when the reader is involved with Adam and hence interested in him. Again Warren indicates the presence of the past by a twisting and turning narrative progression rather than a strict chronological sequence of events. But in *Wilderness* Warren never uses this method to excess, and he does not confuse the reader; in *At Heaven's Gate* and even *All the King's Men* the flashbacks within flashbacks occasionally cause one to lose track of the fictional present. Here, too, this skipping backward and forward in time is convincingly achieved since Warren is as concerned with the state of Adam's mind and his philosophical and spiritual development as he is with the events of the plot. Chapter three, for example, ends with the sailor telling Adam how to jump ship, and four opens with Adam searching for Aaron's house. Warren omits the details of the escape and concentrates upon Adam's reaction to it. This chapter ends with Adam's rescue from drowning; in five he wakes up in an unfamiliar room. Only in a later conversation does Aaron gradually tell him the details of his rescue and arrival. Finally, at the end of the novel Warren connects all the various people Adam had encountered and all the events through which he had lived, not by illogical and incredible relationships and coincidences but rather only in Adam's mind. The other characters are important primarily for their effect upon Adam, for their significance to him. Thus, in the final scene the characters and events live again in Adam's thoughts; Adam's thoughts summarize the novel and illustrate the vital presence of the past.

8

Adam and several other characters learn that man needs a myth, a belief, that he needs to make sense of history and the self, and that illusion can sustain man caught in the ruck of the historical process. Adam knows that in the emptiness of time and the complication of the world, man must have some truth in order to live and to die. He tells Monmorancy's wife, who asks him why he must cross the Rapidan: "A man has to have something. . . . To Live." And ". . . he thought how a man has to have something in order to be ready to die" (p. 26). Nothing can be real without the dream, the myth. "*For a man's deepest dream is all he is*, Adam had said to himself in the night, *and if that is withdrawn can anything else ever be real?*" (p. 89). But what Adam wants and needs is a belief capable of inspiring and promoting action. He rejects Aaron's cynical statement that the only way to know why you do a thing is to do it. He thinks, "The belief did not come out of the action, the action came out of the belief" (p. 68). Like Jack Burden Adam learns the hard way about the value of lies. Because of his hesitancy to tell a true lie, Adam decides Mose had had to kill Jed. After Jed has revealed the puckered "W" branded on Mose's thigh, Mose, in his shame, feels a deep compulsion to salvage some self-respect, some dignity from the full horror of the truth. He implores Adam to believe that the lash marks on his back came from an overseer in Georgia, not a Yankee officer. "You gotta believe me" Mose cried out, the cry torn out of him. Adam looked down at him. " 'I believe you,' he managed to say" (p. 8). But because of his hardness of heart, Adam is unwilling to make Mose believe that he believes in him, and Mose then must justify himself by murdering the man who had revealed his shame. A lie could, perhaps, have prevented this murder.

The adventures of Adam in *Wilderness* underscore Warren's belief in man's urgent need for tradition, for time-honored guides to conduct. *Wilderness* differs from the other novels both in the way of presenting characters acting in accord with tradition and in the traditions which Warren depicts as offering help in adapting purposefully to life. Although frequently relying upon an exemplum to dramatize a story of a person following either the codes of agrarianism or of Christianity, Warren in this novel uses neither the exemplum nor either of these traditions to provide the main character with a spiritual and moral lesson. Here, illumination comes primarily from within Adam himself; we see his struggles to reach his own truth.

But Adam does have two examples of people living by tradition – in this case opposed traditions – to help him achieve his own ideals. There is first the uncle who piously and strictly follows the Judaic tradition; then there is the father who follows liberal humanitarianism. The conflict between these two doctrines informs the entire novel with the sort of dramatic tension Warren so admires. It is the struggle between the law and change, the old court and the new, Judge Irwin and Willie Stark that Warren has been concerned with in all his novels. No character creatively combines the two opposing ideals as does Hugh Miller in *All the King's Men* or Cassius Fort in *World Enough and Time*. In *Wilderness* it is the main character who comes to mediate between them, who synthesizes them. Warren uses the uncle to exemplify one who orders his life by strict adherence to the Jewish tradition, an excellent method of presenting a belief in a stern, Old Testament God, a belief associated in his other novels with the agrarian life. The uncle, then, counsels submission, passive endurance, and patience to wait for the day when, by the example of the Jews, the world will know the law. He obtains a death-bed repentance from Leopold by having him admit that belief in man is blasphemy. He tells him, "I have sat on the floor at midnight with ashes on my head and have prayed that you may die within the law" (p. 7). Emphasizing the glory of God, he believes that the life Leopold lived is foolish and blasphemous. Leopold, on the other hand, believes in the glory of man and works toward achieving liberty and justice; he is willing to fight and to die for his humanitarian ideals. "He had told his son that there was no nobler fate for a man than to live and die for human liberty" (p. 8). He named his son Adam because he wanted man to be fully man, and he taught him Greek and English which he called tongues of liberty. Thus, at the very beginning of his novel Warren has set forth the two conflicting traditions which Adam must bring together in his own life.

Adam finds that neither of these ideals is adequate alone and unmodified. At the death of his father he determines to live by his codes and to throw over the law, which he regards as too slow. "I would work for the day when the world will know Justice" (p. 14). Yet he remains always conscious of his Jewish heritage and never fully breaks with it. He realizes the inadequacy of his liberal idealism when he discovers that he has been devoted to abstractions of the love of mankind and has not really loved men. His first sight of violence, destruction, and suffering seems unreal to him "with no reference to human pain or loss, like a picture" (p. 14). Adam's great moment of truth in the glade consists primarily of his creative combination of both traditions, and it is as subtly and beautifully rendered as any scene in Warren's novels. With his own special boot stolen by the Confederate soldier, Adam takes the boots from the dead Rebel. The dead man, he finds, had taken the boot from another dead man, and now, he thinks, it is his turn. Glancing around the glade, he sees the scattered contents of the kit of religious articles his uncle had given him. At first he fails to recognize them, but then he sees the phylactery, the *tallith*, and the prayer book. These seem to awaken him to a sacramental view of the world as he ritualistically places the boots by the dead Rebel and laments that he had not praised Aaron's maid for repairing the prayer book. He finds that almost unconsciously but with growing realization and understanding he is praying the traditional prayers he had last heard at his father's funeral.

Now he knows what he must do.

He knew that he would have to rise, and go pick up the boots, and put them on, and walk out of the Wilderness. He would walk – hobble, if he could find some way to bind and brace his left foot – out of the forest wearing the boots that had, in the fullness of time and human effort, been passed from one dead man to another. (p. 310)

With this passage the symbolism becomes clear. The boots represent time-honored traditions which men have found valuable in the past. And like traditions they do not fit exactly and may even be quite painful. But just as to Adam any boots are better than none in his present predicament in the middle of a forest, a fire, and a war, so too man in the wilderness of history, crippled by his sinful nature and his human limitations needs guides for his life. At the end Adam has achieved a synthesis of the ideals of his uncle and those of his father: a respect for God, the Law, and the efficacy of prayer, and the humble submission to suffering combined with a true love of men not just mankind and a belief in the dignity and worth of the individual. This is the final goal of all of Warren's characters, but never has it been better dramatized. In this final scene, resembling the quiet resolution of a Greek tragedy, Warren brings everything to a logical and aesthetically satisfactory ending. He has concluded his story at the same time as he has wound up his philosophical themes. In some of his other novels, notably *World Enough and Time* and *Band of Angels*, he had to continue the stories beyond the point where they should have ended dramatically in order to allow his characters to complete their philosophical, spiritual journey. And the final scene, while it is precise enough to be capable of an almost allegorical interpretation, arises convincingly and naturally from the story itself. Adam is no bloodless figure in an allegorical forest; rather he and his situation seem real but freighted with theme, meaning, and significance. Such compression has always been Warren's goal.

Wilderness is thus worthy of being considered one of Warren's most important and successful novels, and it repays careful consideration. It is also in several important respects enough unlike his other novels in method to be almost a new departure. *Wilderness* shows, too, Warren's imaginative grasp and mastery of the facts of the past, in this case the Civil War, the most important event in American history, facts to which he, in fulfilling what he takes to be the writer's highest function, helps give a coloring of tragedy and myth. This shortest of Warren's novels contains highly effective and original dramatizations of his major themes. *Wilderness*, in the final analysis, although it cannot be considered a complete social myth like *The Odyssey* or *The Aeneid*, is certainly one of Warren's best realized "little myths", a work of art in which the artist is seen at full stretch, a novel that perhaps comes closer to realizing Warren's artistic and philosophical intentions than any he has written. It is "A great, multiphase symbol to render his total vision of the world, his sense of individual destiny, his sense of man's place in nature, his sense of history and society".[43]

---

[43]   "Conrad and *Nostromo*", p. 48.

A SELECTED BIBLIOGRAPHY

THE WORKS OF ROBERT PENN WARREN

Accent, IV (Summer, 1944), pp. 251-53. Review of E. E. Cumming, LXI.

At Heaven's Gate (New York, Harcourt, Brace and Co., 1943).

All the King's Men (New York, Harcourt, Brace and Co., 1946).

"*All the King's Men:* The Matrix of Experience", *Yale Review,* LIII (December, 1963), pp. 161-67.

All the King's Men (stage play) (New York, Random House, 1960).

American Prefaces, VII (Spring, 1942), pp. 195-209. Critique of Ernest Hemingway's "The Killers" (With Cleanth Brooks).

"An American Tragedy", *Yale Review,* LII (October, 1962), pp. 1-15.

An Approach to Literature, eds. Cleanth Brooks, R. P. Warren, and John T. Purser, 3rd ed. (New York, Appleton-Century-Crofts, Inc., 1952).

"Arnold vs. the 19th Century", *Kenyon Review,* I (Spring, 1939), pp. 217-21. Review of Lionel Trilling's *Matthew Arnold.*

"Asides and Diversions", *Nation,* CLV (December 5, 1942), p. 625. Review of Edmund Wilson's *Note Books of Night.*

"Autobiographical Notes", *Wilson's Bulletin,* XIII (June, 1939), p. 652.

Band of Angels (New York, Random House, 1955).

Blackberry Winter (Cummington, Mass., Cummington Press, 1946).

"The Blind Poet: Sidney Lanier", *American Review,* II (November, 1933), pp. 27-45.

"The Briar Patch", *I'll Take My Stand: The South and the Agrarian Tradition* (New York and London, Harper and Brothers, 1930), pp. 246-64.

"The Bright Room", *New Republic,* LIV (April 4, 1928), p. 227. Review of John Hall Wheelock's *The Bright Room.*

Brother to Dragons: A Tale in Verse and Voices (New York, Random House, 1953).

"Button, Button", *Partisan Review,* IX (December, 1942), pp. 537-40. Review of Mary McCarthy's *The Company She Keeps.*

"Cass Mastern's Wedding Ring", *Partisan Review,* XI (Fall, 1944), pp. 375-407.

The Cave (New York, Random House, 1959).

"A Christian Education", *Mademoiselle,* XX (January, 1945), pp. 96-97, 155-57.

"Christmas Gift", *Virginia Quarterly Review*, XIII (Winter, 1937), pp. 73-85.

Circus in the Attic and Other Stories (New York, Harcourt, Brace and Co., 1948).

"The Confession of Brother Grimes", *Cronos*, I (Fall, 1947), pp. 29-30.

"Cowley's Faulkner, Part I", *New Republic*, CXV (August 12, 1946), pp. 234-37.

"The Destiny of Hamish Bond", *Sewanee Review*, LXIV (Summer, 1955), pp. 349-81.

"Divided South Searches Its Soul", *Life* (July 9, 1956), pp. 98-99, 101-02, 105-06, 108, 111-12, 114.

"Dixie Looks at Mrs. Gerould", *American Review*, VI (March, 1936), pp. 585-95. (With Cleanth Brooks, Jr.)

"Editorial Announcement", *Southern Review*, VII (Spring, 1942), p. IV (With Cleanth Brooks, Jr.).

"Edmund Wilson's Civil War", *Commentary*, XXXIV (August, 1962), pp. 151-58.

Eleven Poems on the Same Theme (Norfolk, Conn., New Directions, 1942).

"Elizabeth Madox Roberts: Life is From Within", *Saturday Review*, XLVI (March 2, 1963), pp. 20-21, 38.

Faulkner. A Collection of Critical Essays, ed. by Robert Penn Warren (Englewood Cliffs, New Jersey, Prentice-Hall, Inc., 1966).

"Faulkner: The South and the Negro, an Essay", *The Southern Review*, I (July, 1965), pp. 501-29.

"The Fiction of Caroline Gordon", *Southwest Review*, Book Supplement, XX (January, 1935), pp. 93-112.

"Fiddlersburg Preacher", *Esquire*, LX (July, 1963), pp. 55-56.

"A First Novel", *Sewanee Review*, LXV (Spring, 1957), pp. 347-52. Review of Madison Jones's *The Innocent*.

Flood: A Romance of Our Time (New York, Random House, 1964).

"A French View of Jefferson", *New Republic*, LXII (April 2, 1930), pp. 196-97. Review of Gilbert Chinard's *Thomas Jefferson: The Apostle of Americanism*.

"From the Underground", *Nation*, CLXIX (December 3, 1949), pp. 547-48. Review of Elio Vittorini's *In Sicily*.

Fugitive, IV (March, 1925), pp. 29-30. Review of Joseph Auslander's *Sunrise Trumpets*.

"The Gamecock", *New Republic*, LXVI (March 25, 1931), pp. 158-59. Review of Robert W. Winston's *High Stakes and Hair Trigger* and Elizabeth Cutting's *Jefferson Davis*.

"The Gentle Buccaneer", *New Republic*, LVI (September 5, 1928), p. 81. Review of Lowell Thomas's *Count Luckner, The Sea Devil*.

"A Georgian Laureate", *Poetry*, LX (April, 1932), pp. 47-50. Review of *The Poems of Lascelles Abercrombie*.

"Georgian Middle Life", *Poetry*, XLIII (February, 1934), pp. 287-90. Review of Edmund Blunden's *Halfway House*.

The Gods of Mount Olympus (New York, Random House, 1959).

"Goodwood Comes Back", *Southern Review*, VI (Winter, 1941), 526-36.

"Guinea-Fowl", *New Republic*, LIV (May 2, 1928), 330-31. Review of Leonard Bacon's *Guinea Fowl and Other Poultry*.

"Hawthorne, Anderson, and Frost", *New Republic*, LIV (May 16, 1928), 399-401. Review of Herbert Gormon's *Nathaniel Hawthorne*; Gorham Munson's *Robert Frost*; N. Bryilleon Fagin's *The Phenomenon of Sherwood Anderson*.

"Hemingway", *Kenyon Review*, IX (Winter, 1947), pp. 1-28.

"Her Own People", *Virginia Quarterly Review*, XI (April, 1935), pp. 289-304.

"Homage to Oliver Allston", *Kenyon Review*, IV (Spring, 1942), pp. 259-63. Review of Van Wyck Brooks's *Opinions of Oliver Allston*.

"Homage to T. S. Eliot", *Harvard Advocate*, CXXV (December, 1938), p. 46.

"How Texas Won Her Freedom", *Holiday*, XXIII (March, 1958), pp. 72-73, 160, 162-67.

"How Willie Proudfit Came Home", *Southern Review*, IV (Autumn, 1938), pp. 299-321.

Introduction to *A Long Fourth* by Peter Taylor (New York, Harcourt, Brace and Co.), vii-ix.

"James Stephens Again", *Poetry*, XL (July, 1932), pp. 229-32. Review of *Strict Joy and Other Poems*.

"Jeffers on the Age", *Poetry*, XLIX (February, 1937), pp. 279-82. Review of *Solstice and Other Poems*.

John Brown: The Making of a Martyr (New York, Payson and Clarke, 1929).

"John Crowe Ransom: A Study in Irony", *Virginia Quarterly Review*, XI (January, 1935), pp. 93-112.

"John Crowe Ransom: Some Random Remarks", *Shenandoah*, XIV (Spring, 1963), pp. 19-21.

"Katherine Anne Porter (Irony with a Center)", *Kenyon Review*, IV (Winter, 1942), pp. 29-42.

"Knowledge and the Image of Man", *Sewanee Review*, LXIII (Winter, 1955), pp. 182-92.

"The Lady of Lourdes", *Nation*, CLIV (May 30, 1942), pp. 635-36. Review of Franz Werfel's *The Song of Bernadette*.

"Lavender and Old Ladies", *New Republic*, LXVII (August 5, 1931), p. 321. Review of John Peale Bishop's *Many Thousands Gone*.

"A Lesson Read in American Books", *New York Times Book Review* (December 11, 1955), pp. 1, 33.

"The Life and Work of Professor Roy Millen", *Mademoiselle*, XVI (February, 1943), pp. 88, 145-49.

"The Love and the Separateness in Miss Welty", *Kenyon Review*, IV (Spring, 1944), pp. 246-59.

"The Love of Elsie Barton: A Chronicle", *Mademoiselle*, XXII (February, 1946), pp. 161, 282-90.

"Malcolm X: Mission and Meaning", *Yale Review*, LVI (December, 1966), pp. 161-71.

"Melville the Poet", *Kenyon Review*, VII (Spring, 1946), pp. 208-23.

"Merrill Moore's Sonnets", *New Republic*, LXI (January 29, 1930), p. 280. Review of *The Noise That Time Makes*.

"The Middle Flight", *Poetry*, XLV (January, 1935), pp. 226-28. Review of Daniel Long's *Atlantides*.

Modern Rhetoric, eds. Cleanth Brooks and R. P. Warren, 1st ed. (New York, Harcourt, Brace and Co., 1949).

"Moths Against the Screen", *Saturday Evening Post*, CCXXXVII (April 4, 1964), pp. 41-55.

"The Natural History of Ikey Sumpter, Formerly of Johnstown, Tenn.", *Sewanee Review*, LXVII (Summer, 1959), pp. 347-400.

"The Negro Now", *Look*, XXIX (March 23, 1965), pp. 23-31.

A New Southern Harvest, eds. R. P. Warren and Albert Erskine (New York, Bontons, 1947).

New York Times Book Review (June 11, 1950), p. 8. Review of Peter Taylor's *A Woman of Means*.

Night Rider (Boston, Houghton Mifflin Co., 1939).

"A Note on the Hamlet of Thomas Wolfe", *American Review*, V (May, 1935), pp. 191-208.

"A Note on Three Southern Poets", *Poetry*, XL (May, 1932), pp. 103-13.

"Notes", *Modern Poetry, American and British*, eds. Kimon Friar and John Malcolm Brinnin (New York, Appleton-Century-Crofts, 1951), pp. 541-43.

"A Note to *All the King's Men*", *Sewanee Review*, LXI (Summer, 1953), pp. 476-80.

"*Nostromo*", *Sewanee Review*, LIX (September, 1951), pp. 363-91.

"Not Local Color", *Virginia Quarterly Review*, VIII (January, 1932), pp. 153-60. Review of Elizabeth Madox Roberts' *A Buried Treasure*; Caroline Gordon's *Penhally*; Evelyn Scott's *A Calendar of Sin*; William Faulkner's *These Thirteen*, etc.

"Old Words", *Poetry*, XLII (September, 1933), pp. 342-45. Review of Cole Young Rice's *High Perils*.

"Our Literary Harvest", *New York Times Book Review* (June 13, 1943), pp. 5, 18. Review of Edmund Wilson's *The Shock of Recognition*.

"The Patented Gate and the Mean Hamburger", *Mademoiselle*, XXIV (January, 1947), pp. 188-89, 242-43, 245-46.

"Paul Rosenfield: Prompter of Fiction", *Commonwealth*, XLVI (August 15, 1946), pp. 424-26.

"A Poem of Pure Imagination (Reconsiderations VI)", *Kenyon Review*, VIII (Summer, 1946), pp. 391-427.

"Poems by Kenneth Patchen", *Nation*, CLV (July 4, 1942), p. 17. Review of *The Dark Kingdom*.

Poetry, XLIV (September, 1934), pp. 334-37. Review of R. T. Coffin's *Ballads of Square-Toed Americans* and *Yoke of Thunder*.

"The Poetry of Mark van Doren", *Nation*, CLVI (February 6, 1943), pp. 209-11. Review of *Our Lady of Peace* and *Other War Poems*.

"Poets and Scholars", *Nation*, CLV (August 15, 1942), p. 137. Review of Allen Tate's *Princeton Verse between Two Wars*.

"Poor White", *Nation*, CLIV (February 28, 1942), pp. 261-62. Review of Robert Ramsey's *Fire in the Summer*.

"Portrait of La Grand' Bosse", *Kenyon Review*, XII (Winter, 1950), pp. 41-50.

"The Present State of Poetry: In the United States", *Kenyon Review*, I (Fall, 1939), pp. 384-98.

"Prime Leaf", *American Caravan*, IV, eds. Van Wyck Brooks *et al.* (New York, Macaulay Co., 1931), pp. 3-61.

"Principle and Poet", *Nation*, CLIV (April 11, 1942), pp. 438-39. Review of Rolfe Humphries' *Out of the Jewel.*

Promises: Poems 1954-1956 (New York, Random House, 1956).

"Pure and Impure Poetry", *Kenyon Review*, V (Spring, 1943), pp. 228-54.

"The Reading of Modern Poetry", *American Review*, VIII (February, 1937), pp. 435-49 (With Cleanth Brooks, Jr.).

"The Redemption of Temple Drake", *New York Times Book Review* (September 30, 1951), pp. 1, 31. Review of William Faulkner's *Requiem for a Nun.*

"Remember the Alamo!", *Holiday*, XXIII (February, 1958), pp. 52-55, 106, 108-10, 112-13.

"The Romantic Strain", *New Republic*, LIII (November 23, 1927), pp. 23-24. Review of Edith Sitwell's *Rustic Elegies.*

"Sacheverell Sitwell's Poems", *New Republic*, LIV (February 29, 1928), p. 76. Review of *Cyder Feast and Other Poems.*

"The Second American Revolution", *Virginia Quarterly Review*, VII (April, 1931), pp. 282-88. Review of Howard K. Beale's *The Critical Year* and George F. Milton's *The Age of Hate.*

Segregation: The Inner Conflict in the South (New York, Random House, 1958).

Selected Essays (New York, Random House, 1958).

Selected Poems, 1923-1943 (New York, Harcourt, Brace and Co., 1944).

Selected Poems: New and Old, 1923-1966 (New York, Random House, 1966).

"Set in a Silver Sea", *Poetry*, XLVI (September, 1935), pp. 346-69. Review of Victoria Sackville-West's *Collected Poems.*

"A Sheaf of Novels", *American Scholar*, XIV (Winter, 1945), pp. 115-22. Review of Aldous Huxley's *Time Must Have a Stop*, Howard Fast's *Freedom Road*, Harry Brown's *A Walk in the Sun*, Joseph S. Pennell's *History of Rome Hanks.*

Short Story Masterpieces, eds. R. P. Warren and Albert Erskine (New York, Dell, 1954), 2nd ed., 1958.

"Sight Unseen", *Poetry*, XLII (August, 1933), pp. 292-94. Review of Thomas C. Chubb's *Ships and Lovers.*

"The Situation in American Writing, Part II", *Partisan Review*, VI (Fall, 1939), pp. 112-13.

Six Centuries of Great Poetry, eds. R. P. Warren and Albert Erskine (New York, Dell, 1955).

"The Snopes World", *Kenyon Review*, III (Spring, 1941), pp. 253-57. Review of William Faulkner's *The Hamlet.*

"Some Don'ts for Literary Regionalists", *American Review*, VIII (December, 1936), pp. 142-50.

"Some Recent Novels", *Southern Review*, I (Winter, 1936), pp. 624-49. Review of Marjorie Kinnon Rawlings' *Golden Apples*; H. L. Davis' *Honey in the Horn*, etc. Reprinted as "Literature as a Symptom", in *Who Owns America: A New Declaration of Independence*, eds. Herbert Agar and Allen Tate (New York, Houghton Mifflin, 1938), pp. 264-79.

A Southern Harvest: Short Stories by Southern Writers, ed. R. P. Warren (Boston, Houghton Mifflin Co., 1937).

The Southern Review (anthology), eds. Cleanth Brooks and R. P. Warren (Baton Rouge, Louisiana State University Press, 1953).

"Statement Concerning Wallace Stevens' *Harmonium*", *Harvard Advocate*, CXVII (December, 1940), p. 32.

"Statement of Ashby Wyndham", *Sewanee Review*, LI (Spring, 1943), pp. 183-236.

"Straws in the Wind", *Poetry*, XLVIII (June, 1936), pp. 172-75. Review of Ann Winslow's *Trial Balances*.

"Testament of Flood", *The Magazine* (April, 1935), pp. 230-34.

"The Themes of Robert Frost", *The Writer and His Craft*, ed. Roy Cowden (Ann Arbor, University of Michigan Press, 1954), pp. 218-33.

Thirty-six Poems (New York, Alcestis Press, 1935).

"T. S. Stribling: A Paragraph in the History of Critical Realism", *American Review*, II (February, 1934), pp. 463-86.

"Twelve Poets", *American Review*, III (May, 1934), pp. 212-27. Review of Archibald MacLeish's *Poems, 1924-1933*; William Faulkner's *Green Bough*; W. H. Auden's *The Orators*, etc.

"Two for SNCC", *Commentary*, XXXIX (April, 1965), pp. 38-48.

"Two Poets", *New Republic*, LXX (February 24, 1963), pp. 51-52. Review of Alan Porter's *The Signature of Pain and Other Poems* and Eda Lou Walton's *Jane Matthew and Other Poems*.

"Uncorrupted Consciousness: The Stories of Katherine Anne Porter", *Yale Review*, LV (December, 1965), pp. 280-290.

Understanding Fiction, eds. Cleanth Brooks and R. P. Warren (New York, Appleton-Century-Crofts, Inc., 1943; 3rd ed., 1960).

Understanding Poetry, eds. Cleanth Brooks and R. P. Warren (New York, Henry Holt and Co., 1st ed., 1938; 2nd ed., 1951).

"The Unity of Experience", *Commentary*, XXXIX (May, 1965), pp. 91-96. Review of Ralph Ellison's *Shadow and Act*.

"The Veins of Irony", *University: A Princeton Magazine*, nos. 17-18 (Summer-Fall, 1963), pp. 10-12.

Voices, IV (November, 1924), pp. 24-25. Review of John Crowe Ransom's *Chills and Fever*.

Voices, IV (January, 1925), pp. 89-90. Review of Roy Campbell's *The Flaming Terrapin*.

"The War and the National Monuments", *Library of Congress Quarterly Journal of Current Acquisitions*, II (September, 1944), pp. 64-75.

"The Way It Was Written (*Brother to Dragons*)", *New York Times Book Review* (August 23, 1953), pp. 6, 25.

"When the Light Gets Green", *Southern Review*, I (Spring, 1936), pp. 799-806.

Who Speaks for the Negro? (New York, Random House, 1965).
"Why Do We Read Fiction?", *Saturday Evening Post*, CCXXXV (October 20, 1962), pp. 82-84.
"Working Toward Freedom", *Poetry*, XLIII (March, 1934), pp. 342-46.
Review of John Beale Bishop's *Now With His Love*.
World Enough and Time: A Romantic Novel (New York, Random House, 1950).
"The World of Daniel Boone", *Holiday*, XXXIV (December, 1963), p. 162.
"Writer at Work: How a Story Was Born and How, Bit by Bit, It Grew (*Blackberry Winter*)", *New York Times Book Review* (March 1, 1959), pp. 4-5, 36.
You, Emperors, and Others, Poems 1957-1960 (New York, Random House, 1960).

SECONDARY SOURCES

Adams, James Truslow, *America's Tragedy* (New York, Charles Scribner's Sons, 1934).
Adams, Phoebe, *Atlantic*, CCVIII (December, 1961), p. 126. Review of *Wilderness*.
Aldredge, John W., *In Search of Heresy* (New York, McGraw-Hill, 1956).
Alexander, Edward Porter, "The Wilderness Campaign", in *American Historical Association Annual Report for the Year 1908* (Washington), pp. 223-47.
Alexander, Thomas Benjamin, *Political Reconstruction in Tennessee* (Nashville, Vanderbilt University Press, 1950).
Allen, Charles A., "Robert Penn Warren: The Psychology of Self-Knowledge", *Literature and Psychology*, VIII (Spring, 1958), pp. 21-25.
Anderson, Charles R., "Violence and Order in the Novels of Robert Penn Warren", *Hopkins Review*, VI (Winter, 1953), pp. 88-105. Reprinted in *Southern Renascence: The Literature of the Modern South*, eds. Louis D. Rubin, Jr. and Robert D. Jacobs (Baltimore, Johns Hopkins Press, 1953), pp. 207-24.
Aptheker, Herbert, *The Negro in the Civil War* (New York, International Publishers, 1938).
Baker, Joseph E., "Irony in Fiction: *All the King's Men*", *College English*, IX (December, 1947), pp. 122-30.
Barrett, John Gilchrist, *The Civil War in North Carolina* (Chapel Hill, University of North Carolina Press, 1963).
Basso, Hamilton, "The Huey Long Legend", *Life*, XXI (December 9, 1946), pp. 106-08, 110, 112, 115-16, 121.
Batline, Cecil William, *The Crisis of the Confederacy. A History of Gettysburg and the Wilderness* (London, Longmans, Green and Co., 1905).
Baumback, Jonathan, *The Landscape of Nightmare: Studies in the Contemporary American Novel* (New York, New York University Press, 1965).

Beals, Carleton, *The Story of Huey P. Long* (Philadelphia, J. B. Lippincott Co., 1935).

Beebe, Maurice and Erin Marcus, "The Criticism of Robert Penn Warren: A Selected Checklist", *Modern Fiction Studies*, VI (Spring, 1960), pp. 83-88.

Beebe, Maurice and Leslie A. Field, *All the King's Men. A Critical Handbook* (Belmont, California, Wadsworth Publishing Co., 1966).

Bentley, Eric, "*All the King's Men*", *Theatre Arts*, XXXI (November, 1947), pp. 72-73.

——, "The Meaning of Robert Penn Warren's Novels", *Kenyon Review*, X (Summer, 1948), pp. 407-24.

Berner, Robert, "The Required Past: 'World Enough and Time' ", *Modern Fiction Studies*, VI (Spring, 1960), pp. 55-64.

Bigelow, John, *The Campaign of Chancellorsville* (New Haven, Yale University Press, 1910).

Blum, Morgan, "Promises as Fulfillment", *Kenyon Review*, XXI (Winter, 1959), pp. 97-120.

Bohner, Charles H., *Robert Penn Warren* (New York, Twayne, 1964).

Botkin, Benjamin Albert, *A Civil War Treasure of Tales, Legends, and Folklore* (New York, Random House, 1960).

Bradbury, John M., *The Fugitives: A Critical Acount* (Chapel Hill, University of North Carolina Press, 1958).

——, "Robert Penn Warren's Novels: The Symbolic and Textural Patterns", *Accent*, XIII (Spring, 1953), pp. 77-89.

Brantley, Frederick, "The Achievement of Robert Penn Warren", in *Modern American Poetry*, ed. B. Rajan (London, Dennis Dobson Ltd., 1950), pp. 66-80.

Breit, Harvey, "Talk with Mr. Warren", *New York Times Book Review* (June 25, 1950), p. 20.

Bridges, Leonard Hall, *Civil War and Reconstruction* (Washington, Service Center for Teachers of History, 1957).

Brooks, Cleanth, *The Hidden God: Studies in Hemingway, Faulkner, Yeats, Eliot, and Warren* (New Haven, Yale University Press, 1963).

——, *Modern Poetry and the Tradition* (Chapel Hill, University of North Carolina Press, 1939).

Brooks, Jerome Edmund, *The Mighty Leaf* (Boston, Little, Brown, 1952).

Byrne, Clifford M., "The Philosophical Development in Four of Robert Penn Warren's Novels", *McNeese Review*, XX (Winter, 1957), pp. 56-58.

Campbell, Harry Modean, "Warren as Philosopher in *World Enough and Time*", *Hopkins Review*, VI (Winter, 1953), pp. 106-16. Reprinted in *Southern Renascence: the Literature of the Modern South*, eds. Louis D. Rubin, Jr., and Robert D. Jacobs (Baltimore, Johns Hopkins Press, 1953), pp. 225-35.

Cargill, Oscar, "Anatomist of Monsters", *College English*, IX (October, 1947), pp. 1-8.

Carter, Everett, "The 'Little Myth' of Robert Penn Warren", *Modern Fiction Studies*, VI (Spring, 1960), pp. 3-12.

Casper, Leonard, "The Founding Fathers", *Western Review*, XXIII (Autumn, 1957), pp. 69-71. Review of *Promises*.

——, "Journey to the Interior: 'The Cave'", *Modern Fiction Studies*, VI (Spring, 1960), pp. 65-72.

——, "Loss of the Sense of Community and the Role of the Artist in Robert Penn Warren", Ph.D. dissertation, University of Wisconsin, 1953.

——, "The New Criticism and Southern Agrarianism", *Diliman Review*, II (April, 1954), pp. 136-49.

——, "Robert Penn Warren: An Assessment", *Diliman Review*, II (October, 1954), pp. 400-24.

——, *Robert Penn Warren: The Dark and Bloody Ground* (Seattle, University of Washington Press, 1960).

——, "Robert Penn Warren: Method and Canon", *Diliman Review*, II (July, 1954), pp. 263-92.

——, "Trial by Wilderness: Warren's Exemplum", *Wisconsin Studies in Contemporary Literature*, III (1962), pp. 45-53.

——, "Warren and the Unsuspecting Ancestor", *Wisconsin Studies in Contemporary Literature*, II, ii (Spring-Summer, 1961), pp. 43-49.

Catton, Bruce, *America Goes to War* (Middleton, Conn., Wesleyan University Press, 1958).

——, *Glory Road; the Bloody Route from Fredericksburg to Gettysburg* (Garden City, New York, Doubleday, 1952).

Clark, Marden J., "Religious Implications in the Novels of Robert Penn Warren", *Brigham Young University Studies*, IV (1961), pp. 67-79.

——, "Symbolic Structure in the Novels of Robert Penn Warren", Ph.D. dissertation, University of Washington, 1957.

Clarke, Robert Joseph, *The Story of Tobacco in America* (New York, A. A. Knopf, 1949).

Clements, A. L., "Theme and Reality in *At Heaven's Gate* and *All the King's Men*", *Criticism*, V (Winter, 1963), pp. 27-44.

Corson, W. C., *Two Months in the Confederate States, Including a Visit to New Orleans Under the Domination of General Butler* (London, R. Bentley, 1863).

Cottrell, Beekman W., "Cass Mastern and the Awful Responsibility of Time", in *All the King's Men: A Symposium*, eds. A. Fred Sochatoff *et al.* (Pittsburgh, Carnegie Press, 1957), pp. 39-49.

Cowan, Louise, *The Fugitive Group: A Literary History* (Baton Rouge, Louisiana University Press, 1959).

Cowan, Samuel Kinkade, *Sergeant York and His People* (New York and London, Funk and Wagnalls Co., 1922).

Cowley, Malcolm, "Luke Lea's Empire", *New Republic*, CIX (August 23, 1943), p. 258.

Craib, Roderick, "A Novel on Freedom", *New Leader*, XXXVIII (September 26, 1955), pp. 24-25. Review of *Band of Angels*.

Curtiss, Mina, "Tragedy of a Liberal", *Nation*, CXLVIII (April 29, 1939), pp. 507-08. Review of *Night Rider*.

Daniel, John, "Cold Facts", *Spectator* (June 22, 1962), p. 834.

Daniels, Jonathan, "Scraping the Bottom of Southern Life", *Saturday Re-*

view of Literature, XXVI (August 21, 1943), p. 6. Review of *At Heaven's Gate*.

"Dark and Bloody Ground", *Time*, LII (August 24, 1953), p. 82. Review of *Brother to Dragons*.

Davidson, Donald, "The Thankless Muse and Her Fugitive Poets", *Sewanee Review*, LXVI (Spring, 1958), pp. 201-28.

Davis, Joe, "Robert Penn Warren and the Journey to the West", *Modern Fiction Studies*, VI (Spring, 1960), pp. 73-82.

Davis, Robert Gorham, "Dr. Stanton's Dilemma", *New York Times Book Review* (August 18, 1946), pp. 3, 24. Review of *All the King's Men*.

Davis, Washington, *Camp Fire Chats of the Civil War* (Chicago, A. B. Gehman and Co., 1887).

Deutsch, Babette, "Poetry Chronicle", *Yale Review*, XLIII (Winter, 1954), pp. 277-78. Review of *Brother to Dragons*.

Deutsch, Hermann Bacher, *The Huey Long Murder Case* (Garden City, New York, Doubleday, 1963).

Dickey, James, "The Presence of Anthologies", *Sewanee Review*, LXVI (Spring, 1958), 307-09. Review of *Promises*.

Dupee, F. W., "Robert Penn Warren and Others", *Nation*, CLIX (November 25, 1944), pp. 660, 662. Review of *Selected Poems*.

Eaton, Clement, *A History of the Southern Confederacy* (New York, Macmillan, 1954).

Eisenschiml, Otto, and Ralph Newman, *The American Iliad: The Epic Story of the Civil War* (Indianapolis and New York, Bobbs-Merrill Co., 1947).

Eisenger, Chester E., *Fiction of the Forties* (Chicago, University of Chicago Press, 1965).

Ellison, Ralph, and Eugene Walter, "The Art of Fiction XVIII: Robert Penn Warren", *Paris Review*, IV (Spring-Summer, 1957), pp. 112-40. Reprinted in *Writers at Work: The Paris Review Interviews*, ed. Malcolm Cowley (New York, Viking, 1958), pp. 183-207.

Fergusson, Francis, "Three Novels", *Perspectives U.S.A.*, VI (Winter, 1954), pp. 30-44. Review of *All the King's Men*.

Fiedler, Leslie A., "On Two Frontiers", *Partisan Review*, XVII (September-October, 1950), pp. 739-43.

——, "Romance in the Operatic Manner", *New Republic*, CXXXIII (September 26, 1955), pp. 28-30. Review of *Band of Angels*.

——, "Seneca in the Meat House", *Partisan Review*, XXI (March-April, 1954), pp. 208-12. Review of *Brother to Dragons*.

Fitts, Dudley, "Of Tragic Stature", *Poetry*, LXV (November, 1944), pp. 94-101. Review of *Selected Poems*.

——, "A Power Reaffirmed", *New York Times Book Review* (August 18, 1957, pp. 6, 20. Review of *Promises*.

Fjelde, Rolf, "The Ruined Stone and the Sea-Reaches", *Poetry*, XCII (April, 1958), pp. 49-52. Review of *Promises*.

Flint, F. Cudworth, "Five Poets", *Southern Review*, I (Winter, 1936), pp. 650-74. Review of *Thirty-six Poems*.

——, "Mr. Warren and the Reviewers", *Sewanee Review*, LXIV (Autumn, 1956), pp. 632-45.

——, "Poetic Accomplishment and Expectation", *Virginia Quarterly Review*, XXIV (Winter, 1958), pp. 118-19. Review of *Promises*.

——, "Robert Penn Warren", *American Oxonian*, XXIV (April, 1947), pp. 67-79.

——, "Search for a Meaning", *Virginia Quarterly Review*, XXX (Winter, 1954), pp. 143-48. Review of *Brother to Dragons*.

Foote, Shelby, *The Civil War, A Narrative* (New York, Random House, 1958).

Ford, Newell F., "Kenneth Burke and Robert Penn Warren: Criticism by Obsessive Metaphor", *Journal of English and Germanic Philology*, LIII (April, 1954), pp. 172-77.

Forgotson, E. S., "The Poetic Method of Robert Penn Warren", *American Prefaces*, VI (Winter, 1941), pp. 130-46.

Frank, Joseph, "Romanticism and Reality in Robert Penn Warren", *Hudson Review*, IV (Summer, 1951), 248-58.

Frank, William, "Warren's Achievement", *College English*, XIX (May, 1958), pp. 365-66.

Frohock, W. M., "Mr. Warren's Albatross", *Southwest Review*, XXXVI (Winter, 1951), pp. 48-59. Reprinted in *The Novel of Violence in America*, 2nd ed. (Dallas, Southern Methodist University Press, 1957), pp. 86-105.

Garrett, George Palmer, *The Georgia Review*, XII (Spring, 1958), pp. 106-08. Review of *Promises*.

——, "The Function of the Pasiphae Myth in *Brother to Dragons*", *Modern Language Notes*, LXXIV (April, 1959), pp. 311-13.

Garrigue, Jean, "Many Ways of Evil", *Kenyon Review*, VI (Winter, 1944), pp. 135-38. Review of *At Heaven's Gate*.

Geismar, Maxwell, "Agile Pen and Dry Mind", *Nation*, CLXXXI (October 1, 1955), p. 287. Review of *Band of Angels*.

Gerhard, George, "*All the King's Men*: A Symposium", *Folio*, XV (May, 1950), pp. 4-11.

Girault, Norton B., "The Narrator's Mind as Symbol: An Analysis of *All the King's Men*", *Accent*, VII (Summer, 1947), pp. 220-34.

Goodpasture, Albert Virgil, *Life of Jefferson Dillard Goodpasture* (Nashville, Cumberland Presbyterian Publishing House, 1897).

Gordon, Clifford M., "Original Sin: A Short Story", *Explicator*, IX (December, 1950), p. 21.

Gossett, Louise Y., *Violence in Recent Southern Fiction* (Durham, Duke University Press, 1965).

Gregory, Horace, "Of Vitality, Regionalism, and Satire in Recent American Poetry", *Sewanee Review*, LII (Autumn, 1944), pp. 572-93. Review of *Selected Poems*.

Gross, Seymour L., "The Achievement of Robert Penn Warren", *College English*, XIX (May, 1958), pp. 361-65.

——, "Conrad and All the King's Men", *Twentieth Century Literature*, III (April, 1957), pp. 27-32.

——, "Laurence Sterne and Eliot's 'Prufrock': An Object Lesson in Application", *College English*, XIX (November, 1957), pp. 72-73.

Hamer, Philip M., ed., *Tennessee; A History 1673-1932* (New York, The American Historical Association Inc., 1933).

Hardy, John Edward, *Man in the Modern Novel* (Seattle, University of Washington Press, 1965).

——, "You, Robert Penn Warren", *Poetry*, LXXXXIX, pp. 56-62.

——, "Robert Penn Warren's Double-Hero", *Virginia Quarterly Review*, XXVI (Autumn, 1960), pp. 583-597.

Hart, John A., "Some Major Images in *All the King's Men*", in *All the King's Men: A Symposium*, eds. A. Fred Sochatoff et al. (Pittsburgh, Carnegie Press, 1957), pp. 63-74.

Hartt, J. N., "The Return of Moral Passion", *Yale Review*, LI (December, 1961), p. 304. Review of *Wilderness*.

Hassler, Warren W., *Commander of the Army of the Potomac* (Baton Rouge, Louisiana State University Press, 1962).

Hatch, Robert, *Nation*, CLXXXIX (September 12, 1959), p. 138. Review of *The Cave*.

Havard, William C., "The Burden of the Literary Mind: Some Meditations on Robert Penn Warren as Historian", *South Atlantic Quarterly*, LXII (Autumn, 1963), pp. 516-31.

Heilman, Robert B., "Melpomene as Wallflower, or, The Reading of Tragedy", *Sewanee Review*, LV (January-March, 1947), pp. 154-66.

Hendry, Irene, "The Regional Novel: the Example of Robert Penn Warren", *Sewanee Review*, LIII (Winter, 1945), pp. 84-102.

Herschberger, Ruth, "Poised between the two alarms ...", *Accent*, IV (Summer, 1944), pp. 240-46. Review of *Selected Poems*.

Hertz, R. N., "Spiritual Journey, Philosophical Detours", *New Republic*, CXL (December 18, 1961), p. 23.

Hicks, Granville, "Crusader in a World of Chance", *Saturday Review*, XLIV (November 18, 1961), p. 19. Review of *Wilderness*.

——, *Saturday Review*, XLII (August 22, 1959), p. 13. *Review* of *The Cave*.

Hicks, John, "Exploration of Value: Warren's Criticism", *South Atlantic Quarterly*, LXII (Autumn, 1963), pp. 508-15.

Hoffman, Frederick J., *The Modern Novel in America, 1900-1950* (Chicago, Henry Regnery, 1951).

Hudson, Richard B., "*All the King's Men*: A Symposium", *Folio*, XV (May, 1950), pp. 11-13.

Humboldt, Charles, "The Lost Cause of Robert Penn Warren", *Masses and Mainstream*, I (July, 1948), pp. 8-20.

Hynes, Sam, "Quest for the Meaning of Freedom", *New York Times Book Review*, November 19, 1961, p. 58. Review of *Wilderness*.

——, "Robert Penn Warren: The Symbolic Journey", *University of Kansas City Review*, XVII (Summer, 1951), pp. 279-85.

Isham, Asa Brainord, *Through the Wilderness to Richmond* (Cincinnati, P. G. Thomson, 1884).

Isherwood, Christopher, "Tragic Liberal", *New Republic*, LXXXXIX (May 31, 1939), p. 108. Review of *Night Rider*.

Janeway, Elizabeth, "Man in Conflict, Mind in Torment", *New York*

Times Book Review, June 25, 1950, pp. 1, 22. Review of *World Enough and Time*.

Jarrell, Randall, "On the Underside of the Stone", *New York Times Book Review*, August 23, 1952, p. 6. Review of *Brother to Dragons*.

Jones, Ernest, "Through a Glass, Darkly", *Nation*, CLXXI (July 8, 1950), p. 42. Review of *World Enough and Time*.

Jones, Madison, "The Novels of Robert Penn Warren", *South Atlantic Quarterly*, LXII (Autumn, 1963), pp. 488-96.

Joost, Nicholas, "The Movement toward Fulfillment", *Commonweal*, LIX (December 4, 1953), pp. 231-32. Review of *Brother to Dragons*.

——, " 'Was All For Naught?': Robert Penn Warren and New Directions in the Novel", in *Fifty Years of the American Novel – A Christian Appraisal*, ed. Harold C. Gardiner, S.J. (New York, Scribner's, 1951), pp. 273-91.

Justus, James Huff, "The Concept of Gesture in the Novels of Robert Penn Warren", Ph.D. dissertation, University of Washington, 1961.

——, "The Uses of Gesture in Warren's *The Cave*", *Modern Language Quarterly*, XXVI (1965), p. 448-61.

——, "Warren's *World Enough And Time* and Beauchamp's *Confession*", *American Literature*, XXXIII (January, 1962), pp. 500-11.

Kallsen, Loren J., ed., *The Kentucky Tragedy: a Problem in Romantic Attitudes* (Indianapolis, Bobbs-Merrill, 1963).

Kaplan, Charles, "Jack Burden: Modern Ishmael", *College English*, XXII (October, 1960), p. 19-24.

Karanikas, Alexander, *Tillers of a Myth: Southern Agrarians as Social and Literary Critics* (Madison, Wisconsin, University of Wisconsin Press, 1966).

Kazin, Alfred, "A City of the Soul", *Reporter*, XXIV (June 8, 1961), pp. 40-44. Review of *The Legacy of the Civil War*.

——, "The Seriousness of Robert Penn Warren", *Partisan Review*, XXVI (Spring, 1959), pp. 312-16. Review of *Selected Essays*.

Keifer, Joseph Warren, *Slavery and Four Years of War* (New York and London, G. P. Putnam's Sons, 1900).

Kelvin, Norman, "The Failure of Robert Penn Warren", *College English*, XVIII (April, 1957), pp. 355-64.

Kenner, Hugh, "Omnibus review of poetry textbooks", *Poetry*, LXXXIV (April, 1954), pp. 43-53. Review of *Understanding Poetry*.

——, "Something Nasty in the Meat-House", *Hudson Review*, VI (Winter, 1954), pp. 605-10. Review of *Brother to Dragons*.

Kerr, Elizabeth M., "Polarity of Themes in '*All the King's Men*' ", *Modern Fiction Studies*, VI (Spring, 1960), pp. 25-46.

King, Roma A., Jr., "Time and Structure in Early Novels of Robert Penn Warren", *South Atlantic Quarterly*, LVI (Autumn, 1957), pp. 486-93.

Kristol, Irving, "American Ghosts", *Encounter*, III (July, 1954), pp. 73-75. Review of *Brother to Dragons*.

Lane, Calvin M., "Narrative Art and History in Robert Penn Warren's *World Enough and Time*, Ph.D. dissertation, University of Michigan, 1956.

Larew, Charles Lynnal, *Historic Tennessee* (Knoxville, Historic Tennessee Publishing Co., 1937).

Lawson, Albert, *War Anecdotes and Incidents of Army Life* (Cincinnati, A. Lawson, 1888).

Lee, Basil Leo, *Discontent in New York City 1861-1865* (Washington, D.C., The Catholic University of America Press, 1943).

Letargeez, J., "Robert Penn Warren's View of History", *Revue des langues vivantes*, XXII (1956), pp. 533-43.

Linenthal, Mark, Jr., "Robert Penn Warren and the Southern Agrarians", Ph.D. dissertation, Stanford University, 1957.

Litz, A. Walton, *Modern American Fiction: Essays in Criticism* (New York, Oxford University Press, 1964).

London Times Literary Supplement, November 27, 1959, p. 692. Review of *The Cave*.

Long, Huey Pierce, *Every Man a King* (New Orleans, National Book Co., Inc., 1933).

——, *My First Days in the White House* (Harrisburg, Pa., The Telegraph Press, 1935).

Longley, John Lewis, Jr., " 'At Heaven's Gate': The Major Themes", *Modern Fiction Studies*, VI (Spring, 1960), pp. 13-24.

——, *Robert Penn Warren: A Collection of Critical Essays* (New York, New York University Press, 1965).

——, "Robert Penn Warren: American Man of Letters", *Arts and Sciences* (Spring, 1965), pp. 16-22.

"Loss of Illusion", *London Times Literary Supplement*, June 1, 1962, p. 385.

Lowell, Robert, "Prose Genius in Verse", *Kenyon Review*, XV (Autumn, 1953), pp. 619-25. Review of *Brother to Dragons*.

MacDonald, William, *Nation*, CXXXI (July 2, 1930), pp. 22-23. Review of *John Brown: the Making of a Martyr*.

Magmer, James, S.J., *Catholic World*, CLXXXXIV (January, 1962), pp. 244-45. Review of *Wilderness*.

——, "Robert Penn Warren's Quest for an Angel", *Catholic World*, CLXXXIII (June, 1956), pp. 179-83.

Martin, Terence, "*Band of Angels*: The Definition of Self-Definition", *Folio*, XXI (Winter, 1956), pp. 31-37.

——, *New Republic*, CXXXXI (September 7, 1959), p. 20. Review of *The Cave*.

Matthiessen, F. O., "American Poetry Now", *Kenyon Review*, VI (Autumn, 1944), pp. 683-96.

Maxwell, Emily, *New Yorker*, XXXIV (November 22, 1958), p. 214. Review of *Remember the Alamo!*

McCormick, John, "White Does and Dragons", *Western Review*, XVIII (Winter, 1954), pp. 163-67. Review of *Brother to Dragons*.

McDowell, Frederick P. W., "Psychology and Theme in *Brother to Dragons*", *PMLA*, LXX (September, 1955), pp. 565-86.

——, "Robert Penn Warren's Criticism", *Accent*, XV (Summer, 1955), pp. 173-96.

——, "The Romantic Tragedy of Self in *World Enough and Time*", *Cri-*

tique: Studies in Modern Fiction, I (Summer, 1957), pp. 34-49.

McElderry, B. R., Jr., "Robert Penn Warren and Whitman", *Walt Whitman Review*, VIII (1962), p. 91.

McMichael, George, *San Francisco Chronicle* (January 7, 1962), p. 17. Review of *Wilderness*.

Miers, Earl Schenck, *The Great Rebellion* (Cleveland, World Publishing Co., 1958).

Mitchell, Joseph Brady, *Decisive Battles of the Civil War* (New York, Putnam, 1955).

Mizener, Arthur, "Amphibiun in Old Kentucky", *Kenyon Review*, XII (Autumn, 1950), pp. 697-701.

——, "A Nature Divided Against Itself", *New York Times Book Review*, August 21, 1955, pp. 1, 18. Review of *Band of Angels*.

——, *New York Times Book Review*, August 23, 1959, p. 1. Review of *The Cave*.

——, "The Uncorrupted Consciousness", *Sewanee Review*, LXXII (1964), pp. 690-98. Review of *Flood*.

Mohrt, Michel, "Robert Penn Warren and the Myth of the Outlaw", *Yale French Studies*, No. 10 (1953), pp. 70-84.

Moore, L. Hugh, Jr., "Robert Penn Warren, William Styron, and the Use of Greek Myth", *Critique*, VIII (Winter, 1966), pp. 75-88.

Mosley, John Singleton, *Stuart's Cavalry in the Gettysburg Campaign* (New York, Moffat, Yard and Co., 1908).

Nemerov, Howard, "All the King's Men", *Furioso*, II (Fall, 1946), pp. 69-71.

——, "The Phoenix in the World", *Furioso*, III (Spring, 1948), pp. 36-46.

Nevins, Allan, *The War for the Union* (New York, Scribner's, 1959).

"Not Without Blood", *Time*, XLVIII (August 26, 1946), p. 97. Review of *All the King's Men*.

O'Connor, William Van, *An Age of Criticism: 1900-1950* (Chicago, Henry Regnery, 1951).

——, "Robert Penn Warren: 'Provincial' Poet", in *A Southern Vanguard: the John Peale Bishop Memorial Volume*, ed. Allen Tate (New York, Prentice-Hall, 1947), pp. 92-99.

——, "Robert Penn Warren's Short Fiction", *Western Review*, XII (Summer, 1948), pp. 251-53.

Olson, Elder, "A Symbolic Reading of The Ancient Mariner", in *Critics and Criticism: Ancient and Modern*, ed. R. S. Crane (Chicago, University of Chicago Press, 1952), pp. 138-44.

Opotowsky, Stan, *The Songs of Louisiana* (New York, Dutton, 1960).

Parton, James, *General Butler in New Orleans* (Boston and New York, Houghton, Mifflin and Co., 1892).

Patrick, Robert W., *Knapsack and Rifle: Life in the Grand Army* (Philadelphia, Calypso Publishing Co., 1886).

Phillips, William, "Coils of the Past", *Nation*, CLVII (August 28, 1943), pp. 243-44. Review of *At Heaven's Gate*.

Private and Official Correspondence of General Benjamin F. Butler (Norwood, Mass., The Plimpton Press, 1917).

Pulos, C. E., "Warren as Critic", *Prairie Schooner*, XXXIII (Spring, 1959), pp. 1-2. Review of *Selected Essays*.

Purdy, Rob Roy, ed., *Fugitives Reunion: Conversations at Vanderbilt* (Nashville, Vanderbilt University Press, 1959).

Raben, Joseph, "*All the King's Men*: A Symposium", *Folio*, XV (May, 1950), pp. 14-18.

Raiziss, Sona, *The Metaphysical Passion: Seven Modern American Poets and the Seventeenth Century Tradition* (Philadelphia, University of Pennsylvania Press, 1952).

Randall, James G., *The Civil War and Reconstruction* (New York, D. C. Heath, 1937).

Ransom, John Crowe, "*All the King's Men*: A Symposium", *Folio*, XV (May, 1950), pp. 2-3.

——, "The Inklings of 'Original Sin'", *Saturday Review of Literature*, XXVII (May 20, 1944), pp. 10-11.

Rathbun, John W., "Philosophy, 'World Enough and Time', and the Art of the Novel", *Modern Fiction Studies*, VI (Spring, 1960), pp. 47-54.

Reddick, Lawrence Dunbar, "Whose Ordeal?", *New Republic*, CXXXV (September 24, 1956), pp. 9-10.

Report of the Select Committee on the New Orleans Riots (Washington, D.C., Government Printing Office, 1867).

R. G. "Biographical Sketch", *Saturday Review of Literature*, XXXIII (June 24, 1950), p. 12.

Richardson, Maurice, "Dragooned", *New Statesman*, LXIII (June 1, 1962), p. 804. Review of *Wilderness*.

Ridgely, Joseph V., "Tragedy in Kentucky", *Hopkins Review*, IV (Autumn, 1950), pp. 61-63. Review of *World Enough and Time*.

Rolo, Charles, *Atlantic*, CCIV (October, 1950), p. 115. Review of *The Cave*.

Rosenberger, Coleman, "A Bavarian Jew in America's Civil War", *New York Herald Tribune Book Review*, December 3, 1961, p. 4. Review of *Wilderness*.

Rosenthal, M. L., "Robert Penn Warren's Poetry", *South Atlantic Quarterly*, LXII (Autumn, 1963), pp. 499-507.

Rubin, Louis D., Jr., "All the King's Meanings", *Georgia Review*, VIII (Winter, 1954), pp. 422-34.

——, "The Eye of Time: Religious Themes in Robert Penn Warren's Poetry", *Diliman Review*, IV (July, 1958), pp. 215-37.

——, "The South and the Faraway Country", *Virginia Quarterly Review*, XXXVIII (Summer, 1962), pp. 444-59.

——, "'Theories of Human Nature': Kazin or Warren?", *Sewanee Review*, LXIX (Winter, 1961), pp. 500-06.

Ruoff, James, "Humpty Dumpty and *All the King's Men*: A Note on Robert Penn Warren's Teleology", *Twentieth Centuries Literature*, III (October, 1957), pp. 128-34.

——, "Robert Penn Warren's Pursuit of Justice: From Briar Patch to Cosmos", *Research Studies of the State College of Washington*, XXVIII (March, 1959), pp. 19-38.

Ryan, Alvan S., "Robert Penn Warren's *Night Rider*: The Nihilism of the

Isolated Temperament", *Modern Fiction Studies*, VII (Winter, 1961-62), pp. 338-46.

Sale, Roger, "Having it Both Ways in *All the King's Men*", *Hudson Review*, XIV (Spring, 1961), pp. 68-76.

Samuels, Charles Thomas, "In the Wilderness", *Critique*, V (Fall, 1962), pp. 46-57.

Satterwhite, Joseph N., "Robert Penn Warren and Emily Dickinson", *Modern Language Notes*, LXXI (May, 1956), pp. 347-49.

Schoff, Morris, *The Battle of the Wilderness* (Boston, Houghton-Mifflin Co., 1910).

Schutte, William M., "The Dramatic Versions of the Willie Stark Story", in *All the King's Men: A Symposium*, ed. A. Fred Sochatoff et al. (Pittsburgh, Carnegie Press, 1957), pp. 75-90.

Schwartz, Delmore, "The Dragon of Guilt", *New Republic*, CXXIX (September 14, 1953), pp. 17-18. Review of *Brother to Dragons*.

Scott, James B., "The Theme of Betrayal in Robert Penn Warren's Stories", *Thoth*, V (Spring, 1964), pp. 74-84.

Shrapnel, Norman, *Guardian*, December 4, 1959, p. 13. Review of *The Cave*.

Sillars, Malcolm O., "Warren's *All the King's Men*: A Study in Populism", *American Quarterly*, IX (Autumn, 1957), pp. 345-53.

Sindler, Allan P., *Huey Long's Louisiana: State Politics 1920-1952* (Baltimore, Johns Hopkins Press, 1956).

Skillin, Edward, Jr., "Mighty Like Despair", *Commonweal*, XXXVIII (August 6, 1943), p. 398.

Slack, Robert C., "The Telemachus Theme", in *All the King's Men: A Symposium*, eds. A. Fred Sochatoff et al. (Pittsburgh, Carnegie Press, 1957), pp. 29-38.

Sochatoff, A. Fred, "Some Treatments of the Huey Long Theme", in *All the King's Men: A Symposium*, eds. A. Fred Sochatoff et al. (Pittsburgh, Carnegie Press, 1957), pp. 3-15.

Southard, W. P., "The Religious Poetry of Robert Penn Warren", *Kenyon Review*, VII (Autumn, 1945), pp. 653-76.

Southworth, James G., *More Modern American Poets* (Oxford, Basil Blackwell, 1954).

Stallknecht, Newton P., "*All the King's Men*: A Symposium", *Folio*, XV (May, 1950), pp. 18-22.

Stallman, Robert, "Robert Penn Warren: A Checklist of His Critical Writings", *University of Kansas City Review*, XIV (Autumn, 1947), pp. 78-83.

Steere, Edward, *The Wilderness Campaign* (Harrisburgh, Pa., Stackpole Co., 1960).

Steinberg, Erwin R., "The Enigma of Willie Stark", in *All the King's Men: A Symposium*, eds. A. Fred Sochatoff et al. (Pittsburgh, Carnegie Press, 1957), pp. 17-28.

Stewart, James T., "Two Uses of Maupassant", *Modern Language Notes*, LXX (April, 1955), pp. 279-80.

Stewart, John L., "The Achievement of Robert Penn Warren", *South Atlantic Quarterly*, XLVII (October, 1948), pp. 562-79.

——, *The Burden of Time: The Fugitive and Agrarians* (Princeton, Princeton University Press, 1965).

——, "The Fugitive-Agrarian Writers: A History and a Criticism", Ph.D. dissertation, Ohio State University, 1947.

——, "Robert Penn Warren and the Knot of History", *ELH*, XXVI (March, 1959), pp. 102-36.

Strandberg, Victor H., "Theme and Metaphor in *Brother to Dragons*", *PMLA*, LXXIX (1964), pp. 498-508.

Stribling, Robert MacKey, *The Gettysburg Campaign and the Campaigns of 1864 and 1865 in Virginia* (Petersburg, Va., The Franklin Press Co., 1905).

Strugnell, John R., "Robert Penn Warren and the Uses of the Past", *A Review of English Literature*, IV (October, 1963), pp. 93-102.

Tate, Allen, "*The Fugitive*, 1922-1925", *Princeton University Library Chronicles*, III (April, 1942), pp. 75-84.

Thale, Jerome, "The Narrator as Hero", *Twentieth Century Literature*, III (April, 1942), pp. 75-84.

Time, LVI (August 22, 1955), p. 86. Review of *Band of Angels*.

Time, LXXVIII (November 17, 1961), p. 93. Review of *Wilderness*.

"Tobacco War", *Time*, XXXIII (March 27, 1939), p. 73. Review of *Night Rider*.

Trilling, Diana, *Nation*, CLXIII (August 24, 1946), p. 220. Review of *All the King's Men*.

Tyler, Parker, "The Ambiguous Axe", *Poetry*, LXXXIII (December, 1953), pp. 167-71. Review of *Brother to Dragons*.

——, "Novel into Film: *All the King's Men*", *Kenyon Review*, XII (Spring, 1950), pp. 369-76.

Virtanen, Reino, "Camus' Le Malentendu and Some Analogues", *Comparative Literature*, X (Summer, 1958), pp. 232-40.

Wagenknecht, Edward, *Cavalcade of the American Novel* (New York, Henry Holt and Co., 1952).

Wain, John, "Robert Penn Warren: The Drama of the Past", *New Republic*, CLV (November 26, 1966), pp. 16-18.

Wasserstrom, William, "Robert Penn Warren: From Paleface to Redskin", *Prairie Schooner*, XXXI (Winter, 1957), pp. 323-33.

Watkins, Floyd C., "Billie Potts at the Fall of Time", *Mississippi Quarterly*, XI (Winter, 1958), pp. 19-29.

——, "Thomas Wolfe and the Nashville Agrarians", *Georgia Review*, VII (Winter, 1953), pp. 410-23.

Weathers, Winston, " 'Blackberry Winter' and the Use of Archetypes", *Studies in Short Fiction*, I (1964), pp. 45-51.

"The Web of Politics", *Time*, LV (June 26, 1950), p. 98. Review of *World Enough and Time*.

Weissbuch, Ted N., "Jack Burden: Call Me Carraway", *College English*, XXII (February, 1961), p. 361.

West, Paul, *Robert Penn Warren* (Minneapolis, University of Minnesota Press, 1964).

White, Robert, "Robert Penn Warren and the Myth of the Garden", *Faulkner Studies*, III (Winter, 1954), pp. 59-67.

Whittemore, Reed, "Five Old Masters and Their Sensibilities", *Yale Review*, XLVII (Winter, 1958), pp. 281-88. Review of *Promises*.

Wiley, Bell Irvin, *The Road to Appomattox* (Memphis, Memphis State College Press, 1956).

Wilson, Angus, "The Fires of Violence", *Encounter*, IV (May, 1955), pp. 75-78. Review of *Night Rider*.

Woodruff, Neal, Jr., "The Technique of *All the King's Men*", in *All the King's Men: A Symposium*, eds. A. Fred Sochatoff et al. (Pittsburgh, Carnegie Press, 1957), pp. 51-62.

Woodward, C. Vann, *The Burden of Southern History* (Baton Rouge, Louisiana State University Press, 1960).

——, "Reflections on a Centennial: The American Civil War", *The Yale Review*, L (June, 1961), pp. 481-90.

Wright, James, "The Stiff Smile of Mr. Warren", *Kenyon Review*, XX (Autumn, 1959), pp. 645-55.

Zabel, Morton D., "Problems of Knowledge", *Poetry*, XLVIII (April, 1936), pp. 37-41. Review of *Thirty-six Poems*.

Zanger, Jules, ed., *The Beauchamp Tragedy* (Philadelphia and New York, J. B. Lippincott Co., 1963).

Zinman, David H., *The Day Huey Long Was Shot, September 8, 1935* (New York, I. Obolensky, 1963).

STUDIES IN AMERICAN LITERATURE

16. JOHN D. BRANTLEY: *The Fiction of John Dos Passos.* 1968. 136 pp. ƒ 21.—/$6.—

17. GEORGE BRANDON SAUL: *Quintet: Essays on Five American Women Poets.* 1967. 50 pp. ƒ 10.—/$ 2.90

19. PHYLLIS FRANKLIN: *Show Thyself a Man: A Comparison of Benjamin Franklin and Cotton Mather.* 1969. 93 pp. ƒ 21.—/$6.—

22. JONAS SPATZ: *Hollywood in Fiction: Some versions of the American Myth.* 1969. 148 pp. ƒ 28.—/$8.—

23. STEPHEN A. BLACK: *James Thurber: His Masquerades: A Critical Study.* 1969. 128 pp. ƒ 24.—/$ 6.85

26. G. A. M. JANSSENS: *The American Literary Review: A Critical History, 1920-1950.* 1968. 341 pp.
ƒ 38.—/$ 10.90

MOUTON · PUBLISHERS · THE HAGUE